Stravinsky
and the Piano

Russian Music Studies, No. 8

Malcolm Hamrick Brown, Series Editor

Professor of Music
Indiana University

Other Titles in This Series

Stravinsky and the Piano

by
Charles M. Joseph

UMI RESEARCH PRESS
Ann Arbor, Michigan

Produced and distributed by
UMI Research Press
an imprint of
University Microfilms International
Ann Arbor, Michigan 48106

Library of Congress Cataloging in Publication Data

Joseph, Charles M.
  Stravinsky and the piano.

   (Russian music studies ; no. 8)
   Revision of the author's thesis (University of
Cincinnati, 1974)
   Bibliography: p.
   Includes index.
   1. Stravinsky, Igor, 1882-1971. Piano music.
I. Title. II. Series.

ML410.S932J67 1983   786.1'092'4   83-9206
ISBN 0-8357-1426-8

For my daughters
Amy and Jennifer

Contents

List of Plates

Acknowledgments

The origins of my interest in Stravinsky, particularly as it relates to the piano, are traceable to 1968–70, a period during which I was a student of the composer's son, Soulima. In the years that immediately followed, I completed a doctoral dissertation under the supervision of Professor Paul Cooper. To both, I owe a great debt of gratitude. Their encouragement will always be cherished. In the decade that followed my dissertation, my interest in this aspect of Stravinsky's career has continued. Some of my preliminary analytic thoughts, as expressed in my by now dated doctoral thesis, are herein revised. Moreover, since the time of Stravinsky's death, and especially within even the last five years, a considerable amount of information has been made available—information that provides a much clearer perspective within which to discuss Stravinsky's association with the piano.

In this regard, I am especially grateful to Robert Craft, not only for his illuminative writings upon which so much of this study finds its departure, but also for his willingness to share his knowledge of Stravinsky's manuscripts, as well as for his support of this project. Similarly, I wish to thank Professor Richard Taruskin, whose advice and generosity in sharing his own broadly based knowledge of Stravinsky's folk heritage is very much appreciated.

In dealing with those relatively few Stravinsky primary source materials currently accessible, both J. Rigbie Turner, curator of music manuscripts at the Pierpont Morgan Library, and Wayne Shirley, reference librarian of the Library of Congress Music Division, proved to be infinitely patient with my inquiries and requests. Likewise, James Smart and Sam Brylawski of the Library of Congress Recorded Sound Division were most helpful in retrieving and preparing the piano rolls of Stravinsky's music for my personal examination.

Closer to home, I wish to acknowledge Dr. William Hipp, former chairman of the Division of Music, and Dean Eugene Bonelli of the

Meadows School of the Arts, Southern Methodist University, for their support and understanding over the last three years. Particularly, I wish to thank Professor Robert Skinner and Ms. Ruthann Boles of the Division's music library, both of whom were steadfastly helpful in securing needed materials from both the U.S. and abroad. The music examples throughout the book were prepared with great calligraphic care by Michael Levin of Dallas.

I would also like to express my gratefulness to Joan Peyser of *The Musical Quarterly,* Marian Green of *The Journal of Musicology,* and Lewis Rowell of *Music Theory Spectrum,* all of whom in their editorial capacity permitted me to include revised portions of some of my earlier research first appearing in their respective journals. Finally, a list of publishers holding rights to the reprinting of those Stravinsky excerpts appearing in this study follows. Their cooperation in allowing me to incorporate such examples has greatly enhanced whatever small contribution this study may offer.

Charles M. Joseph
Dallas, Texas
April 2, 1983

Reprint Rights Notices

    Ragtime for Eleven Instruments
    Piano-Rag-Music
    All excerpts used by kind permission of J & W Chester/Edition Wilhelm Hansen London Ltd

Belwin Mills Publishing Corporation
    Renard—Kalmus Miniature Score No. 273
    Kalmus Piano Series No. 4064—Tchaikovsky
    Op. 39, #1, Scherzo à la Russe

International Music Company
    Four Etudes, Opus 7 (Edition #1512)
    Five Easy Pieces for Piano Duet (Edition #3074)
    Used by permission of International Music Company

Theodore Presser Company
    Tango—Copyright 1941 Mercury Music Corporation
    Used by Permission Of The Publisher

Faber Music Ltd.
    Scherzo
    Sonata in F$^{\sharp}$ minor
    Reprinted by permission.

Boosey & Hawkes, Inc.
    Petrouchka
    Symphony of Psalms
    Octet for Winds
    Persephone
    Le Sacre de Printemps
    Oedipus Rex
    Serenade en La
    Concerto for Piano and Wind Orchestra
    Duo Concertant
    Movements for Orchestra
    Capriccio for Piano and Orchestra
    Septet
    Sonata for Two Pianos
    Sonata for Piano
    Five Fingers
    Tango
    Reprinted by permission

The author also wishes to include a note of appreciation to the Library of Congress Music Division, and to the Pierpont Morgan Library (the Mary Flagler Cary Music Collection and the Robert Owen Lehman Collection, on deposit).

Introduction

When the history of twentieth-century music is finally written, the pre-eminence of Igor Stravinsky undoubtedly will command a central chapter. Throughout his long career, his work exerted a sustained influence on several generations of musicians and artists. His immortality is virtually assured on the strength of his compositional legacy alone, though his productivity assumed many other forms as well. His diverse abilities not only as a composer, but as a pianist, author, conductor, lecturer and polemicist, have justifiably earned him a notoriety few attain. Moreover, Stravinsky was capable of exchanging any of these hats for another as frequently and as facilely as he seemingly altered his own compositional style. Based on the prima facie evidence bequeathed by a host of contemporary commentators, history's finding of a chameleonic tendency in Stravinsky seems understandable enough, though more and more such a pronouncement must be judged specious. We are now only beginning to realize that, in fact, Stravinsky's "style" never really changed as radically as we may have been led originally to believe. Ultimately, the commonalities of Stravinsky's music, and the various facets of his overall career, far outstrip the more accessible surface differences.

As history so often seems prone to do, we have been willed a series of labels and finely demarcated lines that attempt to partition Stravinsky's career into insular periods. But such efforts approach contrivance and invite an artificiality that conspires against grasping the larger essence of the composer's overall contribution to our century's art. Stravinsky himself loathed placards, especially the tag of a revolutionary which was draped upon his shoulders through the myopia of his contemporary annotators. Revolution simply was alien to Stravinsky's constitution. His was consistently an evolutionary progress, transcending the particulars of any given work or role. Indeed, perhaps too much time has been devoted to categorizing Stravinsky's life into neatly retrievable pigeonholes. If a sharper focus of his achievement is to be gained, then such a processing urge must be resisted. In its place, studies of those cohesive threads that unite rather than divide the various aspects of his music and career must be undertaken if we are ever to grasp the organic nature of his multidimensional creativity. Surely this is what Andre Schaeffner sensed nearly half a century ago in commenting that

> Stravinsky's personality is far too complex for his music to be divisible into distinct styles. Boris de Schloezer regrets the absence of a certain mystery in his late works; but I for one, distrust the apparent clarity which marks all of Stravinsky's music, recent or not. There are many undercurrents of which even the composer himself may be unaware. We are still far from understanding or even seeing clearly into Stravinsky's protean nature. . . . (1936 in *Modern Music*)

Both figuratively and literally, it is suggested that the piano provides one major instrument with which to begin tracing the continuity of Stravinsky's creative efforts, both as a composer and more broadly as a musician. Throughout an ocean of change, the piano endured as a stabilizing, immutable force, and, as such, rests at the very core of all his productivity. From his earliest recollections to Robert Craft's more reliable chronicling of the later years, the piano figured prominently as a central component of Stravinsky's everyday life, and therefore, one might have assumed that the composer would have channeled this attraction into a good many keyboard compositions. This was not the case. Moreover those works that do exist are often viewed with some reservation. Especially given the wide celebrity enjoyed by Stravinsky's Russian contemporaries (Rachmaninov, Prokofiev), as well as by other composer/pianists, Stravinsky's own keyboard *oeuvres* generally have fared poorly:

> Mention must be made of Igor Stravinsky, not because of his piano accomplishment, since it is negligible, but because he is too great to be ignored. Though he was a fine concert pianist, he chose to deny the keyboard the fruits of his genius, writing only a few works and couching them in a somewhat unrewarding style, the neobaroque. . . . His Sonata for one piano [is] dry, perpetually repetitive in rhythm and sparsely written to the point where change in color quality is lacking. His Serenade in A is a bit more varied but not enough so as to render it highly attractive. There are four early studies in romantic style, not outstanding. He writes for the keyboard with the kind of perfection of technique accorded to all his works: it is only that his desired effect does not coincide with that of most musicians and the music-loving public. (Weiser, *Keyboard Music*)

While such a *vox populi* disesteem expresses most pianists' disappointment, it is at the same time a predictable reaction. Measured against such opulently orchestrated ballets as *The Firebird*, for example, a work like the 1921 *The Five Fingers* naturally pales. Stravinsky more than anyone was aware of such inevitable comparisons, as well as the virtuoso's appetite for "immediate triumphs," "sensational effects," and the need to satisfy "the wishes of the public." Yet the fact that the piano works remain relatively obscure or at least do not enjoy the favor of our "music-loving public," surely must not deter one from considering the critical role played by this literature in better understanding certain aspects of Stravinsky's broader development as a composer and musician. Stravinsky wrote piano music all of his life, and though even by the most liberal of enumerations there are fewer than twenty keyboard works, there is a remarkable variety of piano writing within the limits of this repertoire. There are works for solo piano, two pianos, concerti for various kinds of orchestras as well as without orchestra, didactic pieces, transcriptions, and arrangements that surpass the often pejorative connotation associated with such labels. Moreover, Stravinsky's own self-proclaimed stand that composition amounted to a problem-solving proposition suggests an explanation for the paucity of keyboard works. Having met a certain challenge, there was little desire to replicate the problem, and it is particularly in this sense that the piano literature deserves investigation.

Furthermore, seen in proper historical perspective, the chronology and frequency of the writing of piano music suggests that this particular repertoire may have served as a harbinger for the grander and more commonly enshrined Stravinsky works, such as *Histoire du Soldat* or the *Symphony of Psalms*. Indeed, is it not reasonable to speculate the incipient compositional ideas, just beginning to blossom, might first have been tested at the keyboard and that the piano works provide in essence a series of experiments? And beyond such a postulation, it is submitted that many of Stravinsky's nonpiano compositions may well have been first conceived with the actual sound of the piano in mind, as is explored in the final chapter of this study.

In these ways and others, to be examined in the following pages, the piano may be seen as the cornerstone of Stravinsky's formidable career. No other aspect of his life, perhaps not even ballet, so permeates the totality of his creative efforts and thus qualifies as a reliable barometer in considering his long and diversified life. Yet Stravinsky's association with the piano is one that has never really been systematically explored. The comments that follow hope to offer some of the basic tools needed to begin unearthing this critical bond.

1

Foundations and Early Influences

During the late nineteenth century, the Stravinsky St. Petersburg flat overlooking the Kryukov Canal must have been musically animated a good part of each day. At the eye of this activity were the two grand pianos occupying the drawing room just down the hall from the sizeable private library of Fyodor Ignatievich Stravinsky (1843–1902). The family patriarch's devotion to rare books would have easily qualified him as a bonafide bibliophile, though by profession he was a highly regarded bass with the Imperial Opera. From this substantial collection of books and music, the then currently revered opera scores of the Italians, as well as those of Glinka, Serov, and the so-called *Moguchaia kuchka,* doubtlessly found their way to the drawing room and the old Bechstein piano's music rack for repeated trials, before being tucked under Stravinsky's arm for the short walk to the neighboring Marinsky Theatre.

Fyodor Stravinsky's wife, Anna Kirillovna Kholodovskaya (1854–1939), was herself a pianist. Though there were four children to attend, the house servants seem to have discharged their domestic duties adequately, thereby allowing Anna frequent sessions at that same Bechstein piano. It was, in fact, at this very instrument, preserved in the iconography of *Memories and Commentaries,* that the Stravinsky's third son Igor (1882–1971) remembers his first physical contact with music. This tactile imprint indelibly fated him even as a youth. From Stravinsky's statement years later—"I need to touch music as well as to think it, which is why I have always lived next to a piano"—one begins to sense from whence his reliance upon the piano may have arisen.

As one might expect, numerous auditory impressions antedate Stravinsky's youthful pianistic attempts. Through his copious writings, Stravinsky himself has bequeathed a series of colorful memories outlining several contributing ingredients to his early musical awareness. The notion of Stravinsky at age two, for example, demonstrating a rather startling precocity by imitating closely the not-so-simple song of the peasant women returning home from the fields, elicits a rather romantic, if perhaps slightly eidetic image. Yet this memorable event, supposedly having occurred in the village of Lzy during the summer of 1884, is proudly recounted by Stravinsky as having marked the very dawn of his consciousness as a musician. Similar al fresco anecdotes involving various village scenes, red-bearded peasants, and other equally evocative personae have been retold so frequently as not to warrant rehearsing here. Yet throughout these unusually vivid remembrances, there is the omnipresent ethnicity of the natural, the demotic people of Stravinsky's childhood. The environment in which he was reared seems to have provided a remarkable farrago of musical experiences. His regular exposure to the music of the St. Petersburg aristocracy, as well as to the unadorned tunes of the peasantry in Lzy, Pechisky, and later Ustilug, surely exerted a formative influence. Moreover the duality of these musical stimulants was fully assimilated by Stravinsky's acquisitive mind. Especially with regard to the powerful folkloristic elements with which he came in close and constant contact, a latent musical reservoir was stored, then periodically tapped later as it served his immediate compositional needs.

Surely these cherished summer excursions to the country engendered far more than a peripheral force in the boy's musical growth. Just how critical these forces may have been is suggested by Valerii Smirnov, who asserts that the very cornerstone of Stravinsky's first creative forays were constructed upon the wedding songs and circular tunes of the aforementioned locations.[1] But while it is quite likely that even these limited seasonal visits actually eclipsed the daily exposure to music in his parents' home, the effects of the latter must not be dismissed too quickly. That in later years Stravinsky chose not to chronicle in any detail the musical life of his immediate environment as a youth probably owes more to the electively repressed memory of an unhappy childhood than anything else. By his own confession, Stravinsky was neither close to his parents nor two of his three brothers. Stravinsky summarily (and rather poetically) feigns his inability to recall his musical home life inasmuch as "Winter with its curtailing of liberty and amusements, with its rigorous discipline and interminable length, was not likely to make enduring impressions."[2] Years later, however, a more curmudgeonly Stravinsky was far less discreet in dismissing these early years as "a period of waiting for the moment when I could send everyone and everything connected with [my childhood] to hell."[3]

Fyodor Stravinsky's desire to enlist Igor, or for that matter any of his children, as an apprentice was at best minimal. Eventually Igor was given the benefit of piano lessons, and after acquiring sufficient sight reading techniques, the young Stravinsky was even permitted the use of his father's library of scores. But these seem to have been little more than indulgent gestures rather than concerted efforts to channel the young boy's interests towards a professional career. As Stravinsky himself later remembered in the *Journal de Genève*:

> My father's career as a singer did not help me very much, for he wanted me to avoid an artist's life, knowing its difficulties. Neither my piano playing or my essays in composition convinced him that these aptitudes were sufficiently promising to enable me to earn my living in music.[4]

Ostensibly, there is nothing to suggest that Fyodor actually proscribed musical study for his son; to be sure, a familiarity with and even thorough knowledge of music was surely considered admirable, as long as certain implicitly understood boundaries were not crossed. Moreover the very presence of Igor's esteemed father in the household quite naturally could only have exerted some shaping influence, though in all probability whatever musical learning accrued did so indirectly. Only after Igor had tenaciously pursued musical study on his own initiative, extending even into the university years of his legal studies after the turn of the century, did Fyodor finally intercede with his friend Rimsky-Korsakov on his son's behalf. Even when Fyodor in 1901, just a year before his death, did in fact endorse his son's compositional study with Rimsky, by then it could only have been interpreted by Igor as a lukewarm blessing. In the end, it must be said that Fyodor never actively fostered his son's earliest musical ambitions, and in return, the son seems to have viewed his father as a venerated but nonetheless rather distant *paterfamilias*.[5]

If Stravinsky's interpersonal relationship with his well-known father was cool, his feelings for his mother fared worse still. Were it not for the natural bond of consanguity, one wonders if Anna's existence would have won even passing acknowledgment among her son's many remembrances. But there seems to have been a mutual insensitivity. In his recently compiled correspondence of Stravinsky, Robert Craft suggests that of the four children, Igor was "the least favored" by his mother.[6] In later years, when Stravinsky's efforts proved successful in winning Anna's release from her postrevolution homeland, one somehow feels that the impetus for arranging this passage sprung not from compassion or deep affection, but rather from a reflexive filial obligation. Following his mother's arrival in France, Stravinsky by some accounts woefully neglected even the basic necessities of Anna's financial welfare. In this regard, in several letters to

her husband, Stravinsky's first wife Catherine offers a gentle but nonetheless unmistakable admonition:

> I understand [Mama's] fear of not being able to manage with the sum you gave her.
> I also understand *you* but I think you are burdening her. . . . It seems to me that
> you've cut down a great deal on the money for her expenses (June 26, 1935). The poor
> thing barely manages, borrowing from [the housekeeper], giving it back to her, and
> borrowing again (July 6, 1935).[7]

More than any other familial figure in his youth, Stravinsky's mother
remains only on the perimeter of his memoirs. Even so, in her role as a
pianist—albeit a dilettante—surely Anna's playing factors into Stravinsky's early attraction to the piano. One notes, for example, that even the
obvious dearth of references to her in Stravinsky's writings is broken by
his praise for her sight reading facility. Uncharacteristically, there is even
a nominal gratitude expressed in crediting his mother's genetic influence,
since here Stravinsky claims to have "inherited" her talents for reading
at sight.[8] Though her pianistic proficiency seems not to have risen above
the level of a competent technique, nevertheless her repertoire encom-
passed a liberal variety of periods and composers. The easier pieces of
Grieg, Schubert, Schumann, and Chopin, the character pieces of Mendelssohn and of course Tchaikovsky (who seems always to have been
lionized by the Stravinsky family), the easier sonatas of both Mozart and
Beethoven, and finally the standard works of Bach were all included. The
latter compositions particularly were used as finger exercises (the *Inventions, French Suites,* and portions of *The Well-Tempered Clavier*). Stravinsky's friend and confidant, Nicolas Nabokov, adduces that although
Stravinsky never conceded the possible influence exercised by his mother
through her fondness of playing, still the young composer's musical sensitivity, even subliminally, must have been at least partially sharpened by
rehearing this repertoire over the period of several impressionable years.[9]
Finally, though Anna could not of course hope to compete for the musical
respect commanded by her husband in his visibly laureate role as an
operatic celebrity, it may be that it is she, more than Fyodor, who will
provide the immediate link between Igor and his early association with
the keyboard. Accordingly, one hopes that her position will not be undervalued when a full biography of her son is undertaken.

In addition to these representative recollections of his parents, Stravinsky willed several other memories that center around the actual physical taction with the piano. For example, in recalling a marine band that
regularly paraded in the street below his nursery, Stravinsky remembers
attempting to ape the same sounds at the keyboard: "I tried to pick out
at the piano the intervals I had heard—as soon as I could reach the

piano—but found other intervals in the process that I liked better, which already made me a composer."[10] Similarly in 1957, the composer recounts that at age eight, while playing a major scale at the piano, he rearranged the normal order of tones and semitones. Reproached by an uncle who was present at the moment, Stravinsky remembers riposting, "My dear uncle, that's my own invention. Leave me alone."[11]

One observes in both of these *mirabile dictu* narratives the same oracular tone preserved in Stravinsky's relating of the Lzy story during the summer of 1884. Phrases such as "as soon as I could reach the piano" seem carefully orchestrated to suggest a prodigy whose mind's inquisitiveness far surpassed his tender years. Likewise his repartee to what Stravinsky captiously portrays as his somewhat witless uncle, already signals a youthful intractableness as well as an early desire to be viewed as an enfant terrible. Moreover, one must of course be suspect of the potential paramnesia upon which these invocatory tales may be based. By any measure, it would be wise to refrain from ordaining such commentaries with unjustifiable portent. Afer all, is it really so unusual for any child, regardless of what inherent talents exist, to approach the piano in a natural search for new stimuli? Thus these remembrances are entered not as irrefragable proof of some early creative genius, but rather as an approximate yardstick with which to measure the time and general circumstances that first surround the genesis of Stravinsky's interest in the piano. Moreover, though the authenticity of these anecdotes may be unverifiable, recently released sources, including several early letters, seem to corroborate the essence of Stravinsky's accounts. Still, with little more than distant, even if reliable recollections upon which to build, only the most precarious scaffolding exists with which to reconstruct this important early period. Recent Soviet musicological inquiry is often disappointing, sometimes going no further than to lobby for the primary importance of Russian folklorism in Stravinsky's works, an importance that has been recognized for quite awhile now. Thus there currently appears to be little promise in terms of additional source materials that might help to remove the gaping lacuna that prohibits a further understanding of just what transpired during the 1880s.

With the next decade, however, several events begin to cut a path that leads to a sharper view of Stravinsky's childhood, especially as it pertains to his association with the piano; 1891 marked the beginning of formal piano instruction.

When I was nine, my parents gave me a piano mistress. I very quickly learned to read music and, as the result of reading, soon had a longing to improvise, a pursuit to which I devoted myself, and which for a long time was my favorite occupation. . . . I must say that my work at improvisation was not absolutely fruitless; for, on the other hand, it contributed to my better knowledge of the piano, and, on the other, it sowed the seeds of musical ideas.[12]

Here one immediately observes Stravinsky's early cognizance of the catalytic role the piano was consistently to play in awakening his fertile imagination. From the very outset of his keyboard study then, this vital bond between what he termed a "physical medium of sound" and the compositional process is acknowledged. One might also reasonably extrapolate his "longing to improvise" as a consequence of his learning to read music. In later years Stravinsky would often credit the seeds of his initial compositional ideas to such score reading: "I start to look for this material, sometimes playing old masters (to put myself in motion). . . . I thus form my building material."[13] Indeed, Stravinsky's perennial "need" to compose, as he put it, seems more often than not to have been ignited by such pianistic study of models—models that were malleable by his own invention.

An autobiographic letter to G. H. Timofeyev in March 1908 provides an especially revealing content.

I was born in Oranienbaum on June 18, 1882. At the age of nine I began piano lessons from A. P. Snyetkova, the daughter of the violinist in the Maryinsky Theatre orchestra. . . . Hoping to make a pianist out of me, my parents did not stint on the cost of teachers, but gave me the opportunity to study with the very best ones, such as L. A. Kashperova, from whom I took lessons for two years. But I was attracted to composition before that. . . . I did a large amount of sight reading which helped my development . . . and though I improvised endlessly and enjoyed it immensely, I was unable to write down what I played.[14]

In apprising the reader of his preballet vitae, one must remember that here Stravinsky writes as a virtually unknown composer rather than the soon to be heralded young luminary of Diaghilev's *Ballet Russe*. Obviously there was as yet no reason for an image consciousness. Thus in this document the importance with which Stravinsky assesses his early piano training seems to be genuine. Moreover, in comparing this important source with the earlier comments extracted from Stravinsky's autobiographical account, there is an evident congruity. Clearly, in the composer's own estimate, his first formal piano tuition established an important landmark in his youthful musical development. Yet the letter's reference to parental visions of their son as a pianist would seem to contradict earlier statements made herein. Such a sentiment, however, is not repeated in other sources. That Stravinsky himself ever harbored any serious notion of becoming a concert pianist, at least as his parents understood the meaning, is certainly questionable. Nevertheless, there are some indications that Stravinsky took his early study quite earnestly, if not with any appreciable regularity. A recital by Josef Hoffman, for instance, seems to have engendered enough inspiration for the young Stravinsky to renew his enthusiasm for practicing. But such zeal seems to have been fleeting. While little is known about Stravinsky's playing at this time, it does appear that beginning around 1900 he began to collect a fair amount of accompanying experience. Yet the motivation for such playing is attributable to an "economic strategem," as he called it, rather than any genuine ambition to pursue a career as a professional accompanist.[15]

Information about Stravinsky's first teacher, A. P. Snyetkova, is scant. What is known is again only as reliable as Stravinsky's own distant recollections. She was a student at the St. Petersburg Conservatory and had been recommended as a piano teacher by Nikolai Soloviev, a professor of composition and a friend of Fyodor Stravinsky. During the period of Stravinsky's piano instruction, which seems to have lasted about two years, the pupil maintained he learned absolutely nothing from his teacher.[16] In observing that Stravinsky quickly passes over Snyetkova in his letter to Timofeyev, one is led to believe that his later assessment of her importance (as depicted in his interviews with Craft) is probably accurate. By his own confession, Stravinsky was more attracted to improvising than to practicing and so his natural predilection towards self-discovery surely conspired against his passive acceptance of what appeared in his eyes to be pedantry. Indeed, Nicolas Nabokov remembers Stravinsky having confided that he was not at all pleased with his earliest piano studies, though he does seem to have taken some pleasure in the perfunctory finger exercises of Hanon, at least to a greater extent than some of the "short and sweet" pieces for beginners which he was made to suffer.[17]

During the next two-year period, a second piano mistress, Mlle. L. A. Kashperova, exerted a stronger influence over Stravinsky. Kashperova had been a student of the eminent Anton Rubinstein. She herself was a respected pianist in St. Petersburg circles. Predictably, her own musical tastes had been colored by the inviolable principles of classicism espoused by her mentor and his nearly hegemonic Russian Musical Society. The St. Petersburg Conservatory had functioned as a pedagogic wing for the society, propagating the styles of the European masters of classic music rather than Balakirev and his own idealogues.[18] In his later writings, and in his familiar acidulous tone, Stravinsky rails against Kashperova's sectarianism, indicting her as a "blockhead" and charging that "her aesthetics and bad tastes were impregnable."[19] Yet in noting such deprecatory rhetoric, one must be aware of a deep undercurrent; surely this invective emerges from his eventual negativism towards Rubinstein, the conservatory ("that musical prison"), and all that both represented. Many of the predominant figures associated with Stravinsky's youth—his father, Snyetkova, Kashperova, numerous friends, and most especially Rimsky—were all at one time part of the renowned and somewhat exclusive school. But Stravinsky himself was never to win entry into the coterie of this *sanctum sanctorum*. Still, it would seem that such retrospective diatribes could have had little to do with Stravinsky's attitude at age eleven towards Kashperova's teaching. Moreover in the Timofeyev letter, no protest is voiced against his teacher's convictions.

It was towards the improvement of Stravinsky's fundamental piano technique that Kashperova's discipline was most effective. Though Stravinsky claims to have been disinterested in piano exercises (except for the mechanical Hanon etudes), nevertheless his technique advanced rapidly. By age thirteen Stravinsky's piano repertoire included the Mendelssohn Piano Concerto in G minor, some works of Schubert and Schumann, various sonatas of Haydn, Mozart, Clementi, and especially the music of Beethoven. All of these composers were staples of the Russian Musical Society and it is clear that Mlle. Kashperova's own preferences were transmitted to her students. Beethoven seems to have been a central hero as evinced by the frequency of concert programs upon which his music was performed.[20] One biographer contends that Stravinsky's playing of Beethoven piano sonatas seems to have been heightened by the youth's special interest in Beethoven's thematic construction and development, though as yet there is little to support this assertion.[21] Still, Stravinsky's lifelong fealty to Beethoven is traceable not only to Kashperova's teaching but to his own independent exploration of Beethoven's music. Stravinsky's efforts to acquaint himself with the orchestral works of Beethoven at an early age are suggested in a 1907 letter to Rimsky: "I am enjoying Beethoven's symphonies, which I play four-hands with Katia in the evening. I have many thoughts about Beethoven, but I will tell them to you this winter."[22]

Kashperova's pedagogy strongly discouraged the use of the piano's pedals, a caveat that Stravinsky found especially relevant: "I had to sustain with my fingers, like an organist—an omen perhaps, as I have never been a pedal composer."[23] Indeed, the dry, metallic sound of a good portion of his piano music confirms this. Moreover, by many accounts, as a performer Stravinsky employed the pedal most sparingly. Years later, for example, Walter Piston remembered Stravinsky exhorting pianists to play his *Serenade en la* absolutely without the use of pedal; and he himself proceeded to demonstrate to Piston's composition class at Harvard during the 1939 Norton lectures just how this should be accomplished.[24] It was probably during this period of study with Kashperova that Stravinsky began to gain sufficient technique and reading fluency to allow his perusal of the opera scores from his father's library. In addition to the standard literature one might have expected Fyodor Stravinsky to own, the younger Stravinsky professed knowledge of all of Wagner's works, a curious and grand claim to be sure, learning them first in piano reduction then later reading from the orchestral scores. Finally, Stravinsky fondly remembers the enjoyment he derived in playing the four-hand arrangement of Rimsky's operas with Kashperova. Thus the biennium of piano instruction under Kashperova's tutelage seems to have been very productive. If the repertory learned and the proficiency of reading ability Stravinsky suggests he gained is accurate, then clearly he was a more formidable pianist than one might have first supposed. Then, too, his pianistic proficiency could only enhance his improvisational skills; and so by 1895, the piano had evolved not only as the central "physical medium" by which Stravinsky obtained a working knowledge of others' music, but also the primary vehicle by which his own creative energy could now begin to take shape. Ultimately it must be recognized that for whatever shortcomings Stravinsky then or thereafter found in Kashperova, she, perhaps more than any other directly involved figure at that stage of Stravinsky's growth, guided him in acquiring the requisite functional skills that were soon to be employed in his own compositionally nascent discoveries.

A picture of Stravinsky in his St. Petersburg room, taken around 1898 and reprinted in *Pictures and Documents,* reveals portraits of Bach, Beethoven, Schumann, Liszt, and others adorning his desk. It is a clear photographic testament of the extent to which the youth now openly displayed his intensifying interest in music. As this interest ripened during the second half of the 1890s, so, too, did the boy's musical world widen. In large part his pianistic efficacy now permitted a much more intimate contact with the music that had always been in his musical environment. But instead of simply hearing the literature as a casual listener, he could now examine the scores at the keyboard with greater scrutiny.

Even so, it would be fallacious to assume that because of Stravinsky's growing devotion to music, other more broadly artistic endeavors were not pursued with some fervor. Painting, sketching, reading, and even his active participation in various theatrical productions are all mentioned in an informative 1899 letter sent from Ustilug to his parents.[25] Such summers provided a welcome respite from St. Petersburg and the general indifference displayed by his parents towards his aspirations as a professional rather than avocational musician. As he matured, new artistic adventures in the city began to present themselves. While his parents may have lacked enthusiasm for the course upon which Stravinsky was inexorably heading, the boy's uncle Yelachich, Anna's brother-in-law, evidently served as an amiable and supportive surrogate. Again it seems to have been the piano that furnished the tool with which Stravinsky could investigate new literature, this time by reading four-hand reductions with his uncle. Stravinsky remembers him as a passionate dilettante. He speaks of exploring with his uncle, not only Beethoven, but also Brahms, with whom Yelachich was especially enamored. As early as 1894, Stravinsky recalls reading the Brahms symphonies and quartets.[26] It was in fact at his uncle's summer residence in Pavlovka, in 1903, that Stravinsky began his Piano Sonata in F$^\sharp$ minor, an early compositional essay clearly betraying the youth's indebtedness to the piano style of the early Brahms piano sonatas.

In addition to the Germanic musical tastes favored in his uncle's residence, Stravinsky quite naturally also wished to become familiar with the current Russian composers then enjoying such enormous success. Rimsky's compositions easily brought the most respect, and surely Stravinsky knew his scores better than most others. Yet it was Alexandre Glazunov who particularly captured Stravinsky's attention. Glazunov, whose first symphony was premiered by Balakirev in 1882, had become a well-known prodigy at age sixteen. Stravinsky must have entertained thoughts of duplicating such an envious accomplishment.

> Glazunov was almost as much of an idol to me in my fifteenth year as Rimsky himself, that is, until I transcribed one of his string quartets for piano and impulsively took the score to his house to show him. Though I had never been presented to him, he knew my father, in spite of which he received me ungraciously, perfunctorily flipping through my manuscript and pronouncing the work unmusical. I went away thoroughly discouraged.[27]

Having come away from this encounter obviously chapfallen, it is understandable that the impressionable young Stravinsky's once ardent admiration of Glazunov now quickly turned to rancor. After all, such an inimical rebuff, for whatever reason Glazunov may have so strongly expressed it, could not do otherwise than to exacerbate the discomfiture Stravinsky must have already been experiencing about his rather dim prospects as a professional composer.

But beyond this unfortunate meeting, the role of the piano at this stage in the youth's life becomes even more important. Now he began to explore the piano's potential as an aid in preparing transcriptions for his private study. In effect it was an important intermediary step between the first improvisations of which he speaks often and his initial notational attempts at free composition. Moreover this early, and one might reasonably conjecture, imperfect transcription of the Glazunov was to be the first of a continuing series of such efforts; transcribing the music of others as a vicarious means of recreating their compositional process was to become a significant and enduring occupation for Stravinsky, even into his final years.

Of the various influences to which Stravinsky was exposed towards the turn of the century, none seems to have been more broadening than his association with Ivan Pokrovsky. Strangely, there is no mention of Pokrovsky in any of the composer's letters recently released. Yet in Stravinsky's later autobiography, the author speaks in superlatives about his youthful friend, avowing that Pokrovsky "dominated my life from 1897 through 1899."[28] In Pokrovsky, Stravinsky found an informed elder, a member of the current cognoscenti. He seems to have been a stimulating provacateur, a close companion who relentlessly challenged Stravinsky to defend his opinions, to question ideas, to expand his thinking. Pokrovsky introduced the new music of France currently taking hold in St. Petersburg: Gounod, Bizet, Delibes, Chabrier—all tantalizingly foreign to the young Stravinsky. Again it was the piano that helped the friendship to flourish. Once more it was four-hand piano playing that enabled Stravinsky to become familiar with the French literature, thereby stretching the ever-widening boundaries of his musical world.

To this point, the reconstruction of Stravinsky's youthful association with the piano has been by necessity founded upon the admittedly circumstantial evidence of the composer's own recollections, often offered half a century after the fact. But as suggested earlier, fortunately the few letters that have survived from this formative period generally appear to corroborate Stravinsky's own remembrances.[29] Yet without the benefit of more reliable primary sources, especially the music dating from this time, nothing better than fragile conjectures could be offered. Until rather recently, Stravinsky's earliest compositions were thought to have been lost or destroyed. The one major exception is a 1902 song, "Storm Cloud," the manuscript of which remains inaccessible to most Western scholars.[30] However with the resurgence of musicological inquiry following Stravinsky's return to the USSR in 1962 (and even more so since his death), several early piano works, formerly unknown or presumed lost, have now been released by Soviet scholars. Some of the more informative material to emerge from this renewed research appears in Smirnov's *Tvorcheskoe formirovanie I. F. Stravinskogo* [The Creative-Formative Years of Igor Stravinsky].[31] While in good part Smirnov's work draws largely upon the by now standard occidental commentaries offered by Stravinsky long after his departure from prerevolutionary Russia (especially the numerous interviews with Robert Craft), the inclusion of a few fragments of a very early compositional effort provides an important new contribution to the few surviving manuscript sources of this period. As might be expected, the fragments are excerpted from a brief and rather crudely hewn piano piece.

This early—indeed for now the earliest—extant compositional attempt at actually notating an original work dates from October 14, 1898. Stravinsky entitled the work "Tarantella" and goes so far as to name a dedicatee, one D. Rudnev. The work actually appears to be more a series of sketches than a completed composition. With only two short fragments reprinted in Smirnov's monograph upon which to rely, there is little option but to examine the passages given and assume the author's integrity as he further details other sections of the piece not reprinted in his study.

Smirnov's manuscript description deals with many of the most fundamental notational matters summarized herein: first, curiously, the cover page apparently displays a type of facial caricature under which is included a rather florid insigniature—a clear visual testament to Stravinsky's early fondness for drawing. Indeed, Craft suggests that Stravinsky's early letters "refer less frequently to practicing the piano than to painting. . . ."[32] In an 1899 letter to his parents (and so dating from just about the same time as the "Tarantella"), Stravinsky declares "I have made a sketch of a sunset . . . and would now like to have the opportunity to see a number of good pictures so that I can become even more dissatisfied with my own work," a revealing self-critical sentiment in many ways.[33] Yet while his documented sketching interests might easily be accepted as a component of the "Tarantella" manuscript, the musical notation itself, according to Smirnov, is rather surprising. The sixteen year old Stravinsky's notational efforts, scrawled upon a hand-lined piece of note book paper, are apparently very rough indeed. So primitive are these attempts that Stravinsky seems even to have been unsure of notating correctly such rudiments as the time signature. Smirnov further reports that sections of brief sketches are notably incoherent and scattered about the page without any apparent correlation. At times in fact, the left-hand part is missing altogether. Yet somehow Smirnov suggests that despite the crudeness of the calligraphy, signs of Stravinsky's eventually distinctive hand are very evident, though without an examination of the manuscript itself, such a conclusion, especially given the other contravening facts, seems somewhat suspicious. Examples 1 and 2 are the two transcribed fragments of the "Tarantella" as reprinted in Smirnov's 1970 study.

Some of the most endemic characteristics of a typical tarantella dance are quite identifiable in example 1. As could have been anticipated, these are of the most orthodox nature. The 6/8 meter, as well as the harmonically conceived ostinato of perfect fifths, support the simplest of treble

Example 1.   "Tarantella," mm. 1-6

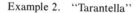

Example 2.   "Tarantella"

patterns. Little more than an elementary familiarity with the dance style is evident. To be sure, the vapidity of any even remotely fresh ideas is perhaps the most distinguishing aspect of these brief six measures. Smirnov does not indicate whether this initial fragment is repeated, extended, or simply isolated. But regardless of its function within the entire piece, these measures are transparently imitative of the folk dance style one can safely assume Stravinsky heard frequently about this time.

Some idea, though little more than a particle, of the harmonic language employed is evident in example 2. In numerous ways this second fragment, taken in apposition with the first, betrays the disjunctive nature of the scattered sketches to which Smirnov refers. Stravinsky's employment of (in order) F natural, F flat, and finally F♯ (bracketed in ex. 2) provides a curious anomaly when compared to the diatonic simplicity apparent in example 1. Yet one must be cautious in prematurely ascribing any refined harmonic control to the young composer based on this single instance. Moreover it is difficult to reconcile the enharmonically structured dominant (spelled F flat, A natural, D flat) occuring on the final pulse of the first measure, which then moves to an area seemingly emphasizing D Major and thus creating a semitone relationship with its auxiliary D Flat chord. Viewed in comparison to the decidedly unexceptional C minor music of the first excerpt, the second fragment assumes a still more suspect hue. Can there be any reasonable explanation for the provenance of this passage other than a rather thinly disguised mimetic attempt to emulate the revered music of Glazunov or Rimsky? Yet if this is the logical conclusion, a study of this imitative effort is not without its own rewards. Based upon even a quick glance, these two fragments easily verify the accuracy of Stravinsky's recollection that "with all the feeble means at my disposal, I assiduously strove to imitate [Rimsky and Glazunov] in my attempts at composition."[34] Stravinsky goes on to admit a particular infatuation with the harmonic palette of Rimsky. Apropos, Smirnov, enjoying a study of the entire manuscript, suggests Stravinsky's understandable desire to replicate as best he could Rimsky's chordal language. Moreover he suggests a similarity between passages of the "Tarantella" and Rimky's opera, *Sadko*. Smirnov speculates, and justifiably it seems, that since Rimsky's recently finished opera had just been published in 1897 in piano reduction, that it is quite possible that the young Stravinsky might have already been familiar with the score. Indeed, it is a plausible theory given the fact that Stravinsky's father played a major role in the original production of the opera, and surely the score went directly into Fyodor's library. That the assimilative musical thirst of the younger Stravinsky could have overlooked the opportunity to study the newly created opera seems unlikely indeed.

The two fragments also offer a clear contrast in the actual pianistic lay of the music. While the first plainly falls within an elementary five-finger pattern, thus averting any need to shift hand position, the second is less gracious. The alternation of the chords in the first measure, amounting only to a D flat chord and its neighbor, is one matter; but the necessity to open quickly the hand position for the D Major chord of the following measure is more difficult, especially given what one would assume to be a fairly quick tarantella pace. Finally, the textural disposition of the inverted D Major chord itself requires a rather extended position and surely reflects the young composer's attempt to reproduce the doublings so common in the musical parlance of his models.

One must of course avoid the temptation to aggrandize this early, inauspicious experiment. Given the brevity of these fragments, it would be unwise to draw anything other than a few simple inferences. Thus, when placed in proper perspective, the "Tarantella" must ultimately be seen as nothing more than a mannered opuscule. Certainly there is nothing whatsoever in these fractional sketches to hint at even a mildly creative incipience. Perhaps, in fact, it is the work's very vacuity, that is, precisely what does not appear, that proves to be most revealing. It is not so much the macaronic attempt to simulate both the compositional formulary employed by Rimsky, as well as a simple peasant dance which is surprising, but rather the unforeseen fashion in which the materials are treated with such apparent callowness. For while the "Tarantella" is easily enough analysed with attention to its obvious faults, one must remember that in view of Stravinsky's espoused musical development from around 1895 onward, it is somewhat odd that such a jejune essay could have been written in 1898. Would not a reasonable expectation have included Stravinsky's ability to manage elementary notational preliminaries, as well as some display of a basic knowledge of developmental techniques, especially given his overtly expressed attraction to improvisation? It is Stravinsky himself who seems to answer these questions in his 1908 Timofeyev letter, written exactly a decade after the "Tarantella."

> The lack of education in theory became even a greater obstacle, however, and though I improvised endlessly and enjoyed it immensely, I was unable to write down what I played. I ascribed this to my lack of theoretical knowledge. Until I began to take lessons in harmony from Akimento, you might say that I ripened in ignorance.[35]

Obviously Stravinsky was aware of his own pronounced shortcomings. Still, with the regular exposure to so much music with which he came in contact through his father, uncle, Pokrovsky, and others, to say nothing of his remarks regarding his early struggle to transcribe a string quartet, the level of competence attained in this little piano piece is quite puzzling. Though we know that by 1898 Stravinsky had been studying piano for several years, establishing with any assurance when the theory lessons to which he refers in the Timofeyev letter began is more difficult to determine. Yet with the "Tarantella" now in hand, it seems very unlikely that on the basis of examining that manuscript, Stravinsky could have initiated his formal theory instruction much earlier than late 1898 or the winter of 1899.

Fyodor Akimento (1876–1945) to whom Stravinsky refers in his letter was to the best of our knowledge his first harmony teacher. A disciple of the new wave of French impressionist music then surfeiting St. Petersburg, Akimento himself was a respected composer, especially with regard to his piano works. With characteristic acerbity, Stravinsky, who seems to have found preterition convenient when it suited him, designates Akimento as an "incompetent pedagogue," though he admits to his own recalcitrance regarding these lessons owing to his "inherent aversion to any dry study."[36] Stravinsky quickly abandoned his work with Akimento and began study with another of Rimsky's pupils, Vasily Kalafaty (1869–1942).

Kalafaty's talents as a teacher of composition were such that he won an appointment to the conservatory faculty in 1900 where he was to become the teacher of Prokofiev. Unlike Akimento, Stravinsky openly admits having profited from his work with this his second theory tutor. Kalafaty's emphasis on contrapuntal exercises proved to be a stimulating discipline for Stravinsky, who apparently had already been pursuing on his own initiative the study of counterpoint prior to these formal lessons.

In remembering his study of counterpoint, Stravinsky assigns an unusual solemnity to this aspect of his theory training, declaring that it laid "the foundation of all of my future technique." But whatever the prominence of counterpoint in Stravinsky's estimate, the value of his work with Kalafaty is undeniable. Just as momentous, perhaps, is the timeliness of Kalafaty's intercession, for his instruction furnished an umbilical line to Stravinsky, nurturing the young composer's ambition at a time when others might have been dissuaded from pursuing composition as a career. In 1901, at the well-intentioned insistence of his parents, Stravinsky matriculated at the university in St. Petersburg where he began a curriculum of legal study.

By his own account, the modicum of interest Stravinsky might have had in the study of law in 1901 began to wane rapidly within a year. At the same time, his interest in music continued to increase and he now seriously contemplated composition as a profession, though there was still little external incentive to do so. A more diligent study of music theory, especially as with the aforementioned contrapuntal lessons under Kalafaty, seems to have gained a regular consumption of time, and it is likely that Stravinsky also expended at least some time now towards free composition. Perhaps the most significant milestone of his university study was the cultivation of a friendship with Vladimir Rimsky-Korsakov, the esteemed composer's younger son. The friendship appears to have been genuine, though one cannot completely rule out some degree of sycophancy on Stravinsky's part. The enterprising young Stravinsky managed to inveigle a meeting with Vladimir's illustrious father sometime during the summer recess of 1902; and there can be little doubt that this encounter marks the most pivotal moment in Stravinsky's aspiring hopes of becoming a composer. Once again, unfortunately, little supporting data has been forthcoming in corroboration of Stravinsky's personal recounting of this meeting.

> I told [Rimsky] of my ambition to become a composer, and asked his advice. He made me play some of my first attempts. Alas! the way in which he received them was far from what I had hoped. Seeing how upset I was, and evidently anxious not to discourage me, he asked if I could play anything else. I did so, of course, and it was then that he gave his opinion.[37]

The content and scope of these first attempts must for now remain unknown. But with the renascent interest in source material retrieval in the Soviet Union, and one hopes its eventual dissemination, perhaps some of these pieces will soon come to light. Even so, based upon what evidence currently exists, a few deductions may be offered.

According to Stravinsky, the portfolio carried to Rimsky's summer estate in Heidelberg included "youthful piano pieces . . . andantes, melodies and so forth."[38] How extensive these piano works were is of course unknown, but it seems improbable that a piece exhibiting the obvious defects of the 1898 "Tarantella" would still have enjoyed a place in Stravinsky's catalogue some four years after its writing. The interim separating the unskilled youth of those days and the student composer of 1902 must have been an eventful one, rapidly changing with the regular and formal learning of fundamental theoretical principles, as well as Stravinsky's continuing exploration of new music. Even an aural appraisal of his aforementioned romance for piano and voice, "Storm Cloud" dating from January 25, 1902, and thus antedating the interview with Rimsky, reveals signs of a fairly quick maturation during this period. This early song demonstrates an assured control of technique and, as one might have anticipated, a certain fluency in writing for the piano. Though the musical ideas are still innately limited and stylized, a firm command in handling these materials is evident. Kalafaty's labors had reaped some success in preparing his student. Moreover it seems reasonable to assume that the piano works Stravinsky played for Rimsky that day were at least as good, if not somewhat improved over "Storm Cloud." Nor is it likely that in his ambition to gain the favor of Rimsky, Stravinsky would offer anything but those pieces which represented him in the most propitious light. Assuming Stravinsky's compositional attempts continued throughout the spring and early summer of 1902, we might then safely equate his most advanced works with his most recent ones. Accordingly, in gaining a window on Stravinsky's progress around that time, it is less crucial to determine the exact pieces represented at that meeting than to evaluate the basic writing style. Thus any music dating from approximately the middle of 1902, either closely before or even immediately following the audition with Rimsky, would at least provide some objectivity in interpreting more reliably Rimsky's reactions as Stravinsky relates them in his own potentially partisan account.

> He [Rimsky] told me that before anything else, I must continue my studies in harmony and counterpoint with one or other of his pupils in order to acquire complete mastery in the schooling of craftsmanship. . . . He finished by adding that I could always go to him for advice, and that he was willing to take me in hand when I had acquired the necessary foundation. Although in my ingenuousness I was somewhat downcast over the lack of enthusiasm the master had shown for my first attempts at composition, I found some comfort in the fact that he had nevertheless advised me to continue my studies, and so demonstrated his opinion that I had sufficient ability to devote myself to a musical career.[39]

These often quoted remarks are replete with unsubstantiated implications of considerable import in accounting for Stravinsky's acceptance into Rimsky's charmed circle. What was meant by sufficient ability? Sufficient enough so that a career change could have been seriously contemplated? Until recently, the paramountcy of this issue could only be viewed in a type of historical vacuum. Without any primary source, and specifically without any music dating from around that summer, no accurate means existed by which one could measure Rimsky's critical assessment, or test the veracity of Stravinsky's interpretation of these remarks. Fortunately, with the publication of Smirnov's research, some progress may be made in clarifying Rimsky's comments. A short piano work entitled Scherzo, unknown until the 1970s, has survived. Dated 1902, it provides the primary source so desperately needed to undertake a fuller study of the events that transpired around the time of Stravinsky's first meeting with Rimsky, as well as furnishing the opportunity to begin examining Stravinsky's early approach to a pianism that will eventually be shown to be notably individualistic.

2

The Preballet Piano Literature

It is for now impossible to determine precisely at what point in 1902 the Scherzo was written. In his editorial preface to the Faber publication of the work in 1973, Stravinsky's biographer, Eric Walter White, suggests that the work might well have been one of those youthful piano pieces that Stravinsky played for Rimsky at Heidelberg that summer.[1] While this contention is quite feasible, its validity remains unconfirmed. Smirnov offers an alternate view, identifying the Scherzo as a post-Heidelberg composition. Specifically, he suggests July to November as a *terminus a quo*; but his justification in so asserting seems almost as tenuous as White's. Smirnov does offer one corroborative fact: it seems that the young Stravinsky presented the autograph manuscript of the Scherzo to the pianist Nicolas Richter in January 1903, though Smirnov does not inform his readers just how he arrived at this determination. If in fact this chronology is accurate, it might lend stronger weight to a later rather than earlier date of composition in 1902; for why would Stravinsky have waited so long to offer the work to his friend if in fact the Scherzo had been completed six or seven months earlier?

    The manuscript, signed and dated by Stravinsky, bears the dedication "A Monsieur Nicolas Richter, temoignage d'un profond respect de la part de l'auteur." It was to be the first of several such tributes to a pianist who remained an ardent supporter of Stravinsky's earliest piano works. The 1903–04 Piano Sonata in F$^\sharp$ minor, and the second of the *Four Studies,* Opus 7 (1908), were also to be dedicated to Richter who in fact premiered the Piano Sonata at one of the Evenings of Contemporary Music (the well-known concert series expressly structured to feature the music of young Russian composers). However there is nothing to indicate that Richter or even Stravinsky himself publicly performed the Scherzo on this series; nor does Yastrebtzev in his *Recollections of Rimsky-Korsakov, Volume II* (Moscow, 1962), mention this work as having been offered at one of Rimsky's weekly composition gatherings joined by

Plate 1. Piano Scherzo (1902), from V. Smirnov's *Tvorcheskoe formirovanie I.F. Stravinskogo*

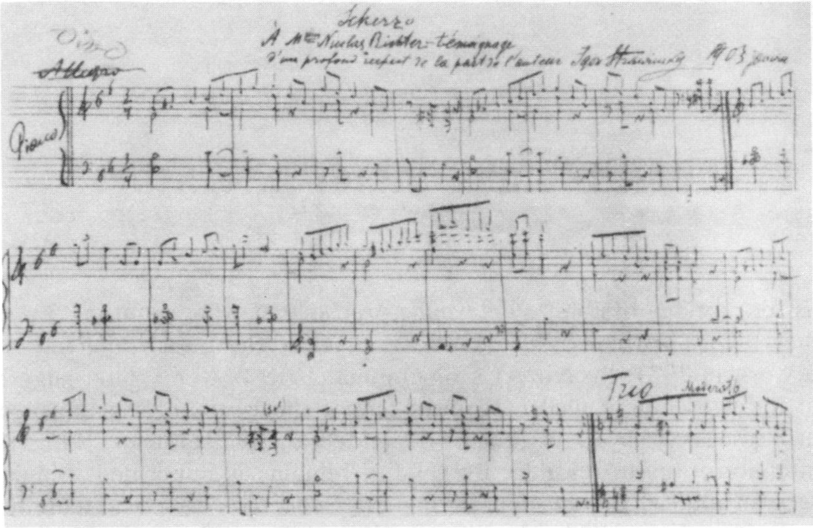

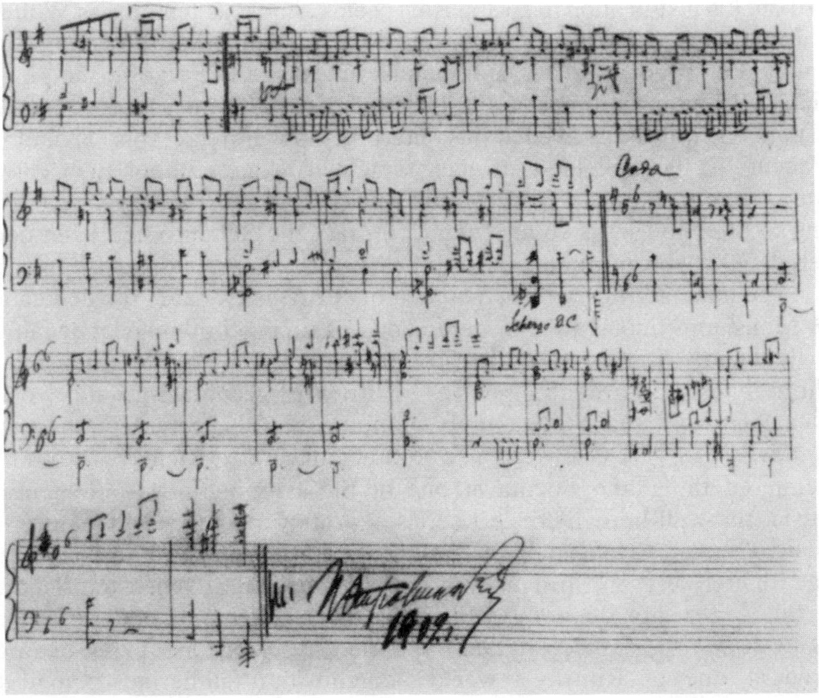

Library of Congress, Music Division

Stravinsky in early 1903. The original tempo as marked on the manuscript was allegro, though it was later altered to vivo. White suggests that Richter might have made the change, a distinct possibility to be sure, though again this must remain a matter of speculation. The revised tempo marking, however, does not appear to be in Stravinsky's hand. Otherwise, the manuscript is extremely clean and sparsely marked. As evident in examining plate 1, neither phrase delineation nor dynamics are indicated.[2]

As with both the early "Tarantella" and "Storm Cloud," this first complete piano opus heavily relies upon the musically mundane traits of Stravinsky's Russian models. Smirnov, in an effort to trace specific sources, suggests the G major refrain from the third act dance of *Ruslan and Liudmilla* (just after rehearsal #49 according to Smirnov). Stravinsky's admiration of Glinka was of course sincere, and there was little attempt to conceal this adulation in his own opera *Mavra*. But any such quotational appropriation in this Scherzo is all but untenable. If there is a wellspring from which this little piece emerges, surely it is Tchaikovsky whose spirit permeates nearly every gesture. While Stravinsky's fondness of Tchaikovsky's piano literature was eventually to be manifested most openly in the 1928 ballet *Le Baiser de la Fée,* there is little doubt that the revered composer's aureole began to influence the impressionable young Stravinsky at a very early point indeed. It is Nabokov again, in his biography of Stravinsky, who speaks in some detail of the way in which Tchaikovsky was championed by the Stravinsky family, and how to a considerable extent Stravinsky instinctively stored the compositional immanence of this music.[3]

But unlike the 1898 "Tarantella" in which blatant borrowing is obvious (if also expatiable), there does not appear to be any specific thematic or harmonic quotation evident in this 1902 work. Rather, as would become a common modus operandi in many of Stravinsky's later works, there is a refashioning of some fundamentally Tchaikovskyan conventions, which through a brief comparison may be easily adduced. Excerpts from two pieces of the Tchaikovsky piano literature, pieces that in all likelihood were known to Stravinsky and his mother, are offered below, along with two sections drawn from Stravinsky's Scherzo.

Example 3 reproduces the codetta of this short piece. Perhaps most perceptible is the continuous pedal figure functioning as a structural underpinning and bringing some degree of unity to the closing section as it reaffirms the G major tonality. A similar approach is adopted in the Scherzo's parallel close, as shown in example 4.

Also relatable are the circled measures of each excerpt. As the diminished seventh sonority of the Tchaikovsky embellishes the closing harmonic progression, so, too, does Stravinsky's striking use of the al-

Example 3.   Tchaikovsky, "Priere du Matin," Opus 39, No. 1 (1878)

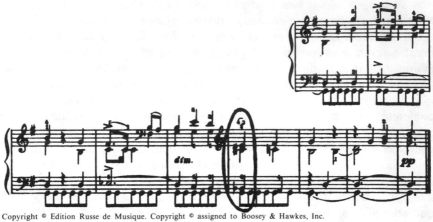

tered dominant, especially by virtue of its agogic accent, heighten the
expectation of a final cadential drive. This French augmented sixth chord,
obviously appropriated from the harmonic vocabulary of the day, was to
become a mainstay in Stravinsky's apprentice works, particularly in such
early pieces as the 1906 *Le Faune et la Bergère* and the 1908 *Pastorale*.

Example 4.   Stravinsky, Scherzo, mm. 71-85

In examining the coda of the Stravinsky, surely one cannot fail to recognize numerous unpianistic configurations. There is indeed an unmistakable orchestral flavor throughout the work, especially in this concluding section. The beginning left-hand gesture as illustrated immediately stratifies two layers of the pedal point, not unlike a typical division of orchestral strings. Even the notation of the figure betrays such a possibility, for the repetition of the upper left-hand pitch D by the printed stroke is by no means a common pianistic notation. The textural disposition of the right hand is no less awkward with its unidiomatic chordal spacing, necessitating a rather quick shifting of hand positions if indeed such chords as the final ones of measures 73 and 75 can be accommodated at all. In many such unconventional ways, this score has the look of a reduction, though of course the fact that it is an authentic piano work is verifiable. Thus if such an early example can be taken as representative of Stravinsky's pianism, a study of the later orchestral reductions for piano may take on an analytic significance unexplored to this point (and a matter to be pursued in the final chapter of this study).

Similarities between Tchaikovsky's "Scherzo a la Russe," and the trio of Stravinsky's own Scherzo also are clear, though they should not be taken too far. Still, certain motivic techniques are shared (see exx. 5 and 6).

Example 5.   Tchaikovsky, "Scherzo a la Russe" (1867)

Example 6.   Stravinsky, Scherzo, mm. 27-35

Reprinted by permission of Faber Music Ltd., London.

In each case the primary motive is a linearly expressed third. The subsequent repetition, extension and overlapping are apparent, and in the Stravinsky Scherzo provide a harbinger of techniques soon to be employed in other more well-known early works, especially as in the opening of the 1908 *Fireworks, Opus 4.* Similar, too, is the motivic migration of this same melodic third between the hands. In the Scherzo this migration has a special formal significance, for it inosculates the separate sections of the bipartite structure in this trio. The E-F#-G third of measure 28 in the right hand eventuates in measure 31 as a nexus, binding together this second half of the trio:moderato. More importantly perhaps, this motive is clearly a derivative of the Scherzo's principal motive stated at the work's outset and exploited throughout the earlier section of the entire work (refer again to pl. 1). Such elementary attempts at a motivic integration clearly promote an architectural concrescence even in a brief work such as this, and signal Stravinsky's awareness of the need for bringing formal cohesion to sectionally structured forms—an awareness that is surely traceable to his careful study of his models. Finally, one observes a shared rhythmic fabric between the Tchaikovsky and Stravinsky motives. The commonality of this *melos* once again probably owes its origins not only to Stravinsky's affinity for the Tchaikovskyan literature, but to other Russian exemplars as well; for example in *Prince Igor* where an identical motive is pervasive.

The harmonic and melodic materials of the Scherzo further reflect the musical language of these same paragons—a language that was *de rigueur* for any young emulative composer. But beyond this anticipated reliance, the technical adroitness of this eighty-five-measure *salonstück,* as White dubs it, cannot be missed. For whatever eclectic characteristics the work displays, characteristics that in this embryonic stage cannot be viewed as imperfections, Stravinsky shapes his materials skillfully, though academically, in the St. Petersburg tradition—a tradition that deified Beethoven and his heirs.

Indeed, for Anton Rubinstein, the founding director of first the Russian Musical Society, then in 1862 the St. Petersburg Conservatory itself, which seems to have begun as a pedagogic wing of the society, it was Beethoven who provided the beacon in a Western European music curriculum. Moreover, during the first decade of the conservatory's existence, the vast majority of its faculty itself was non-Russian.[4] One also notes that Tchaikovsky himself was a member of the first graduating class in 1865, winning the coveted free artist societal standing so sought after.[5] In 1871 Rimsky joined the faculty, thus forging another link between the dual influences of academicism and nationalism, influences that clearly surface in Stravinsky's early works and to some extend even beyond.[6] In this regard the Scherzo's coda particularly suggests an ectomorphic, Beethovenian appearance. Not only is this true by virtue of the aforementioned motivic integration, but more importantly, it is evident by the deeper, psychomusical levels of its expectations, delayed resolutions, and in general the expressed concern with architectonic matters.

Yet of all the parameters to be investigated, none is more revealing than the Scherzo's rhythmic and metric dimensions. It is in this arena that Stravinsky's compositional promise emerges most clearly. Even without the retrieval of this work, one might have guessed an early Stravinskyan penchant for rhythmic imagination. Alfred Cortot, one of the more reliable commentators of the day, suggests that Stravinsky's rhythmic intricacies were precisely what most aroused Rimsky's interest in the young composer's first compositions.[7] As an example, consider the opening four measures of the work, reproduced in example 7.

Example 7.   Scherzo, mm. 1-4

Reprinted by permission of Faber Music Ltd., London.

Certainly the hemiola in itself is far from unprecedented; but its suddenness at the very outset of the work is at least resourceful if nothing else. Moreover, in conjunction with the subsequent use of punctuating rests, a series of syncopes results. Thus when heard contextually, the overall metric ambiguity of this phrase is greatly enhanced. Particularly noticeable are those telling silences that Stravinsky inserts unexpectedly even here at such an early phase of his yet probably untutored compositional development. The harmonic rhythm of this same phrase is also an important contributing factor to this initial gesture. One would quite normally perceive the first pulse of measure one as the presumed tonic though Stravinsky quickly beclouds this issue. The passing A flat, when taken with its adjacent pitch neighbors in the right hand, suggests a phrygian inflection, though it would be wrong to assume that modality is of any major consideration in this work. In hindsight, the first chord appears to function as a submediant, but more importantly, it propels the passage into an ambiguous harmonic realm whose resolution remains undetermined until the very close of the phrase in measure four. Thus, all facets of the gesture are purposefully unsettling, and at this microformal level at least, prove to be clever if not especially innovative.

More importantly, the suspense of this opening phrase is prolonged over half of the initial section of the Scherzo's tripartite structure. Not until measure 13 does the meter settle into a rhythmically unencumbered, stable ternary pattern. Maintaining this metric deception over such a proportionately long period before defining the actual meter is in architectural terms a relatively sophisticated idea for a young, inexperienced composer. It is conceivable, though questionable, that Stravinsky intended to employ a hemiola figure per se, or for that matter even understood the theoretical meaning of the term. But even if we were to assume that he did, it is still more dubious that as a 20-year-old novice he would know anything about such architectonic issues as "the law of good continuation," as Meyer calls it, or realized the psychology of the musical event he had created in this opening passage. The resultant intricacy of the rhythmic, metric, and harmonic design was surely not contemplated in any precompositional sense. More likely, Stravinsky had probably encountered similar passages in the music with which he was most familiar and simply sensed the freshness of the sound as a splendid way of delaying metric clarity and thus creating an effect. Selecting aurally attractive ideas that through their own usage had become synonomous with a particular musical style seems always to have been the first stage of Stravinsky's assimilative process. He quickly transplanted these germinal seeds into his own musical soil; and in recognizing this, one of course quickly grasps one of the basic tenets of his compositional approach. Finally, while little of this transmutational process is to be perceived in the Scherzo, nonetheless some of the fundamental aspects of the language to be eventually transformed are already quite apparent.

It is of course unfortunate that only this single complete piano work survives from this formative period. Still, is there any reason to assume that other pieces written about the same time would have been significantly different? If then, this Scherzo may be taken as an embodiment of Stravinsky's compositional achievement during or around the summer of 1902, what was it that may have prompted Rimsky to encourage the young aspirant to pursue composition professionally? In addressing such compositional relationships as those already discussed, one recalls Stravinsky's witticism regarding the analyst's phobia for "thickly bespectacled hindsight." Yet our own historical perspective permits us a decidedly clearer vantage than Rimsky could have enjoyed. We recognize retrospectively, as of course Rimsky could not, that some of the crude ideas apparent here were to blossom, being refined in the process, and mature as some of the most familiar constructs in the Stravinskyan method.

With these considerations in mind, certain questions naturally arise. Owing to Rimsky's professional association as well as personal friendship with Stravinsky's father, might Rimsky's encouragement have been factitiously motivated if not by nepotism at least by a sense of diplomacy? Stravinsky himself mentions that his father had prepared a letter of introduction that, along with his portfolio of compositions, the young composer carried to his meeting with Rimsky in Heidelberg that summer.[8] It is known that Rimsky chose not to mention Stravinsky's name in his autobiographical *My Musical Life.* In his own *Chroniques de Ma Vie,* Stravinsky quickly dismisses this as an understandable and wise decision made by Rimsky to avoid showing favoritism to any of his students. While Stravinsky's interpretation might first be seen as a cloak aimed at concealing his disappointment, a recently released letter from V. Belsky to Stravinsky, dated November 1928 and so received before Stravinsky's above explanation, does indeed suggest that Stravinsky's assessment of Rimsky's omission may have been correct.

> . . . You play an enormous role in music, and this role was appreciated by another of my unforgettable friends, Nicolai Andreyevich [Rimsky-Korsakov], who doted on you, as you well know. Despite the miserly grip he kept on his favorable opinion, he continually recommended your new works to me, and I recall that he once pronounced to me adamantly: "Igor Stravinsky may be my pupil, but he will never be my or anyone else's follower, because his gift for music is uniquely great and original."[9]

Such indications suggest that Rimsky was at least predisposed to accept Stravinsky as a member of his class. At any rate it would be dangerous to conclude that mere patronization was the overriding factor in reaching his decision. Regardless of personal or professional affiliations, Rimsky's magisterial reputation as a rather harsh critic, not easily inclined to offer casual praise or to acquiesce to external pressure, is, as expressed in the Belsky letter, a matter of documentation. Cortot, too, speaks to this, stating that "Rimsky-Korsakov's judgement was generally practiced without compliance, much to the terror of those who were bold enough to solicit it."[10] More than likely, then, it was the sum of many factors, none the least of which was the identification of at least some potential merit in Stravinsky's first works, that cautiously led Rimsky to encourage the youth to continue with lessons.

Finally, there is a marked similarity to be noted between Stravinsky's development around this time and that of Rimsky's at a similar point in his own youthful career. Rimsky himself acknowledges his ignorance of the most basic compositional fundamentals even at the moment of his appointment to the conservatory in 1871. In fact, Rimsky turned to none other than Tchaikovsky for help in his attempt, as Ridenour observes, "to stay a week or two ahead of his pupils."[11] Moreover, like Stravinsky, Rimsky was a pianist first and was interested in artistic areas beyond his immediate musical environment. He then, perhaps more than many pedagogues of such stature, could at least have appreciated Stravinsky's background and been able to distinguish, in the Scherzo for example, between what constituted inexperience as opposed to ineptitude. In later years Stravinsky was often to impugn his early training, complaining that "I was handicapped in my earliest years by the influences that restrained the growth of my composer's technique. I refer to the St. Petersburg Conservatory's formalism. . . ."[12] To be sure it was not until after Rimsky's death that Stravinsky was fully liberated from what he had perceived to be Rimsky's philistinism.

It was during the spring of 1903 that Stravinsky began attending the weekly master classes held by Rimsky for his composition students. According to Yastrebtzev, Stravinsky was at first only an observer rather than a participant. Whatever he was writing around that time presumably is lost or at least still unavailable. It is not until the early summer of the same year that the charting of Stravinsky's compositional development may be resumed. As with the 1902 Scherzo and "Tarantella" fragments before, it is again a piano work that marks the next important plateau in these formative years. In a letter of June 16, 1903, written from his uncle's estate in Pavlovka, Stravinsky mentions his ongoing devotion to painting and drawing. But he also writes of his satisfaction with progess accomplished on his most recent composition, a piano sonata. The work to which he refers is the Piano Sonata in F# minor, feared lost or destroyed until fairly recently. Like the Scherzo, the Sonata was published in the early 1970s by Faber, along with annotations by White.[13] As the work is viewed now, this 30-minute Sonata smacks of a concocted pomposity, overflowing in its near canonical recitation of most every romantically pianistic ingredient imaginable. Since only a short period of time separates this work from the 1902 Scherzo, one might have anticipated that this later effort would reflect some of those adumbrative Beethovenian glimpses originally exhibited in the Scherzo's coda. In later years Stravinsky himself vaguely recalled the Sonata as an inept imitation of late Beethoven. But this is an *ignis fatuus* if ever there was one, for there is very little indeed that builds from such stock.

More importantly, this Sonata, like so many of Stravinsky's piano works, marks an important historical division in the composer's life. It is with the writing of this work that his regular study with Rimsky may be dated. As he had done the year before, Stravinsky consulted his soon-to-be mentor regarding his new composition.

> In this work I was constantly confronted with many difficulties, especially in matters of form, the mastery of which is usually acquired only after prolonged study, and my

perplexities suggested the idea of my consulting Rimsky-Korsakov again. I went to see him in the country at the end of the summer of 1903, and stayed with him for about a fortnight. He made me compose the first part of a sonatina under his supervision, after having instructed me in the principles of the allegro of a sonata.[14]

Unfortunately, the sonatina appears to have been lost; nor may the extent and nature of Rimsky's guidance be ascertained. However, in his March 8, 1908, letter to Timofeyev, Stravinsky specifically refers to the Sonata in F# minor as a large four-movement work that incorporated "many suggestions by Rimsky-Korsakov."[15] The fact that the Sonata was not completed until the following summer, 1904, and that to our knowledge no other major work dates from this period, suggests that the project consumed Stravinsky's attention and that perhaps Rimsky's counsel was fairly substantive, perhaps even requiring the young composer to revise sections of the work.[16]

Like the 1902 Scherzo, the Sonata is dedicated to Richter, as mentioned earlier. It was he who premiered the composition on February 9, 1905, at one of the periodic meetings of Rimsky's class. Andre Schaeffner, one of Stravinsky's earliest biographers, indicates that the manuscript was given to Richter by Stravinsky as a gesture of gratitude. More importantly, Richter later introduced the work to the highly visible Evenings of Contemporary Music, thereby marking the first known public performance of a Stravinsky opus.

Some of the earliest documents that in one way or another deal with the biographical vitae of Stravinsky's life mention the Sonata, though usually just in passing. In his 1930 monograph, Paul Collaer lists four movements: I. Allegro, II. Andante, III. Scherzo, IV. Final; Collaer also names both Samara and St. Petersburg as the locations at which the work was written. But the manuscript reveals that the scherzo is second in order and that the andante leads attacca into the final. More recent commentators have unhappily conceded the disappearance of this work, though Stravinsky preferred to think of the composition as the "fortunately lost" Sonata. Its rediscovery stems from Balanchine's commemoration of Stravinsky's contribution to the ballet world in the New York City Ballet's tribute, mounted during the summer of 1972. Clive Barnes reported that though efforts to obtain a score from the Soviet Union met with failure, Mrs. Andre Malraux "remembered a facsimile of the score [and] offered to play the second movement, a scherzo, from memory."[17]

Having written only short piano pieces to this point, it was perfectly logical that Stravinsky should now proceed to the challenge of bringing structural cohesion to a larger musical form. Moreover, the writing of a piano sonata was quite a normal assignment in every composer's novitiate.

Thus the "classical bent" in this sonata mentioned by Roman Vlad was surely predictable as a natural consequence of Stravinsky's study with Rimsky. Surely his teacher's inculcation of his own severely classic inclinations doubtlessly affected Stravinsky as it would have any of his students.

Tchaikovsky's Sonata in G Major, Opus 37, written in 1878, was published in 1903 by Jurgenson, the same publisher who would soon engrave Stravinsky's first works, and the similarity between this work and the Stravinsky Piano Sonata is clear. The piano technique required by each work is also alike. Indeed, Stravinsky's pianistic facility raced in advance of his compositional abilities and so while the creative ideas are still at best uneven, the keyboard writing at times exhibits a thorough conversance with the *pro forma* pianism of the day. Thirds, sixths, octaves, and an abundant use of densely compiled chords permeate the work. In texture alone, the difference between the Sonata and the only slightly earlier Scherzo is nothing short of astounding. Particularly in this regard, the spirit of Tchaikovsky is especially present. Moreover, Stravinsky's keyboard style frequently conveys specific textural stratifications that are clearly more conducive to an orchestral realization than a pianistic one (as was true of the Scherzo). If his performance directives are to be interpreted literally, example 8, excerpted from the andante of the Sonata, is virtually unmanageable.

Example 8.   Sonata in F# minor, Andante, mm. 75-77

Reprinted by permission of Faber Music Ltd., London.

The three distinct layers of sound illustrated in the excerpt demand three separate touches. If the sempre staccato is to be strictly heeded, then the damper pedal could not be applied in the passage. Thus not only the ornamental inner layer, but also the uppermost voice, including Stravinsky's phrase delineations, would need to be completely sustained by the fingers without the pedal's aid. Even if Stravinsky, at least at this point of his development, employed the sempre staccato direction as a loosely envisaged performance suggestion, the idea of texturally partitioning the multilayered passage still rests at the musical core of these measures.

By his own admission, Stravinsky chose to consult Rimsky because of the structural problems he was encountering in his attempt to deal with a large, traditional, normative form. Given the aforementioned shortcomings of this work, which in all fairness was Stravinsky's first formidable composition assignment, the opening allegro at least successfully follows the guidelines one customarily associates with the sonata-allegro form. Everything is as it should be: contrasting themes, the proper transitional phrases, an unexceptional but nonetheless structurally conformable development, and even a 30-measure coda that first enlists the movement's opening motive as a unifying device, then finally gives way to a concluding passage, as reprinted in example 9, again reminiscent of the Tchaikovskyan style.

Example 9.   Sonata, Allegro (Coda)

Reprinted by permission of Faber Music Ltd., London.

As in this opening allegro, the other three movements follow the structural format normally associated with their respective macroformal schemes. The second movement, marked vivo, is a scherzo; the andante employs a large three-part form; and the final is a modified rondo. Rather than outline the broad formal outlines of each movement, several representative passages drawn from the interior of each movement, wherein the formal strictures are by nature not so rigid, are offered. Beginning with the final (ex. 10), the transitory passage leading to this closing movement's coda, as well as a portion of the coda itself, are first given.

Example 10.   Sonata, Final, mm. 310-341

Example 10 furnishes a typical display of Stravinsky's harmonic vocabulary and the architectural means by which his ideas are extended.
The harmonic transformation in measures 310-317 of the dominant seventh sonority into a French augmented sixth (enharmonically misspelled)
remained a banality throughout the St. Petersburg years. In the later
works of his apprenticeship with Rimsky, works which by increment owe
more to Stravinsky's invention than to his teacher's, the actual usage of
the same chord types becomes noticably more skillful. In *Le Faune et la
Bergère,* for example,the extraction and subsequent extension of the tritone originally encased in the augmented sixth chord now serves a more
organic function in generating a unified transition, and in so doing already
prefigures many of the transitional sections of the later ballets (ex. 11).

Example 11. *Le Faune et la Bergère*, Opus 2, No. 2 (piano reduction)

Le Faune reflects the deepening effects of the new French music on Stravinsky's post-Sonata compositions. As Stravinsky's compositional horizons expanded, Rimsky's condemnation of what in his parochial estimate was a potentially deleterious musical style held less and less authority. Yet in the Sonata, written only two years before *Le Faune*, there is yet no overt signal of Stravinsky's eventual remonstrance of what he then considered to be his teacher's sancrosanct pedagogy.

The coda of the Sonata, beginning at measure 318 and based upon the primary thematic material of the final, initiates a harmonic sequence revolving around third related movements so common to the Balakirev tradition. A second sequence built upon an equally prosaic harmonic pattern marks the return of the movement's F# major tonality at measure 334. All of these seemingly interminable sequences, through their pedestrian symmetry, ultimately bring about the architectural demise of whatever limited impact the music might have had. The unabated chain of such sequences creates little thrust towards achieving the movement's climax. Compounding this structural weakness is the debilitative fact that example 10 represents only the first third of this 73-bar coda. No less than five additional sequences, all erected upon the grounds of uninventively employed, harmonically tedious stereotypes, contribute to the tumidity of the Sonata's close. In the 1902 Scherzo's coda, the sequence laden, harmonically restricted material was still sufficient to support this more modest work's high point; indeed, it suggested an architectural promise that languishes in the grander proposition of the Sonata. In this respect, Stravinsky's failure is not unlike that of Tchaikovsky's in his own G Major Sonata; for ultimately, the orotund piano virtuosity of each composer's work cannot disguise the tottery structural foundation upon which the music is built.

In approaching this Sonata, surely one of the problems that Stravinsky had to confront was the matter of unifying disparate musical ideas, a concern that was obviously less of an issue in his earlier and more limited piano pieces. Each of the Sonata's four movements' numerous transitional sections provides the opportunity to study the early strengths and weaknesses of Stravinsky's structural control. While some sections, such as the coda just discussed, must be judged inadequate, others are more successful. Especially revealing is the examination of the andante's initial theme, its employment in subsequent sections of the movement, and as a coadunative means of access to the attacca final. Example 12 reproduces the theme at its first appearance.

Example 12.   Sonata, Andante, mm. 1-6

The harmonic and melodic materials, including a profusion of appoggiature hovering above the bass note D, are once again firmly entrenched in the late-nineteenth-century nationalist style. Repetition provides the only means of propulsion. More germane in the architectural scheme is the fragment marked x that serves as the principal transitional motive (see ex. 13). As the first section of this ternary movement closes, it is this same motive that reappears.

A canonic duplet form of this melodic seventh as employed in measures 47-48, next gives way to a slightly altered version of the motive's second cell in measures 49-52, labeled y. The left-hand figure, which directionally mirrors this y cell, is identical to the opening three measures of the andante. The return of the motive's principal x cell, now texturally expanded in measures 53-56, leads directly into the central section of this tripartite movement.

Certainly this elementary motivic fragmentation provided one of the most obvious means of structurally fastening contrasting sections; nor is such a usage surprising since the earlier Scherzo already demonstrates Stravinsky's awareness of motivic integration as a means of unification. But this particular case goes a step beyond: the rhythmic framework supporting the transition also significantly strengthens the elision by a type of motivic metamorphosis. The sixteenth-note figure of measure 44 is retained in the next measure while the principal motive in its fragmented state is announced. This sixteenth-note movement had already evolved as a basic accompanimental pattern earlier in the first section. Thus an over-

Example 13. Sonata, Andante, mm. 42-58

Reprinted by permission of Faber Music Ltd., London.

lapping of two fundamental rhythmic layers occurs. More importantly, the rhythmic fragmentation of the constant sixteenth-note pattern begins to appear in measure 45 immediately after the *x* motive marked in example 13. The reconstruction of the regularity of the sixteenth-note motion reappears in measure 56 after a nine-measure absence, but now is seen in reverse order of the original presentation, that is, a quadruplet of sixteenths followed by the sextuplet on the second pulse of the measure. Also, the sextuplet presages the basic rhythmic figure of the ensuing central section, further joining the first and second sections of this overall three-part form.

The notational placement of the metric change from 6/8 to 2/4 at measure 49 is informative. The adjustment might have been made two measures earlier. Could it be that by delaying the shift for two measures and thereby necessitating the motive's duplet notation, Stravinsky wishes to create the impression of a rhythmic evolution, even though this alteration really amounts to a visual illusion? Such a subtlety, especially in combination with the fragmentation and reconstruction of the motive's rhythmic constitution, may suggest a growing sensitivity to the deliberate pacing of the constituent phases of a large work's transitional seams.

As this transition connects the internal sections of the andante's tripartite structure, so, too, does this same material provide an architectural bond between this third movement and the final. Both in its linear and rhythmic dimensions, the closing material of the andante is clearly derived from the passage just discussed in example 13. In successive stages, this same material that of course had originated from the very opening of the andante now evolves into the principal theme of the closing movement. The first of this transformation's three metamorphic phases is offered in example 14.

Example 14.   Sonata, Andante, mm. 145-153

Reprinted by permission of Faber Music Ltd., London.

The pitch direction of both lines in measures 146-147 is analogous to the previously labeled *y* cell in example 13. The left-hand material is identical to that of the opening of the andante. The most significant aspect of change is what may first appear to be an inappreciable alteration, viz. the introduction of the dotted eighth and sixteenth figure in measure 146. Through the process of diminution, the idea is continued as it migrates to the left hand in measure 148. The derivation of this motive from the pitch content of the previous measure's bass line provides yet another link. Next, in examining example 15, the relationship of these ideas to the second phase of the transition becomes clear.

The continuance of what is destined to be the unifying rhythmic motive of the dotted figure established in example 15, and as observed in other parts of the Sonata, are now sequentially extended and texturally expanded. The poco a poco agitato heralds the final phase of the transition

Example 15.   Sonata, Andante, mm. 154-161

as it swells pianistically to the allegro final. The incipit of this final exhibits both a linear and rhythmic bond with the transitional motive; for though the rhythmic values are now doubled, the pulse remains constant because of the gradually accelerating tempo. Moreover a similarity between the opening motives of this fourth movement and that of the opening allegro exists in that both share common rhythmic and melodic properties (ex. 16).

Example 16.   Sonata, Andante and Final (transition)

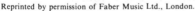

Such motivic transformations seem somewhat contrived and stamp this Sonata as a student effort. Yet in placing the work in historical perspective, one must look beyond the transience of chromatic dominants, the strained use of motives too overburdened to be structurally effective and the ubiquitously employed, cliché-ridden harmonic sequences. The fundamental tools used by any increasingly aware composer in engineering a more formidable compositional proposition such as this Sonata are, if at times unpolished, still operative. Indeed, motivic extraction, fragmentation, and overlapping were, in a more finely honed state of course, to endure long after Stravinsky shed the mantle of this early decadent style of piano writing.

While each of the Sonata's movements share the shortcomings of his inexperience, the second movement, vivo, in some important respects rises above the work's general mediocrity. Specifically, this obtains in the movement's classic scherzo-trio plan. The writing is more pianistic, the rhythmic dimension fresher, and the motivic employment more assuredly handled. Again it is especially the spirit of Tchaikovsky that imbues the movement with a buoyancy not to be found in the three more weighty movements of the work. Example 17 reprints the opening gesture.

Example 17.   Sonata, Vivo, mm. 1-24

Reprinted by permission of Faber Music Ltd., London.

Perhaps most conspicuous is the notated duple rather than more orthodox triple meter for this scherzo. Additionally, the rhythmic grouping of the principal motive into four note groups enhances a degree of temporal ambiguity not unlike that encountered in the opening measures of the 1902 Scherzo. There is also a more compelling motivic direction in these first measures, culminating with the agogically accented G$^\sharp$ of measure five. It is, in fact, just this kind of directional thrust that goes largely wanting in the thematic architecture of the other three movements. Moreover, several structurally vital compositional seams are negotiated here with a deftness not seen elsewhere in the Sonata. The elision of measures 13 and 14, uniting the close of the principal theme and its renewal by repetition, provides just such an instance. Here the final E of measure 13 serves a dual function; not only is it the expected resolution of the four-note pitch set that had been rising and falling regularly in the immediately prior bars, it also ushers in the theme's renewal as well. Even this ensuing repetition outstrips the rather pedantic use of others that plague so many passages in the overall work. The arpeggiated bass line of measures 17-22 provide a subtle but nonetheless effective variation of the idea's original appearance in measures 5-11. Finally, the trio section (ex. 18), though it is not marked as such, suggests yet another instance of Stravinsky's early affinity for rhythmic and metric equivocalness.

Example 18.   Sonata, Vivo, mm. 146-151

Reprinted by permission of Faber Music Ltd., London.

The institution of the triple meter provides a point of contrast to the earlier duple pattern; but Stravinsky appears to add another stratagem. For if the performer heedfully executes the composer's carefully drawn phrase delineations, each of the two principal divisions illustrated in the passage will create a quarter note grouping of 4 + 5 instead of what normally would be the perceptually expected 3 + 3 + 3 pattern. As in the 1902 Scherzo, such delusions, particularly at this early formative stage, are surely the product of an intended capriciousness, and like other emulative aspects, learned more by example than anything else. But still, this movement more than the other three, seems more genial, more *dégagé*, in a fashion much like Stravinsky's later and more mature scherzo works. One notes, for example, the success of such later, though still preballet compositions, as the *Scherzo Fantastique* and *Fireworks*. Also, in evaluating his student's early Symphony in E Flat, Rimsky, while providing considerable revisional suggestions for three of the work's four movements, had little to say about the writing of the scherzo section.

In many ways, the same structural principles that were first tested at the piano in the F# minor Sonata were to be applied immediately to this Opus 1 Symphony, begun in 1905 and completed two years later. With this work, Rimsky's instruction turned predominantly to matters of instrumentation. But even so, the piano remained the central vehicle in Stravinsky's instruction. It is not surprising that the surviving composing score should be for two pianos since Rimsky encouraged Stravinsky to work at the keyboard.[18] In this score, Rimsky's critical remarks are most often penciled in and offer not only advice in regard to instrumentation, but occasionally suggest ideas for the recasting of melodic lines and textural matters. Indeed this early two-piano score of the Symphony was in Stravinsky's opinion worthy of being published on its own strength, as he would often conclude with other piano scores of his later orchestral works. In a letter to Rimsky dated July 1, 1907, Stravinsky, who here seeks advice about the publication of the Symphony, informs his mentor that he had just written to the son of H. J. Zimmerman, a potential publisher, suggesting that "they purchase the whole work, the orchestra as well as the piano, though it was understood that only the piano score would be published."[19]

Stravinsky's study with Rimsky continued until his teacher's death in June, 1908. Though we have come to associate this student-teacher relationship as one primarily founded upon Rimsky's imparting of the principles of orchestration, in fact his influence extended in other directions as well. Stravinsky's 1908 *Fireworks,* a work which Rimsky did not live to hear (though he was familiar with Stravinsky's plans for this important piece), embraces in large part an octatonic pitch vocabulary, reflecting Rimsky's own interests in symmetrically constructed pitch collections towards the end of his own compositional career. About the same time, Stravinsky's continued devotion to the keyboard now produced a genuine set of piano pieces worthy of remaining in the repertoire, and also destined to be his first published opus.

The *Four Studies,* Opus 7, are authentic concert etudes, born of the virtuoso metier and demanding a considerably mature pianistic technique. They were composed in Ustilug the summer of 1908 where Stravinsky had been spending this time of year since his marriage in 1906 to Catherine Gabrielovna Nossenko. It was in fact in 1908 that they built their own home, whereupon Stravinsky moved his favorite Bechstein piano from St. Petersburg to this summer residence. Each etude is inscribed to a friend who had occupied an important role in Stravinsky's St. Petersburg life: the first in C minor is dedicated to Stephan Stepanovich Mitusov, the co-librettist for *Le Rossignol,* the opera begun that same summer in Ustilug; the second in D major was written for Nicolas Richter; the third in E minor and fourth in F♯ major were intended as tributes respectively to Andrei and Vladimir Rimsky-Korsakov. Each of these four lays stress upon a particular aspect of nineteenth-century pianism. Generally, the writing bespeaks a pianistic fluency, though the work is not without its awkwardness. Stravinsky himself performed the set in 1908, thus attesting to both his prowess as a pianist and desire to be seen as an executant in behalf of his own compositional cause.[20] Published by G. P. Jurgenson two years after its completion, the collection quickly captured rather widespread success at the time. In a letter of 1915, for instance, the Indian composer Sorabji wrote to Stravinsky in praise of the work, commending him on his "technical mastery of the piano" and entreating him to add further to the literature.[21]

The harmonic and melodic language of opus 7 differs little from the other works of the same period. The second and fourth etudes share a common tripartite structure, each creating tension by exploiting a thickly chromatic vocabularly, usually over dominant pedals. Their *perpetuum mobile* character unabashedly emphasizes an effulgent display of pianistic facility, each exhausting the virtuoso's arsenal of rapid repeated figurations, dramatic leaps, thirds, sixths—the very bag of tricks that Stravinsky was to shun in his piano works of the neoclassic years. The opening measures of the second etude in D major (see ex. 19), for example, are representative of this still academically devised, vestigial conservatory music, the last of Stravinsky's St. Petersburg compositions about which such can be said.

Example 19.   Etude in D major, Opus 7, No. 2, mm. 1-6

The third etude, marked andantino, incorporates many of those harmonic devices that typify Stravinsky's works before *The Firebird,* and to a more limited extent are perpetuated even in that ballet. The profusion of augmented and neapolitan sonorities, the pervasiveness of added ninths and in general, the evasion of tonic resolutions throughout the etude, characterize this ternary designed form. The closing gesture provides a concise catalogue of such traits (see ex. 20). The cadence is of special interest for it provides one of the earliest opportunities to trace Stravinsky's fastidious attention to detail.

Example 20.   Etude in E minor, Opus 7, No. 3, mm. 34-39

Copyright © 1953 by International Music Co. Copyright renewed. Used by permission.

The autograph manuscript is beautifully preserved and held by the Pierpont Morgan Library.[22] An examination of the score exhibits several erasures. Easily detectable, these alterations indicate that at an earlier stage, Stravinsky's conception of the florid gesture emanating from the penultimate measure's tonic E was slightly, though still significantly, different. Taking into account these erasures, a transcription of these measures reads as shown in example 21.

As apparent in example 21, this earlier, less sinuous version in its harmonic-linear implications is directionally quite clear. Yet the final version embellishes the melodic curve by adding appoggiature, thereby creating a more correlative relationship with the prevailing contour of the entire etude. The placement of the dissonance on the especially strong second and fourth pulses was surely carefully calculated for just this effect. Meliorations of this sort are frequently found in Stravinsky's piano

Example 21.   Etude in E minor, mm. 38-39 (transcription)

autographs, demonstrating his discriminating re-evaluation of compositional details at the very last moment.

Numerous other discrepancies are to be observed in comparing the
same autograph with the Jurgenson edition and subsequent engravings.
Two variances in performance directions are particularly striking. The
sempre poco marcato ed espress of the opening measure may well have
been an editorial amendment. The autograph bears the exhortation, m.g.
toujours en dehors—a common directive in Stravinsky's early works. In
all probability this editorial alteration, aborting the French in favor of the
more neutral Italian usage, was enacted to avoid whatever perjorative
implications might be associated with this modernist touch. Secondly, the
perdendosi of the penultimate measure (again referring to ex. 20) is not
to be found in the autograph. One suspects that this particular enrich-
ment, like the similar insertion of a rubato in measure 31 of the first etude,
was a purposeful machination, if not dictated by Jurgenson, then perhaps
included as an advisement in the proofs. The second etude provides yet
another example; the original allegro designation had by the time of engraving swelled to allegro brilliante. Thus in the case of the *Four Studies*
at least, it would appear that even at this early stage of his productivity
and especially conceding the avowed romantic quiddity of this collection,
Stravinsky himself at least originally chose not to inflate his ideas with
romantic excess; rather, such sentiments may have been inflicted upon
him.

As Tchaikovsky's music had deeply affected the earlier piano works
of Stravinsky, it is the presence of Alexandre Scriabin that is felt throughout these pieces. So transparent is this influence that Stravinsky himself
admits, "I [was] influenced by Scriabin in one very insignificant respect,
in the piano writing of my *Etudes,* Opus 7. But one is influenced by what
one loves, and I could never love a bar of his bombastic music."[23] Yet
despite this professed contempt, Scriabin had been a powerful figure during the first decade of Stravinsky's compositional growth. Stravinsky first

met Scriabin in Rimsky's home, where Scriabin was a frequent visitor. Later, Stravinsky was to attribute Scriabin's immense success in St. Petersburg circles around 1905 solely to his "phenomenal abilities as a pianist," rather than to any genuine compositional skill.[24] But at the time of Scriabin's eminence, Stravinsky was in fact thoroughly acquainted with his music, especially the piano literature. In a letter to Jurgenson dated April 4, 1913, Stravinsky, who was then in the throes of preparing the original production of *Le Sacre,* still found time to request copies of Scriabin's most recent composition, the 1912 Opus 65 Etudes. In September of the same year, Stravinsky is known to have procured copies of Scriabin's Sixth and Seventh Piano Sonatas.[25] While such purchases confirm Stravinsky's knowledge of these later Scriabin works, with both Stravinsky and Scriabin attending Rimsky's class around 1903, it is all but certain that Stravinsky was also acquainted with Scriabin's earlier works.

For example, the resemblance between Scriabin's early piano sonatas, particularly the third in F♯ minor (1897) and Stravinsky's own sonata of the same key, is unmistakable. Both share what Asaf'yev would doubtlessly have called that certain "Belaiev look." More specifically, Stravinsky seems to have constructed the aforementioned conjunction of his work's final two movements upon the same unitive idea employed by Scriabin at the parallel juncture of his own sonata. Moreover, Scriabin's third movement closely relies upon the reinstitution of material originally appearing as the initial motive of his sonata's first movement (ex. 22).

Example 22.   Scriabin, Sonata No. 3 in F♯ minor

A similar melodic motive appears again in Scriabin's 1903 Opus 42 Etude, No. 2—a work that Stravinsky may well have heard soon after it was written. In fact when a comparative analysis of Scriabin's Etude in F# minor, No. 2, and Stravinsky's Etude in C minor, No. 1, is undertaken, Stravinsky's begrudged confession of an "insignificant influence" stands as a muted understatement indeed. For in this case, Stravinsky's replication of the Scriabin work is categorically *in flagrante delicto*. The opening measures of each work are provided in examples 23 and 24.

Example 23.   Scriabin, Etude in F# minor, Opus 42, No. 2

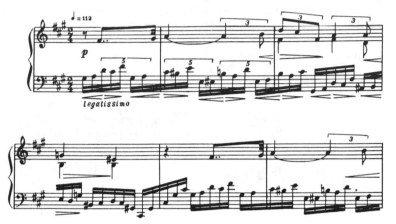

Example 24.   Stravinsky, Etude in C minor, Opus 7, No. 1

Both accompanimental figures share a common rhythmic motion as well as an ascending architectural shape. Also, the melodic line of each is similar in pitch content, contour, and rhythmic pattern. Moreover the analogy may be carried beyond these similarities, for both works share a structural pacing within their larger tripartite design. Example 25 illustrates the structural turning point of the Scriabin whereupon the central section of the piece gives way to a recapitulation of the first section. The abrupt cessation of the persistent rhythmic quintuplet, the use of the initial melodic motive here expressed over a neapolitan chord, and the general retardation of pacing all serve as an archetype for Stravinsky's own architectural conception so apparent at an analogous juncture in the C minor etude as given in example 26.

Example 25.   Scriabin, mm. 19-23

Example 26.   Stravinsky, mm. 31-34

Finally, in the resumption and development of the initial quintuplet motive in the returning first section, a similarity of cadential gestures may also be observed. Pianistically the correspondence is clear, though the

Plate 2.   Etude in C minor, Opus 7, No. 1

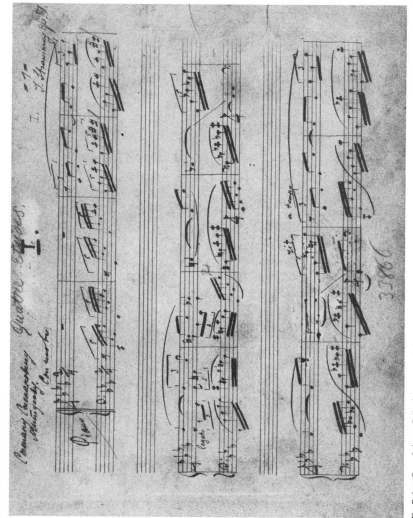

Plate 3.   Etude in C minor, Opus 7, No. 1

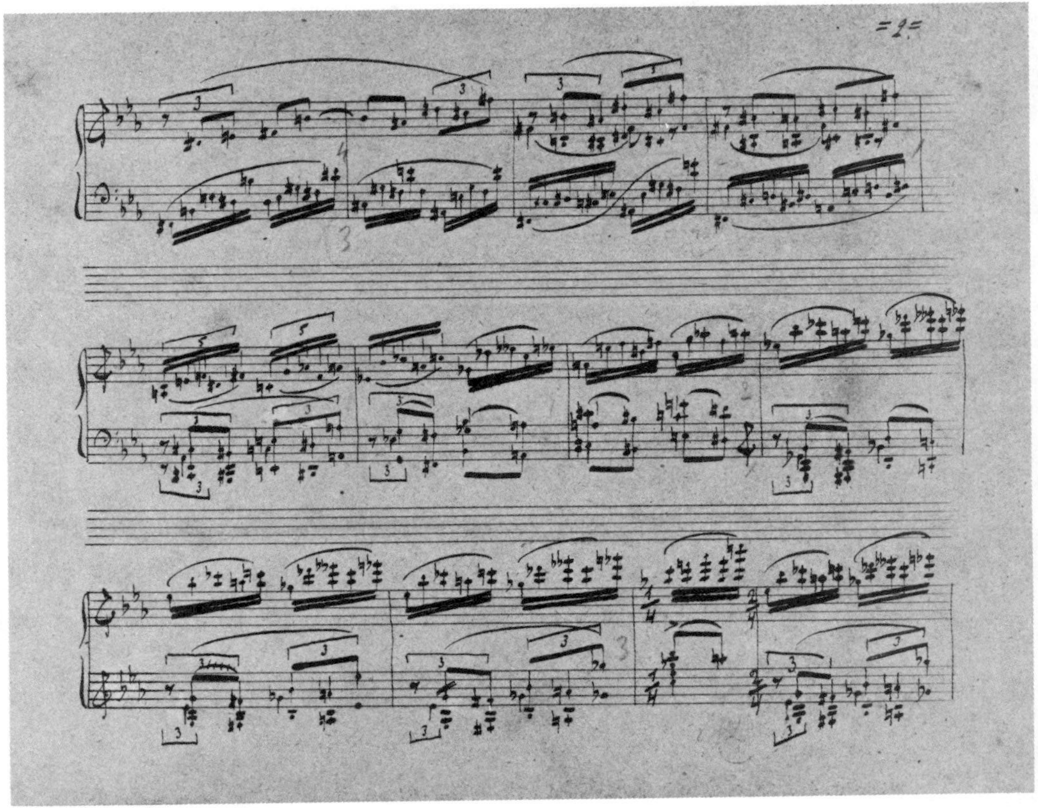

Plate 4. Etude in C minor, Opus 7, No. 1

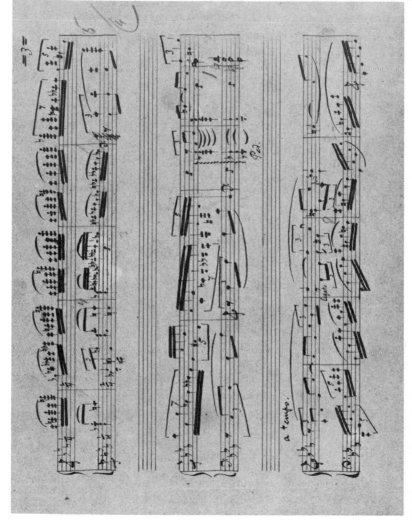

Plate 5.   Etude in C minor, Opus 7, No. 1

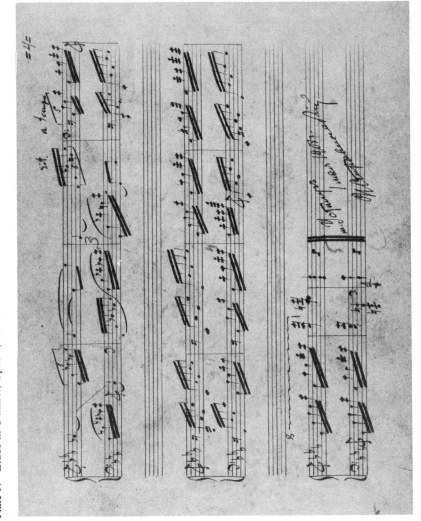

Stravinsky etude exhibits a much more expansive sweep. The resonating low octave C in the final measure of the Stravinsky piece was in fact added in pencil in the autograph, a final crowning stroke to this thoroughly epitomized Scriabinesque model (exs. 27 and 28).

Example 27.   Scriabin, closing section

Example 28.   Stravinsky, closing section

Stravinsky was 26 years of age when these etudes were written. He stood at the threshold of his own career, independent of those ties that had come to be confining and only shortly before had bound him by deference to Rimsky's adamant views. At such a crossroads, surely Stravinsky must have experienced an understandable ambition to make his own professional way by seeking public recognition. Just as certainly, the extraordinary plaudits Scriabin was currently capturing must have partially induced Stravinsky to seize the crest of Scriabin's success by writing an ectypal set of concert etudes that would have been marketable, and thus publishable. Yet for whatever compositional resemblances result, it is the dissimilitude of the works that is more revealing in charting Stravinsky's growth as his own ideas developed.

Returning then to a comparison of the Scriabin etude with Stravinsky's, consider now the central section of the Stravinsky, measures 11-13, as illustrated in plates 2-5. One must look beyond the harmonic language, as was the case in the earlier Sonata in $F^{\sharp}$ Minor, to observe the fundamental techniques of fragmentation, extension, and overlapping, which now enjoy a degree of cultivation once absent in the sonata of only four years earlier. Indeed, many of the compositional seeds that were to bloom in the forthcoming ballets, especially in the structuring of ideas rather than the ideas themselves, are suggested here. As a specific example, the rhythmic and metric scheme of measures 22-30 (ex. 29) provide the wherewithal for articulating the zenith of the accumulating motion in this middle section finally released as the thematic material returns in measure 29. The incessance of the fundamental quintuplet motive is texturally expanded to both hands in measures 27-28 creating a heightened sense of tension, and thus expectation, before the plunging septuplet figure of the following two measures ensues. More importantly, the inclusion of the metrically unanticipated 1/4 bars at measure 23 and 25 indicate asymmetrical units unprecedented in Stravinsky's preballet works.

Finally, the autograph at the Morgan Library exhibits erasures that reveal an earlier structural unfolding of an important juncture quite different from the final version in measure 10. As example 30 illustrates, the earlier plan employed the unifying quintuplet on the first left hand pulse only with a clear cadential implication on the tonic as suggested by the linear disposition of the second pulse. Stravinsky's revisions as shown in the example 31 transcription allow for the uninterrupted flow of the quintuplet, built above the harmonically supportive French augmented sixth sonority. An elision is effected, thereby enabling a degree of structural homogeneity often missing in works prior to this set.

The *Four Studies* appear on the eve of Stravinsky's meteoric rise to artistic acclaim. His renunciation of the stylized pianism that so

Example 29.   Etude in C minor, mm. 22-30.

Example 30.   Etude in C minor

Example 31.   Etude in C minor (transcription)

thoroughly grips opus 7 was swift and irrevocable. Not without justifiable reason, Stravinsky could easily have continued manufacturing such idiomatically popular pieces, as many of his contemporaries were content to do. Yet like the Piano Sonata in F# minor, these etudes should not be judged as harshly as Asaf'yev does in declaring them "more dead than alive."[26] Rather, they should be viewed as a passage, a crucial egress that leaves behind the once deeply inculcated conservatory tradition, or as Satie once epigrammatized it, Rimsky's westernized "scholastic mania." Naturally the juvenilia of these St. Petersburg years pales in history's estimate. But the eclat of the Diaghilev years should not blind us to the considerable strides Stravinsky made in a decade marked at one end by the 1898 "Tarantella" and at the other by the 1908 *Four Studies*. Finally, throughout this compositionally incubative period, it is these few scattered pieces of piano literature that begin to provide some insight in eventually measuring just how great a distance Stravinsky first had to travel in preparing for the opportunites just ahead.

3

Shorter Works from the Swiss Exile

Following the *fin de siècle* fashioned *Four Studies* of 1908, Stravinsky's star ascended swiftly. His sudden rise from near obscurity to international notoriety was largely attributable to the providential intercession of Sergei Diaghilev, whose timely appearance at the 1908 premiere of Stravinsky's luminously orchestrated *Fireworks* proved to be the catapult in launching Stravinsky's career. So favorably taken by the young composer's colorful flare for scoring was Diaghilev that he invited Stravinsky to prepare two orchestrations for a forthcoming production of the then fledgling *Ballet Russe,* Diaghilev's young troupe that sought (and essentially succeeded) to renovate the art of ballet as it was then known. Laying aside his partially completed opera *Le Rossignol,* begun in Ustilug about the same time as the *Four Studies,* Stravinsky naturally accepted the influential impressario's enticing offer.

Surely Stravinsky sensed the inestimable artistic kudoos to be won in writing music to be danced by the likes of Pavlova, Karsavina, and especially Vaslav Nijinsky, whose instant acclaim in 1907 at the Marinsky Theatre had already firmly established him as a leading St. Petersburg figure by the time he joined Diaghilev's tour. More opportune still was Stravinsky's chance to observe and be observed by Fokine, and particularly Benois, respectively the choreographer and designer with whom Stravinsky would soon again collaborate in the 1910 *The Firebird.* Though being entrusted with such a responsibility must surely have provoked an understandable apprehension, Stravinsky really had little choice but to accept Diaghilev's momentous commission.

Two piano pieces of Chopin were assigned: the Opus 32, No. 2 Nocture in A Flat; and the familiar Opus 18 Grand Valse in E Flat. The nocturne was to provide the music for the ballet's opening scene, originally entitled *Chopinianna,* while the valse served as the finale. Until recently, the manuscript of Stravinsky's orchestration had been in the private possession of the Diaghilev heirs; however in November 1981, the original performing score of the valse was placed on auction by the Berlin firm of J. Stargardt.[1] The manuscript of the nocturne seems to have been lost. Perhaps the most striking feature of the valse is the rather surprising inclusion of the piano itself, prefiguring by several years its use in the 1911 *Petrouchka,* a work in which the piano as part of the orchestral tutti was then considered to be novel. Stravinsky's contribution, like those of the other Russian composers contracted by Diaghilev for this production, was incorporated into the now retitled ballet *Les Sylphides* and mounted in the spring of 1909 at the Theatre du Chatelet. With this auspicious inauguration, a 20-year association between composer and entrepreneur began. That Stravinsky's compositional emergence should be predicated upon the successful orchestrating of piano pieces by Chopin, the very composer declared verboten by Kashperova, is rather ironic. But even more remarkable is the fact that the Diaghilev-Stravinsky alliance, founded upon the staging of such palatable music, would only a few years hence produce an artistic colossus of such iconoclastic impact as *Le Sacre du Printemps.*

Indeed, *Le Sacre,* as part of the celebrated trinity of ballets that quickly followed *Les Sylphides* during the fertile quadrennium 1909–1913, remains the most heralded watershed of Stravinsky's octogenary career. But other than the initial 1909 Chopin transcriptions for *Les Sylphides* which enabled Stravinsky to join Diaghilev's rarified coterie, one might first assume that Stravinsky abandoned the piano in favor of the orchestral forces now at his disposal. With successive commissions to undertake major creative collaborations now afforded by the Diaghilev covenant, what real compositional incentive could there be for the ambitious and increasingly visible Stravinsky to continue writing piano pieces in the antiquated mold of the Opus 7 *Four Studies*? Then, too, for the first time in his young career, Stravinsky was now faced with the practical exigency of composing towards a deadline. After all, it must be remembered that in the early stage of his association with the *Ballet Russe,* Stravinsky was very much an obligee, especially regarding his role in the composing of *The Firebird.* Thus despite whatever ebullience he was experiencing in having been chosen to compose the music for his first complete ballet (though he was not Diaghilev's first choice), surely his euphoria was tempered by the realization of production pressures. His self-confession is to the point: "Although alarmed by the fact that this was a commission for a fixed date, and afraid lest I should fail to complete the work in time—I was still unaware of my own capabilities—I accepted the offer."[2]

Such factors surely contributed to what appears to have been a near total immersion in the project. Not only did Stravinsky prepare the score, but he also frequently attended rehearsals, assumed the role of repetiteur, and in every way plunged supererogatively into the business of staging the ballet. It is not surprising therefore, that little time remained for the writing of nonballet works during these years. Only three piano-voice works of comparatively modest proportions appeared: settings of poetry by Verlaine and Balmont respectively in songs of 1910 and 1911; and the curiously nontonal *Three Japanese Lyrics* of 1912/1913. Finally, the often (and unfortunately) disregarded cantata *Zvezdoliki* (1911/1912), dedicated to Debussy, dates from this period.

Yet in all of these works, especially the three ballets, the piano's role should not be undervalued. The primacy of its service in the morphosis of *The Firebird* and *Le Sacre* will be examined in chapter 7. Obviously the history of *Petrouchka* cannot be properly recounted without considering its transformation from *Konzertstücke* to ballet. Nor is Stravinsky's reliance upon the keyboard restricted to this genre or time. The stylistically pivotal *Three Pieces for String Quartet,* begun in 1914, betray a decidedly nonidiomatic lay no doubt owing in part to Stravinsky's dependence upon the familiar patterns of the keyboard, as may be easily confirmed by considering the two piano reduction of the revised 1918 quartet score reproduced in *Pictures and Documents.* Most evidently, the protracted maturation of *Les Noces,* with Stravinsky's employment of various keyboard instruments (including harpsichord) at different points along the journey to its eventual use of four pianos, signals the composer's continued interest in the piano in a more broadly utilitarian capacity than the narrowness of solo literature. Finally Stravinsky's enchantment with mechanical pianos (also once employed in *Les Noces*) may be traced to this period. Diaghilev's company had actually employed the instrument for rehearsals, and so Stravinsky was exposed to the intriguing possibilities of writing for the instrument long before his documented transcriptions for the Pleyela appeared in the 1920s. When the aggregate of these events and compositional efforts are compiled, it would seem ill-judged to interpret this period as one in which Stravinsky's appraisal of the piano's usefulness faded. For rather than indicating any marked disaffection towards the keyboard itself, the period simply, but crucially, now reflects the piano's more functional employment. The romantically intumescent concept of the piano as some *ne plus ultra* purveyor of virtuosity no longer could sustain Stravinsky's broadening artistic concerns. His clear renunciation of what had increasingly descended into the wholesale production of a rather effete brand of piano literature soon led to a refurbishing of his own keyboard approach. More and more, the piano served Stravinsky in a new way: as a testing grounds, a vehicle with which the primordium of his compositional ideas could first be fashioned, if only crudely, then later refined.

Though Stravinsky's self-imposed exile to Switzerland is most often dated from 1914, he was in effect an emigré much earlier; he had been passing the greater part of each year there since 1910. His frequent junkets to neighboring metropolitan music capitals for performances of his ballets contributed to an expanding global awareness. Yet even in the guise of the urbane cosmopolite he fancied himself to be, Stravinsky's deep-seated Slavophilism remained inextirpable. While only the seasonal trek to his cherished aestival estate in Ustilug tangibly bound him to his native land, the escalating political fomentation then stirring in pre-Lenin Petrograd seems more than anything to have sparked significantly his fervor for Russian folklorism: "My profound emotion on reading the news of the war, which aroused patriotic feelings, and a sense of sadness at being so distant from my country, found some alleviation in the delight with which I steeped myself in Russian folk poems."[3]

Even as a child, Soulima Stravinsky, the younger of the composer's two sons, remembers that during the war years, his father undertook an operose investigation of folk song, surrounding himself at the piano with the various topical books, anthologies of published tunes, and available recordings, some of which had been requisitioned from Russia after Stravinsky's departure.[4] Recent evidence demonstrates, however, that this sudden devotion to folklorism was not all that new, but rather indicative of a resurgent interest in the study of such autochthonous source materials. The revealing photograph of a young Stravinsky (first reproduced in his elder son Theodore's iconographic album *Catherine and Igor Stravinsky*) transcribing from dictation the tunes of a blind mojik, distinctly testifies to an ardentness in such studies years before his exile. Even earlier, his transcription of 16 folk songs from a Russian anthology of Georgian folklore, copied around 1904 and recently reprinted in *Pictures and Documents,* furnishes striking visual verification of this interest even at the outset of his apprenticeship with Rimsky.[5]

The composer's reliance upon and application of such materials is most evident in the works written during the Swiss years, such as *Renard* and the thoroughly folkloristic *Les Noces.* But Stravinsky's renewed esteem for the music of his youth, specifically Glinka and Tchaikovsky, may also be surmised from Soulima's recollection of his father's piano arrangement, now presumably lost, of a type of cavatina from *Russlan,* transcribed in 1916 as a gift for Soulima, marking the son's first piano instruction. The slightly earlier piano work, *Valse des fleurs,* completed on September 30 (not August 30 as is often reported), 1914, according to Soulima pays homage to Tchaikovsky "a la *Nutcracker.*" But here, however, Soulima's memory may be in error, for an examination of the manuscript shows the music to be unlike anything Stravinsky had written to that point and clearly not in the mold of his more obviously Russian *Pribaoutki* or *Les Noces*.[6] The recent premiere of an excerpt from *Boris Godunov,* transcribed for piano in 1918, further attests to the exiled composer's yearning for things past.[7]

While these three instances, each in its own way, imply a certain reactionary impulse on the part of a disconsolate composer who by now had become a victim of a growing isolation, a third piano work more explicitly demonstrates Stravinsky's reprehension of an ideological movement destined to expatriate him, at least geographically, from his homeland. Derisively entitled *Souvenir d'une marche boche,* the holograph of this 1915 work has survived.[8] Cast in the most ordinary ternary structure, this 37-measure inchoation seems recklessly bent on drowning in its own dullness, shunning even the meagerest of efforts to salvage any sort of compositional substance or respectability. Indeed it is disrespect itself, as the "boche" epithet suggests, that is exhibited in the caliginously repetitive initial idea, and presumes Stravinsky's intentional meretriciousness. A short F major trio seems to mock the "Vivace alla marcia" sentiment of Beethoven's opus 101, and here strangely adumbrates the goose-stepping impiety included one war later in Stravinsky's *Symphony in Three Movements.* Yet it is not so much the inanity of the piece that is enlightening as it is its raison d'être; at the moment when Stravinsky's fortunes had sunk to a musical, financial, and emotional nadir, the *Souvenir* served an analeptic function.

Despite his proclaimed arousal of "patriotic feelings" in his *Chroniques,* as well as the more reliable series of letters recently released by Craft, Stravinsky's voluntary exile to Switzerland had often been erroneously interpreted by his contemporaries as symptomatic of his political insouciance. But it is quite clear that his long harbored anti-German sentiment ran deep and here surfaces in this calculated, maladroit parody. For example, Stravinsky's September 20, 1914, letter to his friend Leon Bakst divulges: "My hatred for the Germans grows not by the day but by the hour."[9] Doubtlessly this diatribe is ascribable to Stravinsky's outrage over the minacious power being exercised by agents in Switzerland, who while making little pretense of conspiring with Lenin, sought to undermine the sizeable resident Russian colony.[10] Less than a year after the letter to Bakst, the respected littérateur Edith Wharton approached Stravinsky with the proposal:

> Monsieur Bakst has led me to hope that you would give a page of music for "Le Livre des Sans Foyer." Your manuscript will be part of a large collection in a volume that I am preparing for the benefit of the refugees, and I will be personally very proud to have you on my list of writers and musicians who have shown their concern. I am enclosing our little circular, et vous prie, Monsieur, de croire à mes sentiments très distingués, Edith Wharton, August 12, 1915.[11]

Stravinsky complied. A facsimile of the *Souvenir* did appear in Wharton's *The Book of the Homeless* published in 1916 and sold for the benefit of the protectory caring for the orphans and children of the Flanders Rescue Committee. Soulima remembers that the work was written on the spur of the moment. Nonetheless, it provided the composer with a catharsis through which he could vent his political views publicly, yet from a safe distance. One suspects that owing to the *Souvenir's* rather egregiously expressed irreverance, Stravinsky prudently chose to withhold the work from commercial release.

The adversities brought about by the war conspired against Stravinsky's blossoming career at the very moment he stood poised to profit most from his Parisian triumphs. Commissions for future projects were not forthcoming; copyright for earned achievement meant nothing. His contemplation of new endeavors now necessarily had to allow for the pragmatic contingencies dictated by the *res augusta domi* atmosphere into which he was thrust. Any thoughts of continuing to write for such grand ensembles as the *Ballet Russes* surrendered to a forced temperance. Moderation supplanted opulence as Stravinsky's creative options narrowed. But beyond such constraints, other attitudinal considerations influencing his compositional approach must be taken into account. For example one must weigh Stravinsky's frequently expressed nostalgic allusions to his "sadness at being so distant from my country." Familial circumstances had also changed. His children now numbered four and either by his own volition or perhaps as a prisoner of the wartime confinement, Stravinsky seems to have devoted a good bit of his compositional energy towards nurturing their musical rearing.

The composer's productivity during this period reflects the amalgam of these forces. Dimensionally modest works, often referentially Russian and frequently written for or about his children, clearly preponderate his writing. (The two notable exceptions, *Le Rossignol* and *Les Noces,* were in fact completions of earlier projected works.) Among these en famille works, several include the piano: *Three Little Songs* ('Recollections of My Childhood') whose melodies were sketched in 1906, though the piano accompaniment was added in 1913; the aforementioned *Pribaoutki* (1914); *The Cat's Cradle Songs* (1915/1916); the musical fable *Renard* (1916) which uses cimbalom, though Stravinsky approved the substitution of a piano; *Three Tales for Children* (1916); and the 1917 *Berceuse* written for his daughter Mika. Moreover Stravinsky wrote two sets of easy but deceptively important piano duets and a short solo entitled *Valse pour les enfants.* [12]

The earliest of these completed piano works (for there were several abandoned efforts) is the *Three Easy Pieces* for piano duet, written in late

1914 and early 1915. A sketch of another duet, recently reprinted in Craft's first volume of Stravinsky's correspondence, dates from 1913 and is closer in spirit to the second set of completed duets, finished in 1917.[13] It is in fact similar to the Napolitana of that collection, though the sketch is actually a bit more involved, including a metric change for one measure, than the 1917 publication. Perhaps suffering from its contemporaneity with the more well-known *Renard* and *Les Noces* (the first tableau of which was completed in 1915), the *Three Easy Pieces,* like the second collection of these miniatures, has for a long time been unjustifiably relegated to the fatefully hermetic category of musical diversions. Though published as the last of the three, the polka, signed November 15, 1914, was the first to be written. According to Craft this little 32-measure burlesque occupied Stravinsky's attention for what would seem at first to be a rather inordinate amount of time. Apparently a two-hand version was first completed. Then after the duet score was written in November, Stravinsky again recast the work in yet another solo version, or at least began to do so on March 23.[14] The duet score is dedicated to Diaghilev, though the manuscript of the earlier solo does not bear such an inscription. Nevertheless, this music hall piece, as Stravinsky described it in a letter to Ansermet, has become eternally immortalized through the composer's musical portrayal of its dedicatee as a splendiferous circus ring-master, thoroughly savoring the powers appertaining to his station as a powerful regisseur. In his *Dialogues,* Stravinsky recalls in some detail the circumstances surrounding the preparation of the duet and its first private performance:

> I wrote the Polka first as a caricature of Diaghilev. . . . The idea of the four hand duet was a caricature also, because Diaghilev was very fond of four-hand playing. The simplicities of one of the parts were designed not to embarrass the small range of Diaghilev's technique. I played the Polka to Diaghilev and Casella in a hotel room in Milan in 1915, and I remember how amazed both men were that the composer of *Le Sacre du printemps* should have produced such a piece of popcorn. For Casella, however, a new path had been indicated, and he was not slow to follow it; so-called neoclassicism of a sort was born in that moment.[15]

Stravinsky's retrospective prophecy of neoclassicism's birth is in fact not to be dismissed too quickly as some amusing *obiter dictum.* Under closer scrutiny, unmistakable portents of the catechrestically dubbed neoclassic movement become apparent and thereby corroborate the significance of these works in tracing Stravinsky's stylistic development. Moreover the dramatic *volte face* from *Le Sacre* to the harlequinism of the polka was not ephemeral. For this new compositional embarkation seems to have been judged substantive enough that upon returning to

Clarens, a second duet dedicated to Casella was added. Perhaps in recognition of Casella's perspicacity in grasping the kernel of this "popcorn,"
Stravinsky dedicated a march to the Italian composer. Eventually this
duet, dated December 19, 1914 (and the most compositionally revealing
of the three) was released as the first of the collection in the 1917 publication of Ad. Henn, Geneva.[16] There are no indications that this duet was
first conceived for a solo pianist. The final piece, entitled Waltz, was
completed on March 6, 1915. Dedicated to Satie, whose sardonic wit
haunts the entire set, this concluding duet foreshadows the stylized waltz
of *Histoire du Soldat* written three years later. Apparently this particular
duet, like the polka, was originally intended as a solo piece.[17]

    Stravinsly was particularly enamored with piano waltzes about this
time. In addition to the earlier cited *Valse des fleurs* and the later solo
waltz *Valse pour les enfants,* Stravinsky began at least four other waltzes
for four hands, though only the duet for Satie was published. All of these
aborted efforts seem to have been written for children and from the few
sketches included in appendix G of Craft's first volume of Stravinsky's
letters, each appears quite like the one chosen for the *Three Easy Pieces.*
Moreover the very fact that so many of these diversions, as they are
tagged, were undertaken, as well as the quantity of sketch materials themselves, surely suggests that Stravinsky approached these vignettes with
the same characteristic industriousness he brought to the larger creations
of only a few years before.

    The prima part of each of the *Three Easy Pieces* is virtually charged
with all the essential musical materials. Conversely, elementary triadic
patterns constitute the whole of the seconda (this appears to be generally
true in the sketches for the incomplete waltzes as well). In each case
these accompanimental patterns provide a rhythmic and harmonic underpinning tantamount to a traditional piano waltz's left hand figurations.
Stravinsky's professed deference to Diaghilev's limited pianistic gifts at
least partially accounts for the utter simplicity of the lower duet part. Yet
even a cursory look at the respective ostinati (ex. 32), suggests that simple
though they be, the textural disposition of each would quite likely, or at
least more facilely, dictate a distribution between both hands.

    This being the case, the seconda's execution not only could have
been accommodated by Diaghilev's modest technique, but even by an
untutored child incapable of dealing with even the most elementary concepts of shifting hand position, or for that matter even reading notation.
Soulima, then approaching the age of five, claims to have been the intended recipient of this propaedeutic; and considering Stravinsky's pa-
ternal devotion to his children about that time, it is quite conceivable that
these rudimentary ostinato figures were designed with his son in mind

Example 32.   Ostinati for *Three Easy Pieces*

March

Waltz

Polka

rather than, or at least in addition to, Diaghilev. The physically untaxing manner of alternating the figures between hands would easily have permitted the boy to join actively rather than vicariously in the process of making music at an early stage. The relationship of Stravinsky with his son Soulima rests beyond the province of this study, though it cannot be ignored completely. Soulima was to become a protégé and accorded every advantage of study with the finest pedagogues of the day: Naprovnik, Phillipe, Cortot, Boulanger. He would later join his father as an equal partner in the duo piano works and as a soloist under the composer's baton in performances of the Piano Concerto and *Capriccio*. But curiously, there was never to be a formal dedication of any composition to Soulima. Even in what would seem to have been the most obvious instance, the 1935 *Concerto for Two Solo Pianos,* a work whose genesis is inextricably bound with Soulima's pianistic collaboration with his father, Stravinsky chose to withhold such personal tribute. Yet Soulima was entrusted with such important matters as preparing the piano reduction for the *Symphony of Psalms* and *Persephone*. He also recorded what for many are still the definitive performances of his father's piano music. But by the time Stravinsky discussed his four-hand works with Craft in *Dialogues,* the unfortunate estrangement between father and son that widened in the years following Soulima's own immigration to America in 1948 now disallowed any reference to Soulima in connection with these duets.

However, in the *Five Easy Pieces* of 1917, Stravinsky identified Theodore and Mika, his two eldest children, as the inspiration for this second set of duets, though Craft indicates that the collection was actually inscribed to Mme Eugenie de Errazuriz whose interest in Stravinsky's music continued for several years.[18] In any case, it was his own children whom he surely had in mind when he later stated that the duets were written for "amateurs little practiced in the use of the instrument," and that his pedagogic intent was to create "a real sense of performance participation." In contrast to the 1915 set, here the seconda task demands greater technical skill. At times, as in the Española, the writing is extended and provides a good example of the quirky writing commonly associated with his future piano works. Especially apparent in this the second duet is the *fioratura* style, programmatically intentional of course, which later effloresces to an even more florid level of pianism in the adagietto of the 1924 Piano Sonata. The prima part is primarily a melodic one, often for one hand, though sometimes doubled at the octave. With minor exceptions, and even then the problem is easily surmountable, the melodic patterns conform to a simple five finger piano position. Indeed, Craft reveals that ideas for the opening fanfare of the second piece in the aptly titled 1921 *The Five Fingers* dates from as early as March 1915.[19] Examples 33 and 34 provide representative passages of melodic figures easily handled by the smallest of hands.

Example 33.   Napolitana

Example 34.   Galop

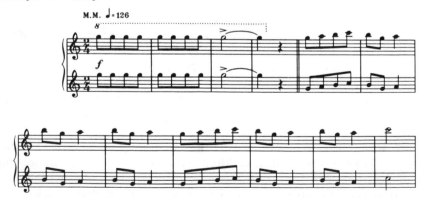

As in the *Three Easy Pieces,* the published score does not adhere to the actual order of composition. The galop for instance, which appears last, was written on February 21, 1917, though the sketches predate the finished work by at least a year. As with all the others, Stravinsky eventually orchestrated this duet. He later recalled that Ravel reacted to his conducting of the piece rather glibly: "Ravel . . . advised me to play it faster—the fastest possible—tempo, but I think that is because he mistook it for a cancan."[20] But in the sketches for the galop, Stravinsky apparently marked a borrowed tune used for the melodic basis of the work—"Cancan." The balalaika is third in order and according to the composer "not borrowed," though such disclaimers were commonly voiced about other works shown to be based on paraphrase. The most stylized of the five are the aforementioned Española, second in published order, and the fourth duet entitled Napolitana. These are really musical memorabilia from Stravinsky's recent travels to Spain and Italy. Finally, though Stravinsky states that the opening andante was written last and "tacked on like most preludes," the dating of the manuscript establishes this as the first of the set to be completed on January 4, 1917. The opening ostinato of the andante's seconda, marked by its alternating D and E minor implications, exhibits many of the texturally inventive dispositions more closely allied with Stravinsky's neoclassic instrumentations than piano scores. The segregation of the right hand's oscillatory fourths from the repetitive left hand linear sevenths, for example, is indicative of Stravinsky's experimenting with traditionally unpianistic textural ideas in the search for fresh combinations of sound. Even the essentially superfluous middle stave contributes to the separation of these two distinct layers, as example 35 illustrates.

Example 35.   Andante

Of the children's literature from this period, the only solo piano work is the *Valse pour les enfants,* probably composed in early 1917 as well. Following its appearance in the May 21, 1922, issue of the Parisian daily, *Le Figaro,* the work went commercially unpublished until its recent inclusion in Soulima's anthology of his father's shorter piano works.[21] Since the piece was written five years before its printing in the Sunday issue of *Figaro,* it is quite likely that this work, like the two sets of duets before, was originally intended as a pedagogical gift for his children. That Stravinsky chose to release the work to the newspaper only years later might be interpreted as one of his frequent attempts around that time to ease the exigent "pecuniary difficulties," as he labeled them, that he faced as late as 1922.

Though by most standards the slightness of this 56-measure work suggests only a modicum of effort, several epigraphic signs indicate that the *Valse* was more than a lark. For example, on its appearance in *Figaro,* the inscription read: "*Valse pour les enfants,* improvisee au *Figaro* par Igor Stravinsky . . . une valse pour les petits lecteurs du *Figaro.*" But these prefatory remarks seem to have been the product of an editorial fabrication, for Stravinsky took umbrage with them on at least two accounts: Soulima, for example, in his edition of the work reports that Stravinsky appended to his own copy of the *Valse* the explicative annotation, "Pas du tout improvisee, tout ce qu'il y a de plus composee!" And Craft indicates that on a copy of the newspaper itself, Stravinsky not only comments that the work was thoroughly composed, but that it was not written for *Figaro* but for his own family.[22] Moreover, sketches do exist and at the work's final measure, Stravinsky marks the exact length of the *Valse* as 52 seconds, thus suggesting that the duration was of some concern to him in his construction, not unlike the later callibrations of Bartok's pianistically didactic *Mikrokosmos.* Finally, in both spirit and structure, the piece shares a kinship with the waltz from the earlier *Three Easy Pieces.* Unfortunately, this little solo is almost forgotten totally or at least summarily dismissed as nothing more than a musical amusement.

Eclipsed on one side by the grand and utterly Russian works of the same period, especially *Renard* and *Les Noces,* and on the other by such a luminary landmark as *Histoire,* the *Figaro* piece, like the duets, pales as trifles. Their *jeu d'esprit* parody of Western European musical conventions is so infectiously amusing, so undisguisedly pellucid, as to occlude anything so pontifical as the rigours of structural analysis. The very thought of dissecting them invites a tilting at windmills allegation. After all, why would such wittingly sapid and avowedly caricatural *facetiae* pretend anything even remotely cryptic or portentous? History's pronouncement, then, rings consistent in proclaiming these miniatures to be only the products of a harmless contrivance. A contemporary Soviet view, for example, implies that the duets are only incidental creations, reminiscent of the minuets and ländler of the Beethoven-Schubert era. As such, they warrant no better than passing mention for the sake of biographical completeness.[23] Robert Siohan, in one of the many standard biographical surveys of Stravinsky, espouses a similar view in dismissing the literature as "brief parerga thrown off as a temporary escape from Stravinsky's overwhelming occupation with folklore."[24] But the myopia of these precipitously fatal verdicts is lamentable. Such judgments can only lead into a convenient cul-de-sac, and so enisle these piano works from the mainstream of Stravinsky's development, thereby fostering an undeserved imparity. Nor do such suppositions address the embedded Russian features of Stravinsky's neoclassicism, especially in terms of a linear-harmonic content, indeed an important structural aspect of that period that until recently has been virtually ignored.

As a comparison, consider that history's appraisal of Schoenberg's much discussed *Sechs Kleine Klavierstücke* (1911) has fared far better. Opus 19, like Stravinsky's duets, offers a collection of vignettes shaped within the restricted and controllable environment of the piano. Each collection appears at an analogous point in the composers' career: both were written en route to what has been mistakenly perceived as an insularly stylized period, that is, serialism and neoclassicism. Yet while the Stravinsky set continues to suffer the commonly expressed traducements mentioned above, the import of Schoenberg's opus 19 as a strategic moment in his evolution, remains a staple in any analyst's study of this century's literature. But one must appreciate the crucial beginning advantage enjoyed by the Schoenberg: it is a pure work, unfettered by the impedimenta of artifice so overwhelming in the Stravinsky works. The Schoenberg piano pieces are immediately scrutable from a neutral, tabula rasa viewpoint. The Stravinsky duets, however, are all but blinding in their formulary of stereotyped tunes and rhythms. Thus, it would seem that if the purported shallowness of Stravinsky's overtly fashioned stylizations is to be proven illusory, and in its place a more substantive compositional cohesiveness revealed, then the substructural regions of these polkas and waltzes, especially in respect to the construction of the all important intervallic relationships within, must be explored not with an analogical eye towards comparison with their models, but with the same exegetic resoluteness mounted in tracing the nontonal cellular pitch content of Schoenberg's work. Indeed, just as analysis of this kind holds the potential of unlocking the secrets of Schoenberg's sophisticated network—secrets which may be discovered only by entering the penetralia of each work—so, too, it is contended that the hidden coherence of Stravinsky's miniatures is retrievable once one decides to pass beyond the imposing banality that initially surfeits us. Moreover, the fact that numerous sketch materials as well as discarded fragments survive, seems to indicate that Stravinsky labored over their construction rather than effortlessly tossing each off without some compositional plan.

In order to test this hypothesis, a detailed investigation of the march from the 1915 *Three Easy Pieces,* held to be a representative example of the children's literature dating from this period, is first pursued. The first 10 measures are submitted as example 36.

Example 36.   March, mm. 1-10

Used by kind permission of J&W Chester/Edition Wilhelm Hansen London Ltd.

While a comparative study of Stravinsky's treatment of borrowed materials should not be the sole destination of analytic pursuit, neither should it be ignored; for it is clear that Stravinsky employed model tunes and rhythms in many of the pieces of this time. In the case of the march, the six measure introductory fanfare as well as the ensuing theme, owe their origins to an identifiable source. According to Craft, Stravinsky purchased an anthology of *Old Irish Folk Music and Songs* in London a year or so before the duets were begun. Tune No. 486 (ex. 37) of this collection provides Stravinsky with his melodic material and the similarities between the original and its imitation are evident, both rhythmically and linearly.[25]

With the acknowledgment of this source made, it is wise to move quickly to other matters that though less obvious as a means of creating coherence are in fact more essential. As an introductory example, con-

Example 37.   Irish Folk Tune (#486)

sider the clearly defined stylized rhythm elicited by the opening passage of the March. It is just what one would expect of such a tantura. But this should not be allowed to mask the more important cellular interval of the clearly stated perfect fourth (and hereafter its complement, a perfect fifth) that eventuates as one of the cornerstones of the piece. By the third measure, the repetitive fourth spawns an assurgent gesture that in itself is sparked by its own quartal incipit. The temptation to view simplistically the juxtaposition of the opening interval with this new fourth merely as a clash has often proved too alluring to resist. Thus history has become the benefactor of such beguiling analyses as "The biting irony of these pieces is expressed mainly by means of a series of modal and tonal shifts; roguish off-key effects, twisting and slipping pitches."[26] Such an observation implies a type of cavalier, happenstance approach, primarily aimed towards creating what has come to be recognized as a neoclassic imprint, a rub, and nothing more. The purpose here is not to dispute whatever aural impressions result, for these are perceptual rather than conceptual concerns, but rather to argue that these are achieved in a very orderly, calculated fashion. Simply stated, one idea does not preclude the other, and in fact, it is perhaps the compatability of sounding "roguish" but being part of the essential pitch vocabulary that goes to the core of this passage.

When the opening G-C dyad of the left hand is combined with the first entrance of the F-B flat fourth in measure three, an ordered tetrachordal projection results. That is, the symmetrical array of the G-C-F-B flat pitches produces a distinctly quartal sound that Stravinsky enhances by the articulation of accents and the first use of a triplet. But more importantly, by estimating the total universe, limited though it be, of pitch aggregates potentially available within this tetrachordal resource, three protean sonorities, or subsets as they hereafter will be labeled, may be identified. Not only are these three subsets a potentiality in the theoretical sense, but they are in fact a recurring element of the overall pitch vocabulary of the march. Since the following study will be largely concerned with the employment and subsequent transformation of these three saturative sets of pitches, hereafter referred to as pitch-class sets, it is desirable to identify each by a simple alphabetic label. Example 38 offers a summary of the intervallic cells within this opening combination of the two fourth structured dyads. The three cells marked *A, B, C* (ex. 38) are in fact the only possible subsets of the generative tetrachord, given the important proviso that each cell is transposable. The identification of this resource is not only important in that it provides some insight into the pitch content itself, but it further proves valuable in understanding the fundamental constructs employed in creating an architectural whole.

Example 38.   Subsets, cells A,B,C

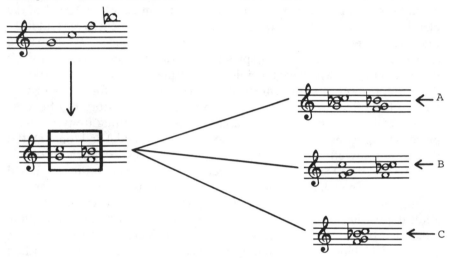

In examining the subsets, no attention is given to dyads since such two-note structures seldom enter into a discussion of the architecture as units in themselves. More often they function as fragments of a tetra-chordal cell or the three-note (trichord) cells. First then, consider the constitution of cell *A*. There are two possibilities as listed in example 38, each comprised of a perfect fourth that enfolds both a minor third and whole step. Since it is only the position of the internal third that differs, rather than any change in intervallic content itself, both are reducible to the same pitch-class set. The *B* cell also has two forms for the same reason as *A*, and here is distinguished by two perfect fourths partitioned by a whole step. The third cell, *C,* is simply a union of both the *A* and *B* cells. These three cells when taken together as a resource, constitute one of two seminal pitch banks from which Stravinsky draws regularly throughout the March.[27]

While these three cells by far furnish the principal pitch source for the March, a second potential resource warrants attention. Returning to the initial melodic gesture of measure three (refer again to ex. 36), and in accordance with the symmetrical array of perfect fourths employed to the juncture discussed above, the opening F-B flat dyad of the right hand might have been logically extended to include next an E flat as the next ordered perfect fourth. But the unexpected E natural which appears produces a tritone relationship with its adjacent B flat. The fact that the E natural, like the two preceding pitches, is marked by an accent and falls within the triplet figure, clearly indicates that Stravinsky thought of the three pitches of the figure as some complete unit. Thus rather than simply dismissing the E natural as a colorfully vagrant moment, it seems more reasonable to consider the pitch within its own context. Yet it is precisely this kind of errant pitch that annotators revel in labeling as a piquant effect when attempting to account for Stravinsky's pitch vocabulary during this period. The deviant E would be viewed by many as no more than an adscititious impulse meant merely to amuse, and an example perhaps of Stravinsky's "twisting and slipping" pitch approach. Because these pitches do not conform to what is still assumed as a triadically based system, frequently such pitches are conveniently excluded from harmonic analyses. Yet whatever the aural impression created by this E natural, the fact is, stretching a perfect fourth to a tritone is not at all peculiar to this particular stylized idiom. Indeed it is commonly found throughout the Stravinsky literature.[28] Such appearances were probably consciously wrought, and occur long before the a posteriori "wrong note" theories of Stravinsky's pitch usage came into vogue, bringing in their wake some misperceived notions about Stravinsky's mutant pitch mannerisms.

Not only must the resultant tritone relationship engendered by the contiguous B flat and E be considered, but just as importantly, it must be realized that these two notes are part of a larger linear gesture that culminates with the climactic G. These three pitches as a unit form a diminished triad, the same sonority that soon pervades the balance of the composition as the seconda's ostinato. Moreover, given the diatonic implications of an Irish tune employed within the context of a traditional march framework, one could hardly expect that tertian constructs such as a diminished triad, would not in someway play a contributive role in enhancing the piece's stylization.

Yet it is not so much the vagrant E natural that goes to the heart of the issue as it is the B flat. Specifically, it is the potential of the B flat to function sumultaneously within both tertian and quartal pitch orbits that signals a fundamental structural technique used to reinforce those links that bind separate parts of the architectural whole. Indeed, it is this functional dualism that most characterizes a central aspect of a structural concinnity even in such a modest work as this. The ability of a single pitch to act as a pivot provides the link by which the composer at least begins to bring some degree of coalescence to seemingly appositive harmonic-linear ideas. Compared to a work with which it is contemporary, such as the aforementioned opus 19 of Schoenberg, the function of the E in the march is not unlike the identification of invariant pitches or pitch-class sets found to be useful in understanding the structural bonds of Schoenberg's atonal compositions. Within the diminutive world of such piano duets as this, one cannot fail to recognize the same technique of architectural coherence addressed long ago by Edward Cone as "interlocking," that fundamental tenet usually associated with Stravinsky's more dimensionally significant efforts, though no less effective, or for that matter essential, in bringing order to the microcosm of the march.[29] The use of the B flat as a fulcrum, enabling access to both pitch resources, as well as the resulting pitch cells themselves, are expressed schematically in example 39.

Example 39.

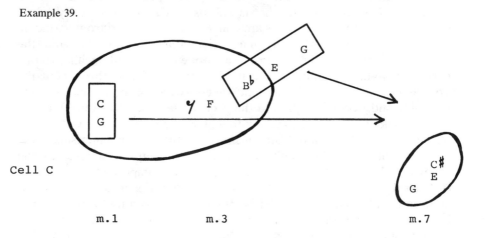

Cell C

m.1   m.3   m.7

With the fundamental properties of the pitch vocabulary employed in the march outlined, their application and development may now be pursued.[30] Three sections of the march are offered, selected on the strength of their structural contribution to the macroformal framework. First, the transition from the introductory fanfare through the initial statement of the borrowed tune (measures four through nine, see ex. 36 once again) is submitted. The intrusion of what first appears to be an unrelated idea occurs in measure six above the by now established stability of the G-C perfect fourth. In relation to the even tessitura of the left hand ostinato material heretofore, the spatial, as well as the sudden dynamic contrast of this figure clearly places an emphasis upon this new material. Yet in terms of both pitch content and interlock, it is not at all unprecedented, for its relationship to the previous material is easily demonstrable. The pitch material of this figure, B flat-D flat-E flat, is only a transposition of the earlier labeled cell *A,* with the lowest note B flat acting as a pivot (as it did in measure three in a different, linear context). While the chromatic B flat finds precedent, the D flat and E flat should not be interpreted as roguish inflections since in fact they stem logically from the B flat. Moreover this same pitch, here seen as the lowest member of cell *A,* also functions in an interlocking manner with the G-C retained interval below; and when these three pitches are formed as a unit (i.e., G-C-B flat) yet another instance of one of the three basic cells, cell *B* in this case, occurs. In this light, it would seem reasonable to conclude that Stravinsky's use of the B flat as the crucial pitch member of this configuration was much more than a mere product of chance.

The articulation of an important new passage follows in the next measure, and though texturally disparate, it is in fact related to the introductory measures just discussed. The seconda's ostinato and the embellished tune are comprised of pitch resources consentaneous with the tertian pitch content already presented. Of specific interest is the pitch level of the tune's entry on A, the first note of the right hand in measure seven. To be sure, the sound of this unanticipated A seems to conjure thoughts of one of those "ironic tonal shifts" that refractorily resist explanation. Yet in attempting to find some coadjunative point between measures six and seven, it is again the by now familiar B flat, here acting as an important directional tone, that provides the most immediate link in resolving to the A and coherently initiating the next section of the work. Also, the A of measure seven may be reconciled with the G-C interval of the left hand, measure six; for together they form another example of cell *A.* Both analyses offer the kind of organically smooth, though aurally disjunct structural concrescence of the transition. The entrance of the seconda's ostinato, beginning with the low G, may also be related to the G-C fourth employed to this point in the prima's left hand, thus providing another link. All aspects of the measure six to seven commisure are summarized in example 40. When the totality of pitch materials is considered, a resultant octatonicism becomes apparent.

While it is known that Stravinsky completed the march on December 19, 1914, only recently Craft has reported that on that same day Stravinsky

> made a fair copy on printed music paper, adding a measure (sustaining the C and G in measure 4), changing flats to enharmonic sharps, repeating the dotted rhythms in measure 4 (replacing the sixteenths), and implementing other improvements as well.[31]

Example 40.

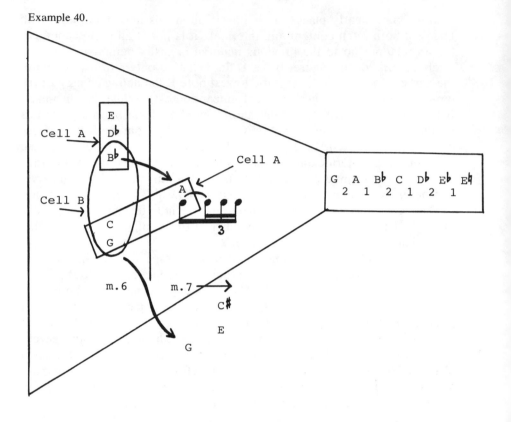

The emendations to which Craft refers are indeed significant in studying the transitional section discussed above. The incorporation of the dotted rhythms in measure four clearly develops and perceptually reinforces
the same figure of the opening measure, while the sustaining of the predominant G-C fourth for a full added measure (the new measure five)
permits a durational expansion of utmost importance. By lengthening the
G-C dyad and reinstating the duple meter, the arrival of the B flat-D flat-
E flat cell *A* in measure six seems to be more evenly paced and so creates
more of an impact than had it been hurried into a temporal position immediately following the melissma of the right hand's measures three and
four. Such a slight but nevertheless crucially architectural refinement
clearly evinces the care with which Stravinsky considered the structural
junctures of each passage (and here is reminiscent of the same discrimination used in altering a similar elision in the early Opus 7 Etude, No. 1).
Moreover, the fact that Stravinsky elected to change the orthography of

sharps and flats demonstrates his concern for the directionality of pitches as they infer certain resolutions within the harmonic context of the piece. One notes, for example, the specific, and perhaps at first appearance, rather unorthodox spelling of the middle layer ostinato beginning in measure seven (ex. 41). This passage, as marked by the directional arrows, offers a good example wherein Stravinsky's flats to sharps amelioration is quite thoughtful.

Example 41.   March, mm. 7-9

The retention of the B flat spelling from its former use is evident. The C$^\sharp$ of the middle strata, instead of the D flat of measure six, was probably altered so that it would conform with the C$^\sharp$ of the melody and also because of its eventual movement towards a D pitch priority at the close of measure nine. Likewise, the respelled D$^\sharp$ in place of its original E flat enharmonically indicates a resolution to E, a priority pitch of the diminished triad ostinato, as well as an important melodic note. Finally, the G$^\sharp$, which in fact is the only new chromatic inflection present, seems preferable to an A flat spelling, since the pitch A is the beginning place for the Irish tune seen in the highest layer of the example.

But while such an enharmonicism offers an explanation for the notation Stravinsky eventually selected, it does not address the compositional use of these middle layer pitches themselves; in examining each component of this transition, they, too, must be held accountable lest they succumb to the indefensible catch-all of a loosely envisaged pandiatonicism. As marked in example 41, all four pitches of the middle strata function directionally; yet as an autonomously structured, tetrachordal pitch-class set, they replicate in transposed form the two overlapping dyads first encountered in measure three. Thus the ostinato of the middle layer beginning in measure seven is another instance of cell *A* (measure three, F-G-B flat-C = measure seven, G$^\sharp$-B flat-C$^\sharp$-D$^\sharp$ = cell *A*). Moreover, when either of the two alternating dyads of this layer are combined with the notes of the lower ostinato that sound at the same moment, a major and minor third respectively result, thus juxtaposing the tertian-quartal dichotomy of pitch resources (D$^\sharp$-G-B flat = major triad, C$^\sharp$-E-G$^\sharp$ = minor form as articulated on first two eights and thereafter in measure seven).

The architectural coherence that accrues as a result of what would seem to be a premeditatively fashioned pitch vocabulary primarily constructed upon these three cells is not so distant from a similar reliance upon such cells in Schoenberg's early piano works. While obviously it would be foolish to peruse too closely these similarities (though the technique of developing pitch-class sets is in some ways surprisingly analogous), Schoenberg's opus 19 miniatures do employ many of the identical sets apparent in the march. Equally important, the same overlapping of these trichordal cells often spawns a developmental path that will prove vital in creating an overall unity in the composition.[32]

A second example from the march, here extracted from a middle section of the piece, is reprinted in example 42 as another instance of a transitional unity.

Example 42.   March, mm. 18-23

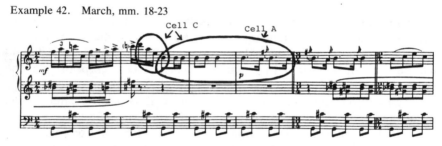

Used by kind permission of J&W Chester/Edition Wilhelm Hansen London Ltd.

The triadically conceived outer layers, which frame the continuing cell *C* of the middle strata, moves directly to the first pulse of measure 19 whereupon the F Major arpeggiation is abandoned in favor of a descending projection of fourths. When reduced, this figure (as circled in the example) is again equivalent to the same cell *C* (transposed of course) of the middle ostinato which now is halted. A further link is forged with the repeated pitch B (the final note of the cell just mentioned) in combination with the following two pitches A-F$^\sharp$, thus yielding the pitch-class set F$^\sharp$-A-B, or once again cell *A*. The reassertion of the middle layer cell *C* in measure 20, now overlapping with the continuing cell *A* above clearly produces a stronger cohesion at this recapitulative point. Indeed the entrance of the middle layer ostinato in measure 22 instead of measure 23 creates the same type of smoothly seamed interlock one has come to expect of Stravinsky in uniting larger sections of an architectural scheme.

Finally, the closing gesture of the march provides a third example of the duet's employment of these cells and triads towards creating an architectural homogeneity (ex. 43).

Example 43.   March, mm. 37-42

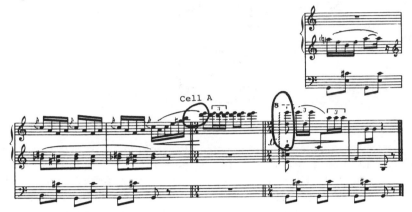

The F major triad, having appeared earlier in measure 18 (ex. 42), represents another triadic use now employed above the ostinato in measure 37. In this instance it appears to be isolated. But as the cell *C* pitch-class set returns in measure 38, the same F triad now migrates to the highest textural layer. This layered additive process, so characteristically Stravinskyan, is easily recognizable. In the next bar, the broken triad gives way to the arpeggiation of thirds which concludes measure 39 while simultaneously leading to a restatement of the martial figure in measure 40, in its triplet disposition, reminiscent of the opening fanfare. The D-E dyad, if extended back one note to include the final B of the interlocking figure in measure 39, produces an additional instance of cell *A*. These three notes share a familial relationship, especially since they immediately appear on the first beat of the penultimate measure (circled in the example). But the elaborate catenation of these final two measures far surpasses this solitary link. The closing cadential gesture exposes a labyrinth of quartal cells and overlapping triads. Example 44 schematizes these final measures by partitioning the pitch-class sets into the numerous instances of cell *A* as articulated by rhythmic, linear and spatial emphases. Further, the reductions show an overlapping C#-E dyad extracted from cell *A* as a shared property within the triadically persistent diminished triad of the seconda.

Example 44.

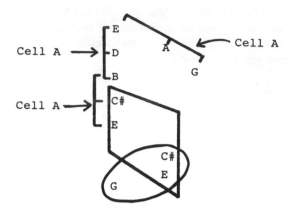

These same materials and constructive techniques so pervasively apparent in the march are also evident in both the waltz and polka. Moreover, the somewhat later *Five Easy Pieces* though perhaps architecturally less inventive, still exhibit the basic three cells first seen in the earlier set of duets. Two representative passages extracted from the fourth of the five duets, the Napolitana, are submitted in examples 45 and 46. Example 45 offers the opening measure, while example 46 reproduces the cadential gesture.

Example 45.   Napolitana (Seconda)

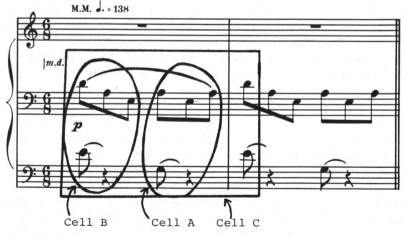

Example 46. Napolitana

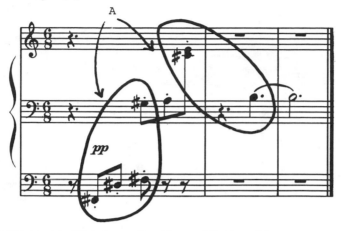

If such cellular units are truly ubiquitous, then these pitch-class set patterns should appear not only in the eight elementary duets, but also in other works contemporary with these two collections. This is in fact the case in the aforementioned waltzes that Stravinsky chose not to complete. For in the sketches that Craft reprints, numerous instances of cells *A* and *B* permeate the melodic materials. Moreover, even a brief study of the 1917 *Valse pour les enfants* fulfills the same expectation. The opening 17 bars of this *Figaro* waltz are reproduced in example 47. The ostinato, here restricted to the conjunct notes of a simple five finger pattern, like the duets of the same period, precludes a hand position shift, thus once again anticipating a fundamental pianistic premise of the later *The Five Fingers*.

The actual segmentation of this left-hand ostinato amounts to the subdivision of a pentachord that produces cells *A* and *B* as marked. The linear projection of these same intervallic cells onto the right hand is frequently employed as a source of short melodic ideas. A comparison of the right-hand figures in measures six and seven respectively with the harmonic content of cells *A* and *B,* as labeled in measures one and two, indicate a harmonic confluence quite typical for this work and others of the same period. Furthermore, the transposed and ordered pitch materials of cell *B* are more expansively used in an overlapping fashion in measures 13-15. Because of the symmetrically equidistant scheme resulting from the use of a major second plus a minor third, the imbrication obtains as shown in example 48.

Example 47.   *Valse pour les enfants*

Example 48.

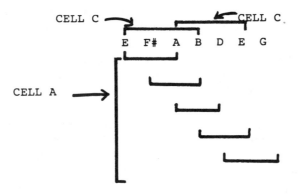

Finally, the pitch content, owing to the inherently segregated textural fabric of the work, might seem unrelated to the left hand ostinato. But in fact the melodic line emphasizes the same seminal pitches of the ostinato itself. The complete linear resource of the right hand, ordered in example 49, demonstrates that the second and seventh tones are the only degrees occasionally inflected, as circled.

Example 49.

$$E \quad \boxed{F \quad F\sharp} \quad (G) \quad A \quad B \quad \overset{(C?)}{} \quad \boxed{D \quad D\sharp} \quad E$$

The parenthesized pitch G plays a less vital function in the total pitch vocabulary, but does constitute the pitch acme in measure 15 (refer to ex. 47). The pitch C is altogether absent, producing a basically hexachordal scale. Moreover, by its absence, the C is removed from the prevailing diatonic environment as a potential tonal center. By elimination, as well as by a noticeable rhythmic articulation throughout the work, the pitches E, A, and B enjoy a priority and so duplicate the essential cellular units of the ostinato (transposed). If these three pitches are added to the G and the uninflected D and F, the hexachordal resource becomes D-E-F$\sharp$-G-A-B, another instance of a symmetrical array with the semitone dividing the scale evenly—a specific linear approach that will be pursued in subsequent piano and nonkeyboard works.

In observing the proliferation of these cells and techniques, the temptation to seek complete conformance at every moment must be resisted. As in most cases, and certainly similar to the early nontonal experiments of Schoenberg, there seems to be some license apparent in the pitch vocabulary of these transitional works. Even so, there is little doubt that the three cells identified to this point function almost as an insignia of a developing pitch system that eventually provides the foundation for the works of the future. That such patterns never seem to have been explored in much depth, though of course their existence has been acknowledged, is perhaps at least partially due to the overwhelming aural disorientation between these thinly shaped piano miniatures and the grand productions of only a few years earlier. Yet the actual selection of the specific pitch materials used in the duets and the *Valse* finds its roots in the melos of Russian folk song upon which we know Stravinsky had been drawing, indeed relying, for the past several years. In his biography of Stravinsky, White rightfully acknowledges these same insignia cells (as well as compiling a list of transmutations of the cells) as a resource in the hallmark of Stravinsky's Russian heritage, *Les Noces*. One should be wary, however, of attempts to relate such cellular pitch-class sets directly to inferences of modality, as has often been the case. To be sure, a clear residual modality is apparent, but in *Les Noces,* as in these piano pieces, this results from a use of folkloristic tunes that happened to employ modal patterns. Thus it seems to have been the patterns themselves, rather than the de facto modality displayed, that primarily attracted Stravinsky.

In his study "Russian Folk Melodies in *The Rite of Spring*," Richard Taruskin outlines numerous melodic prototypes employed by Stravinsky in that ballet drawn from the anthologies of Istomin-Liapunov, Zemtsovsky, Juszkiewicz, Rimsky, and others—anthologies known to have been in Stravinsky's possession.[33] As Taruskin convincingly demonstrates, Stravinsky's reliance upon such folk models provided the "emancipation" in breaking new ground with *Le Sacre* while clinging to the roots of his heritage. But more relevant here is the fact that the same insignia cells that rest at the foundation of these enchorial sources were to be efficaciously and pervasively employed in works far beyond the St. Petersburg years. One begins to sense that the insular compartmentalization of Stravinsky's so-called stylistic periods is perhaps more the product of history's mythopoeic reflex than an objective search for those common properties that transcend the particulars of a work or "ism." Thus, in substantial measure, the linear-harmonic staples of Stravinsky's earliest neoclassic works do not constitute a diametric turn away from the folkloristic models of earlier years, but in fact suggest a steadily evolving style that emanates from the basic pitch cells of these models and is carried into the duets and children's literature of the Swiss exile. That these unjustly maligned duets have been judged as chic, rather than substantive, should not denegrate their importance at a crucial crossroads in the composer's development. Artifice, mimicry, and ritual seemed always to attract Stravinsky, and a study of works even aesthetic eons apart, such as *Le Sacre* and the *Three Easy Pieces,* begin to reveal similarities, at least in their respective substrata where the most basic of compositional elements are examined.

While the identification of such Russian folk models as those quoted by Taruskin provide the putative wellspring for works like *Le Sacre,* such a discovery might have been predictable, despite Stravinsky's avowed ignorance of such a reliance. More importantly it seems, and certainly unforeseen, is the assimilability of the cellular bases of these same materials, as well as their harmonic-linear manipulations into valses, marches, and other such frivolities. What transpires is in fact a transfiguration of fundamentally indigenously Slavic pitch-class sets, by extraction from a normally linear context, into a totally stylized western dance form with some emphasis on not only linear but also vertical constructs as well. Essentially this differs from Stravinsky's application of tetrachordal or pentachordal motivic fragments within such works as *Petrouchka* or *Le Sacre* where a more independent counterpoint arises. Nonetheless, the cells themselves are analogous. As an example of this congruence, consider the correspondence of the insignia cells identified in measures six and seven of the March from the first set of duets with two very familiar precedents (ex. 50).

Example 50.

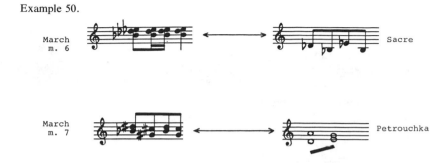

In offering such analogies, one is reminded of Stravinsky's stupefaction at Diaghilev's and Casella's horrified response upon the first hearing of the Polka of 1915. Yet the bonds between the aurally incongruous works as those quoted above are stronger than some might wish to concede, especially those who prefer to characterize Stravinsky as a chameleon. The filling of new bottles with old wines is surely nothing new, but in this instance, it is the curious blend of pitch-class set derivatives from one culture within the stylized mode of another that signals the significance of these piano pieces so often undervalued.

Amongst the panegyrical tributes following Stravinsky's death, the portent of this literature was aptly summarized by Leo Kraft in noting that "from the four hand pieces of 1915 to be exact, Stravinsky deliberately moved into another, a wider tradition, that of Western European music from the Middle Ages to the present."[34] Connections having been drawn to antecedent compositions, what relationships might exist between these piano pieces and the more established works—"the ones we care about most," as van den Toorn comments—which soon followed? Could these pieces have functioned as harbingers for subsequent, grander creations? Such a thesis is by no means new. In his often overlooked and by now dated biography of Stravinsky, Frank Onnen suggested just such a possibility:

> It is noteworthy that almost every major work by Stravinsky is preceded by a minor composition for a smaller ensemble (song, piano piece, quartet) in which one can find treated in skeleton form the very technical or musical problems which later occupied the composer on a larger scale.[35]

One notes for example, that the preliminary ideas for the musical fable *Renard* are to be found on the reverse side of a manuscript leaf for the *Valse pour les enfants.*[36] The similarity between the insignia cells of that piano work and the extracted motive from *Renard,* as seen in both the clarinet and cimbalom, is evident in example 51.

Example 51.   Renard, March (Allegro)

Relationships between the pitch content and process of the piano pieces and works written several years later, especially *Histoire* for example, are also quite clear. In this regard, Stravinsky's own assessment of the importance of the piano as a shaping force is acknowledged (to be examined in chap. 7). Several passages from *Histoire* are herein submitted towards addressing this potential relationship. To begin, consider the initial passage of *Histoire's* opening scene, "The Soldier's March," in comparison to the pitch content and techniques of the similarly stylized march of the 1915 duets. Example 52 reprints the well-known contrabass ostinato that serves as the fundamental harmonic underpinning for the entirety of the work.

Example 52.   *Histoire du Soldat* ("The Soldier's March")

The martial rhythm of this scene, like the middle strata ostinato of
the duet, is of course of only secondary importance since it forms a
component of the highly recognizable stylization. A more revealing similarity is both works' shared use of cell *A* as a staple in their respective
pitch systems.[37] Moreover, while the ostinato's string figuration appears
unpianistic by most standards, one must remember that Stravinsky's approach to the keyboard was an unusual one to say the least; and in fact
the extended interval of a major ninth, employed as a pianistic ostinato
was rather common in his solo piano literature. Example 53 illustrates a
passage from the later *Piano-Rag-Music* (though some sketches for this
work actually date from the time of *Histoire's* writing, as will be discussed
in the next chapter) which not only displays the same textural disposition
as the contrabass figure, but also provides yet another instance of a familiar pitch-class set.

Example 53.   *Piano-Rag-Music*

Used by kind permission of J&W Chester/Edition Wilhelm Hansen London Ltd.

Materials common to both works undergo similar transformations as
well. Example 54, which extracts a few measures of *Histoire* at a slightly
later and structurally important division, provides a clear instance of
shared architectural techniques (the example employs a piano reduction).

Example 54.   "The Soldier's March" (piano reduction)

Cell B   Cell C   Cell A

Rehearsal 3 marks the first cadential gesture of the piece, resolving to the A-E fifth above the continuing ostinato. The juxtaposition of these textural layers results in the labeled cells. The triadic arpeggiation commencing at measure 20 recalls the tertian-quartal dichotomy of the duets when viewed with the measures just completed. Additionally, three observations are appropriate: 1) the outlining of the triads in measures 20 and 21, built on A and B major sonorities, alternate at the distance of a whole tone, the same distance at which the triads of several of the duets, for example measures 7-12 of the march, rotate; 2) the stress effected by both rhythmic and melodic emphasis provide an articulation of cell *A* when the initial notes of each triad are combined (as circled); 3) the frequent metric shifts of the passage find precedent, too, in the march from the *Three Easy Pieces,* the only instance among the eight duets of which this can be said.

Example 55 provides a further combination of tetrachordal and trichordal pitch-class sets between the contrabass ostinato and the protagonistic violin. All three cells are apparent. The alternation of cells *B* and *A* become especially interesting in their union resulting in a hexachordal resource, D-E-F#-G-A-B, that is, the same symmetrical array observed as the harmonic-linear vocabulary for the earlier *Valse pour les enfants.*

Example 55.

The same hexachordal pattern, which in each case conspicuously averts an implied leading tone, is again apparent in the closing gesture of example 56, the final cadence of the "Music to Scene I." Here the symmetrical array, G-A-B-C-D-E, provides the material for a clear G priority in the ostinato and an embellished A triad in the violin, thus resulting in the alternation of sets again at the distance of a whole tone. The numerous overlapping instances of cells *A* and *B* in the closing violin melisma lead directly into the nostalgically expressed "And now I ask you, what am I to do." "Music to Scene III," which as reprinted in example 57, continues to employ the same cellular pitch elements as circled. Even the levels of entry as marked in the example provide an instance of cell *B*.

Example 56.   Music to Scene I

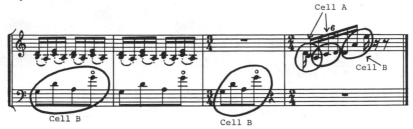

Example 57.   Music to Scene III

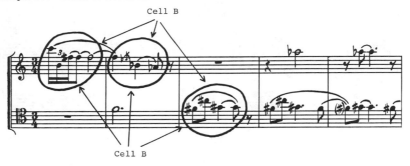

The germinal nature of these cells as they function in the piano pieces discussed in this chapter, must ultimately be judged static, providing instances of a generally evanescent, vertical use, rather than the focus of any extended development, Nevertheless, their potential as a principal component of the structural network one associates with the more readily perceived linear works of later years is already apparent. By the early 1920s, Stravinsky had indeed taken such a course in works like the *Octet* and Piano Sonata which were now almost suddenly contrapuntal. His evolution towards a systematic harmonic centricity, a polarity as it was loudly ballyhooed, is marked by a convergence of harmonic-linear definers that include the traditional elements of directional tones and the consequent onset of at least a temporary harmonic functionality, especially at cadential moments. As an example (more fully explored in chap. 5), consider the brief excerpt from the 1923/24 *Concerto for Piano and Winds* shown in example 58.

A clear progression towards the E at rehearsal 23 is observed. The stratification of the passage reveals several layers that converge on the polar pitch which in turn acts as an extended dominant preparation for

Example 58.   Piano Concerto, I., mm. 150-152

the movement's priority pitch A, which is rearticulated at the recapitulation as expected. The insignia cell *A* is apparent (as circled) in both the
pianistic display of the linearly conceived right hand, as well as the verticalized constructs in the orchestral lines. The left hand of the solo, as
boxed, indicates an uninterrupted linear descent towards the same E,
also reinforced by the chromatic fall of the piano reduction's left hand.

By the time of this piano concerto, completed nearly a decade after
the duets were conceived, the "period of experimentation" as Craft justifiably tags it, had given way to such mature works as this. Now the
cellular base flows more steadily into the linear mainstream, though as
seen above, it still retains a motivic identity that would continue to serve
the composer for many years. To suggest that works like the piano concerto owe their inception to the same roots as those of a work like *Les
Noces* would be to overstate the case. But to say that works like the *Octet*
or *Symphonies of Winds* are not intimately related to the piano duets of
the Swiss years (whose roots are traceable to the more folkloristic creations examined) would be to make an equally narrow conclusion. While
it has not been the purpose here to place the total burden of Stravinsky's
neoclassic development upon the thin shoulders of a few genotypical cells,
still it is suggested that the initial phases of this aspect of Stravinsky's

broadly based compositional evolution, pitch-wise, extends back further than many have perhaps previously considered.

While the identifiable use of paraphrased folk tunes in works like *Le Sacre* aided Stravinsky in his liberation from the "academic post-kuchkist milieu," as Taruskin so colorfully describes it, the same elemental pitch arrays of those resources once again seem to have armed the composer as he set out upon a journey that led to the monuments of the 1920s. That these same pitch elements become increasingly unidentifiable at the surface (for reasons of "style," as already addressed), slipping further and further into the deeper, infrastructural regions of the architecture, certainly has little to do with the vital support system they continue to provide. In this regard, one should not be mislead by Stravinsky's attempt to extricate himself, at least publicly, from his folkloristic heritage. His overtly expressed disclaimers regarding a reliance upon folk melodies in *Le Sacre* and even his purported disappointment in Bartok's employment of folk elements, seems to have been no more than a concerted foil as he went about burning the bridges that might have imprisoned him to a public image he wished to shed. His conversion to the European neoclassic cause was calculated to be ostentatious. Yet for whatever momentary success his efforts achieved, ultimately, the deeply ingrained pitch language of earlier years remained at the center of his evolving compositional approach.

In his stimulative monograph, *The Harmonic Organization of The Rite of Spring,* Allen Forte cogently suggests a fundamental relationship between the pitch elements, and their control in that ballet, with some of the early atonal experiments conducted by Schoenberg and his disciples. Forte goes on to mention that "from our contemporary vantage point [The Rite] has more in common with those works than with the later works of its composer—in particular, with the so-called neoclassical works, at least as we understand them now."[38] His suggestion is well taken, especially as it applies to the Viennese connection. His wisely stated proviso regarding our current and perhaps still myopic understanding of the preneoclassical works is also to be considered seriously. For as this understanding broadens, surely further bonds between Stravinsky's once thought disjunctive stylistic periods will be revealed. In any such examination to be undertaken, a study of the piano literature from these years should provide a vital link in formulating future connections.

4

Stravinsky and the Music of Ragtime

Like so many of Stravinsky's works, *Histoire du Soldat* marks both a plateau and a crossroads. In one sense it is a creative point of arrival, a redoubtable attainment that had been in the process of a steady development ever since the seemingly trifling piano duets were first imagined only a few years earlier. In retracing Stravinsky's steps en route to that ill-defined compositional period of neoclassicism, *Histoire* now appears as a fruitful summation of those controlled experiments originally tested within the finite, near private laboratory of the 1915 and 1917 duets. This is especially so in its codification of a rather rigorously erected pitch system whose musically etymological derivation springs first from a deracination, then occidental stylization of some ineradicable, and to use Stravinsky's own word, "aboriginally" Slavic wellspring.

One suspects, however, that the musical world was for the most part oblivious to the funneling journey leading to this 1918 landmark. The public needed only to realize that *Histoire* was an explicitly discernible gateway, "a final break with the Russian orchestral school" as Stravinsky would later declare *per dictum*. [1] Indeed, even barring such a retrospective pronouncement, the world of 1918 could hardly mistake *Histoire* for anything but the emancipating setting of a fresh compositional sail. Finally, in some ways *Histoire* seems to have provided the propitiation needed to regain the *réclame* that had been gradually eroding during the interregnum of Stravinsky's devotion to children's literature. Thus *Histoire* was contemporarily viewed in some quarters as a recrudescence, a redemptive escape from what many misperceived as the composer's rather arid odyssey following the earlier triumphs of Paris.

In approaching several of the formative aspects of *Histoire*, the role of the piano goes far beyond the underlying pitch structure examined in the duets. For example, there is an unmistakable pianistic stamp to much of this nonkeyboard work. The contrabass figure that permeates so much of the "Music to Scene I" as discussed earlier, implies an easy accommodation by Stravinsky's left hand, especially insofar as he inveterately conducted such pianistic, and so in a very basic way, physical searches at the keyboard. The similarity to the ostinato figure in the later *Piano-Rag-Music* has also already been noted. This string figure is reprinted once again in example 59.

Example 59. Music to Scene I

Used by kind permission of J&W Chester/Edition Wilhelm Hansen London Ltd.

Yet in this instance, there is little need for conjecture as to its origins. Consider first the apparent pianistic roots of the above passage as employed in the voice and piano song "Tilimbom," the first of the *Three Tales for Children* written on May 22, 1917, at least a year in advance of *Histoire.* Secondly, in the little voice and piano *Berceuse* written seven months later, on December 10, the identical motivic idea now harmonically shaped, illustrates yet another pianistic harbinger of the *Histoire* ostinato. Finally, one might also observe that all three passages replicate the insignia cell *B* earlier identified as a nuclear pitch construct in the piano duets. Both the rhythmic and textural disposition of these piano accompaniments clearly anticipate the later string transformation.[2]

Example 60. Tilimbom and Berceuse

While such specific evolutionary tracks reveal in a very tangible way the piano's direct infusion into the sculpturing of Stravinsky's compositional materials, especially regarding the shaping of lines and textures, the importance of the piano, and especially the composer's fascination with mechanical pianos around this time, should not be confined only to instances of such narrow congruence.

Stravinsky's attraction to player-pianos of all kinds, and as a result his dedication of "hundreds of hours of work" in preparing as many as 77 "pleyelization rolls," as he referred to them, is a part of the composer's productivity that continues to remain only on the periphery of his biography. While such an investigation exceeds the limits of this study, its history cannot be ignored altogether. It is felt appropriate, therefore, that a brief diversion aimed towards addressing a few aspects of this part of Stravinsky's career is warranted.

Just before *Histoire*, Stravinsky had written an *Etude for Pianola*, dated September 10, 1917. In his biography of the composer, White states that according to Paul Collaer, the work was dedicated to Madame Errazuriz. But in a June 1919 letter to Ansermet, Stravinsky is quick to point out ". . . please make careful note of the following: no one commissioned the *Etude for Pianola*."[3] There is little doubt that the inspiration for this curiosity stemmed from Stravinsky's 1916 visit to Madrid where he became enchanted with the *fioriture* ornamentation in the music that he heard. Indeed, the work was later orchestrated under the title of *Madrid* and along with the orchestration of the 1914 *Three Pieces for String Quartet,* combined to form the 1928 *Four Etudes for Orchestra.* Moreover, *Madrid* was later transcribed by Soulima for two pianos. The original score of the *Etude for Pianola* remains unpublished; but according to Craft the first notations are found amidst various entries for dance pieces, and even a tune later used in *Histoire.*[4] Much of the *Etude's* style is in fact similar to that of *Histoire*.

Stravinsky enjoyed championing the "unplumbed possibilities" of the pianola, as he addressed them in a 1925 interview:

> There is a new polyphonic truth in the player-piano. There are new possibilities. It is something more. It is not the same thing as the piano. The player-piano resembles the piano, but it also resembles the orchestra. It shares the soul of the automobile. Beside the piano it is practical. It has its utility. Men will write for it. But it will create new matter for itself. Not a new manner, no, New matter. . . .
>
> I was the first to try it. That was in 1917 in London. I wrote a study that was not for the piano, but for the player-piano and nothing else—an attempt to see what could be done with the whole keyboard available to one's will.[5]

If in addition to creating a new automated art form, Stravinsky intended to stem the "notorious liberty" of some performers by guaranteeing his own interpretations of his compositions as transcribed for pianola, then such a time consuming project might have been at least theoretically justifiable. But the pianola itself was not so rigidly mechanical that the performer could not still interpret Stravinsky's transcriptions. Indeed, the pianolist must control the tempo by a hand lever and the dynamics with the pressure of his feet. As Ansermet comments in a June 12, 1919, letter to Stravinsky "I have had two meetings with the expert *pianoleur.* He played your piano roll for me several times. . . . Unfortunately I heard the piece on a very bad instrument, and to make matters worse, the expert made *rubati.*"[6]

Nonetheless, Stravinsky did sign a contract with the Pleyel Company of Paris to transcribe his complete works for the Pleyela mechanical piano. Moreover in 1924, Stravinsky next signed an agreement with the Aeolian Company to record for that company's Duo-Art Reproducing Piano.[7] Once again a sizeable amount of Stravinsky's time during the 1920's would be committed towards the fulfillment of this contract.

As an example, the Library of Congress Division of Recorded Sound holds the complete Duo-Art pianola rolls for *The Firebird*. (Actually a disc recording was released of these rolls in 1975 by Klavier Recordings.) Craft addresses this set of six rolls in *Pictures and Documents,* observing that the running commentary that appears on the rolls themselves, and prepared by Stravinsky himself, is "startlingly literary."[8] Each roll begins with an autobiographical commentary translated by Edwin Evans; but the analysis of *The Firebird's* music itself, in addition to Stravinsky's narrative, also includes rather superficial observations on the composition's themes, harmonies, rhythms and orchestration. The intended audience of this is immediately obvious. An editorial preface as printed on the unfolding roll advises:

The Thermophrase lines and marginal notes in red continue to point out structural and other technical details of the music.	A Running Commentary in black is now added to the roll. It describes point by point the action of the Ballet so enabling the listener to follow it in imagination.

It is not intended that all these markings should be observed at any one reading of the roll. The listener should give attention at first to the Running Commentary (in black) and afterwards, if he wishes, to the markings (in red) of a technical nature.

Following these opening remarks, the music begins, accompanied at each moment by these red and black descriptions. A sampling of these observations follows:

(IN RED)	(IN BLACK)
'Cellos and Basses	Black Mystery broods over the bright flowers of the

	Magic Garden of Kastchei the immortal embodiment of all that is evil.
Violas added	The place is haunted by memories of grim spells,
Trombones give the Thirds in reversed order	eerie sounds coming from unseen shapes fall upon the ear and strange beings are moving
Interplay of Thirds on Bassoons and Clarinets	invisible in the shadows
Bassoons, Horns And Basses	Heavy footsteps betray their presence.

Plates 6 and 7 illustrate many of the typical markings to be found on the rolls. In addition to the perforations, one observes part of the commentary style described above, as well as some "pictorial decorations" as they are called, by V. Polunin, "artist to the Russian Ballet."[9]

Plate 6. *The Firebird*, Duo-Art Pianola Rolls

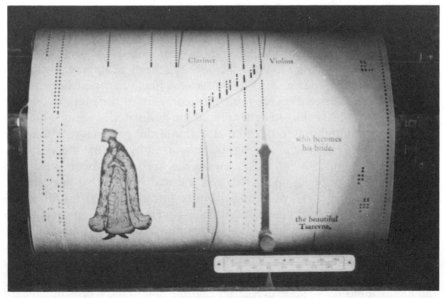

Plate 7.   *The Firebird*, Duo-Art Pianola Rolls

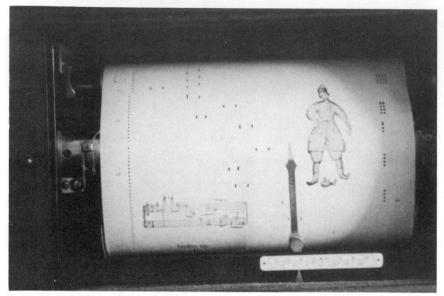

Library of Congress, Division of Recorded Sound

Returning to 1918 and *Histoire,* as the piano had provided the younger Stravinsky with a stimulative, tactile tool in experiencing the music of his then immediate compass, now again it steered him through his ever-widening exploration of foreign musical waters. Nowhere is this more apparent than in Stravinsky's immersion into the music of ragtime. This new infatuation appears evident first in the caricatural "Ragtime" the last of *Histoire's* three dances. With this work, a brief examination of Stravinsky's interest in rag music as it involves the piano may now be pursued.

Until the relatively recent rebirth of curiosity in the ragtime era, the music of that time remained generally on the perimeter of serious inquiry. The occasional and only tangential attention it did gain, more often than not promoted a superficial glazing, often marred by factual inaccuracies. Likewise, Stravinsky's attraction to rag has frequently been misunderstood, sometimes being dismissed as a musical bauble that appealed to him only fleetingly. Yet what may have begun as an amusing diversion soon surpassed a mere episodic enthusiasm. His adaptation of rag conventions were to extend immediately beyond *Histoire's* "Ragtime" into the *Ragtime for Eleven Instruments* completed later in 1918, as well as in the 1919 *Piano-Rag-Music.* But Stravinsky's interest was not to be ephemeral. He clung to some of the more conspicuously aural aspects of the highly identifiable style even after ragtime had in the words of Edward

Berlin "ceased to be the emissary of American popular culture."[10] More-over Stravinsky was noticeably unconcerned with ragtime's demise at the very moment it captured his own charm. Craft reports that in a critical review of *Histoire's* premiere, one commentator wrote "Sociologists are predicting that this American dance step will soon be abandoned, but Mr. Stravinsky's answer is, 'It is sufficient to be true in 1918.'"[11] Indeed, the audibly omnipresent patterned syncopes of rag remained useful to Stravinsky throughout the 1920s and the high tide of his neoclassic works. As a single example, a representative excerpt from the 1923/924 Piano Concerto is offered as example 61.

Example 61.   Piano Concerto, I. mm. 87-95

By the time the concerto was written, Stravinsky had gleaned a full decade's familiarity with the diversity of rag styles. His knowledge was acquired from various contacts, though Stravinsky himself offered dis-crepant accounts of his introduction to what he typically often termed jazz. The proliferation of ragtime in the United States in the early years of this century had quickly spread to Europe, and with the transport of the American military force during the war, there was simply no escaping it. Cortot somewhat derisively quipped that both American jazz and chewing gun had become equally indispensable to the French.[12] Not only was it a commonplace among the cafe circuits that Stravinsky is known to have frequented during his pre-exile days, but it had become a musical dalliance as well, "le temps du chiffon" as it was described by the French, and played for the amusement of the *beau monde*.

Surely Stravinsky was allured by rag's foreign swagger, just as he had been fascinated by the native music of Italy and Spain. But Stravinsky's knowledge of American popular music preceded works like the Napolitana and the *Etude for Pianola,* works which were in effect musical tributes written upon returning from his excursions to these countries. Nor can one discount Stravinsky's familiarity with rag as treated by other European composers for whom he held respect. As a specific example, in his second book of *Preludes.* Debussy parodies the rhythmic fiber of rag in the sixth piece of that collection, "General Lavine—eccentric." This collection, published by Durand in 1913, was presented to Stravinsky ("surtout pour amuser Igor Stravinsky" so the inscription reads) in June of that year.[13]

Yet if there is a single figure to whom Stravinsky's direct exposure to ragtime is attributable, it is Ernest Ansermet. As the conductor for the premiere of *Histoire,* Ansermet had won the favor of the composer— indeed a rarity in the annals of Stravinsky's brabbles with a legion of besieged maestros. While accompanying Diaghilev's entourage to America in 1916, Ansermet had gone so far as to intercede for Stravinsky in negotiating the possible publication of the earlier of the two sets of piano duets.[14] Upon returning to Europe, Ansermet presented the composer with a package of several scores including American piano rags, piano rag reductions, and also some instrumental parts for rag ensemble scores. Stravinsky recalls the event in his autobiographical account:

> At my request, a whole pile of this music was sent to me, enchanting me by its truly popular appeal, its freshness and the novel rhythm of which so distinctly revealed its Negro origin.[15]

Unfortunately, Stravinsky educes somewhat of a chronological muddle at this point in his remembrances, for he implies that his knowledge of these notated rags came only after *Histoire* and just before the *Ragtime for Eleven Instruments.* Not only does Ansermet's earlier transatlantic delivery repudiate the romantic notion that Stravinsky neither studied nor even saw notated rag scores, as has sometimes been contended, but it clearly places the composer's documented introduction to such notations well before *Histoire* may even have been contemplated.[16]

In *Dialogues* Stravinsky refers to this "bundle of ragtime music" as having been brought to him in 1918 before *Histoire*. More reliable are two sources that record Stravinsky's views about rag closer to the approximate time that Ansermet visited him. In a November 1917 issue of *Current Opinion,* Stravinsky is reported not only to have been vaguely familiar with rag, but that "he collects examples of it with assiduity."[17] Earlier still, Stanley Wise in a 1916 interview for the *New York Tribune* quotes Stravinsky directly:

> I know little about American music except for the music halls, but I consider that unrivaled. It is a veritable art, and I never can get enough of it to satisfy me. I am convinced of the absolute truth of utterance in that form of American art.[18]

It was not until 40 years had passed that Stravinsky, in *Expositions and Developments,* confesses knowledge of the printed scores Ansermet carried, though even now he pleads a different ignorance:

> My knowledge of jazz was derived exclusively from copies of sheet music, and as I never actually heard any of the music performed, I borrowed its rhythmic style not as played but as written.[19]

Yet as early as 1914 while still in Paris, Stravinsky collected phonograph records of jazz, as he called it. In the following year, having taken up residence in Morges, he in fact procured a phonograph machine.[20] Moreover Craft reports that Ansermet delivered not only rag scores in 1916, but specifically "a fresh supply of ragtime records," which apparently Stravinsky remembered with delight.[21] If in fact this chronological reconstruction is accurate, then it would appear that Stravinsky must have been quite conversant with both the look and authentic performance practice of rag much earlier than is generally believed. In addition to seeing and listening to ragtime, there can be little doubt that Stravinsky became more intimately acquainted with the compositional nuts and bolts of its construction by actually playing the music at the piano. His appetite for rag, to which he alludes in the above cited interview, was nothing short of insatiable. His son Soulima, even as a child, retains a vivid memory of his father seated at the keyboard as he constantly experimented through improvising in the search for fresh ideas. Soulima amusingly recalls that his father's fondness for rag was contagious. Soulima himself fell victim to the rage, freely improvising at the keyboard much to the detriment of his own assigned piano etudes, so much so in fact that it eventually forced his admonishing grandmother to enforce a retributive "scales only" six-month penance.[22]

Though the improvisatory nature of rag apparently mesmerized Stravinsky, the attraction ran deeper. Stravinsky seems always to have been taken by the implicative processes of music. Musical conventions and their contextual expression frequently served as a compositional desideratum and the blending of stylistic paradigms—paradigms which during his apprentice years subjugated rather than liberated his creative will— now increasingly emerged as the very cornerstone in many of his compositional blueprints during the period. Comparisons of Stravinsky's ragstyled music with its American precursors are of course inevitable and can prove quite enlightening in studying Stravinsky's transformative approach. But in suggesting that "Stravinsky and jazz were engaged in exactly similar enterprises," one writer presents a too commonly held belief that exceeds relevant comparison by crudely analogizing the blue notes of jazz and Stravinsky's "wrong notes."[23] Richard Middleton's Jungian apologia for an "ontogenetic and phylogenetic equivalence" virtually precludes the possibility that Stravinsky could effectively employ elements of parody without foresaking his own compositional integrity. Indeed, Adorno and his disciples' villification not withstanding, it seems to be Stravinsky's efficacy in mixing a diversity of materials into his own language that perhaps best bespeaks the essence of his neoclassic works. With these introductory remarks given, attention may now be turned towards an examination of Stravinsky's three ragtime pieces themselves.

Mention has already been made of the pianistic tenor that underlies several sections of *Histoire*. Nowhere is this more evident than in the "Ragtime." This is clearly illustrated by the opening passage wherein the unfurling of the double stops in the fiddle and the contrabass octaves closely resemble a pianistic scoring. Moreover, such a distribution of parts is not only a near generic emblem of piano rags, but also typical for piano reductions of ensemble rags with which Stravinsky would probably have been familiar since such reductions are known to have comprised part of Ansermet's bundle. How premeditatively instrumental was *Histoire*? Such passages as those reprinted in example 62 suggest a certain reliance upon Stravinsky's thoroughly ingrained pianism.

Histoire is of course a thoroughly idiomatic chamber work in its final conception; but nevertheless, Stravinsky himself admits that in the early stages of *Histoire's* precompositional gestation, the notion of significantly integrating the piano into the instrumentation was seriously considered:

Although the piano [had] much more varied polyphonic qualities and offers many particularly dynamic possibilities, I had to avoid it for two reasons: either my score would have seemed like a piano arrangement—and that would have given evidence of

Example 62.   *Histoire du Soldat*, "Ragtime"

Used by kind permission of J&W Chester/Edition Wilhelm Hansen London Ltd.

> a certain lack of financial means, not at all in keeping with our intentions—or I should
> have had to use it as a solo instrument, exploiting every possibility of its technique.
> In other words, I should have had to be specifically careful about the "pianism" of
> my score.[24]

Such explications seem to border on the defensive and hint at a certain supracompositional extenuation, perhaps one that Stravinsky necessarily had to consider at that time. Yet within a year of *Histoire's* premiere, a piano arrangement did appear in a transcription which included violin of course, and clarinet, no doubt partially employed as an homage to Werner Reinhart for his timely subvention of *Histoire's* production. Though by any measure this arrangement is indeed a transcription, its own separate musical merits should not be prematurely deprecated as so often seems to have been the case. Far from being as one biographer complains "thoroughly disagreeable and an error in musical taste," this version of *Histoire,* like so many of Stravinsky's inappropriately labeled piano reductions, reflects an extraordinarily natural pianistic temper, indebted no doubt to Stravinsky's use of the keyboard in the original compositional process. Shortly after the premiere of this transcription, the Rumanian ethnomusicologist Constantine Brailoiu perceptively noted the naturalness of the arrangement in reporting that

> the recomposed suite became, in effect, a new work. . . . On musical evidence alone,
> it would be almost impossible to discover which version came first: and the same is
> true of the other works by Stravinsky which exist in two instrumental forms.[25]

Though the predominance of piano rags among the music of the ragtime era is often assumed, Berlin points to the speciousness of this claim. He reports as one indication of this misconception, that in exam-

ining more than 200 articles addressing rag music during the period 1896–
1920, only 16 even mention piano rags.[26] The vocal forms of rag seemed
to enjoy a greater vogue, though it was the ragtime band that most captured the fancy of its audience. Thus ensemble rags probably would have
provided a rather well-known precedent for Stravinsky's second attempt
in this form. More importantly, while some biographers state that Stravinsky was ignorant of such ragtime ensembles prior to *Ragtime for Eleven
Instruments,* the contravening fact that Ansermet carried the individual
instrumental parts of ensemble rags to Stravinsky, parts which Stravinsky
subsequently wrote out in score on his own initiative, suggests that Stravinsky was quite familiar with specific models.

The scoring of *Histoire's* "Ragtime" called for seven instruments. In
Ragtime for Eleven Instruments (hereafter referred to as *Ragtime*) it in-
creases to eleven players with the concertante cimbalom serving as the
primary addition. The composer's expressed intent in composing *Ragtime*
was to create "a composite portrait of this new dance music, giving the
creation the importance of a concert piece, as in the past, the composers
of their periods had done for the minuet, the waltz, the mazurka, etc."[27]
The cimbalom had previously been used in *Renard* (as well as other
works). It continued to fascinate Stravinsky. Not only is there an important part for cimbalom in *Ragtime,* but Stravinsky claims to have composed sections of the work at the cimbalom itself, thus utilizing the
instrument in the same manner with which we have come to associate the
piano. Later, in *Dialogues,* Stravinsky not only recalls its influence in
1918, but reveals how its idiosyncratic quality continued to attract him a
decade later in another piano work, the 1929 *Capriccio.* Stravinsky, as he
was wont to do with any new experience, became absorbed, not only by
the cimbalom's novel sound, but by its construction and the requisitie
playing techniques needed in adequately managing a performance. Upon
witnessing a demonstration of the instrument in Geneva by the cimbalist
Aladar Racz, Stravinsky purchased a cimbalom, took several lessons from
Racz, and apparently even acquired some basic skills for maintaining the
instrument's repair.[28] Ultimately, however, writing for the cimbalom proved
impractical due largely to the dearth of competent players. By the time
of a 1930 performance of *Ragtime,* Stravinsky, having failed to commission a cimbalist, advised the conductor Paul Sacher to attach a nail or
tack to each hammer of the piano in the hope that this would serve as a
satisfactory substitute.[29] Craft reports that in a July 9, 1930, letter, Stravinsky acknowledges the at least rough equivalence of this contrivance
in producing "a comparable effect" in a later performance in Paris.[30] Yet
Stravinsky's heraldry of the cimbalom's virtues tends to disguise the uninterrupted significance of the piano in his compositional process, including its undivulged role in the *Ragtime* itself.

Until now, it has been suggested that the *Ragtime* was the second of Stravinsky's three rags to be composed. This historical supposition would seem to be well founded, especially in that Stravinsky himself dates the writing of this composition immediately after the completion of *Histoire*: "I began the *Ragtime for Eleven Instruments* in October 1918 and finished it on the morning of the Armistice."[31] Here Stravinsky undoubtedly refers to the completion of the instrumental score, dated precisely at eleven o'clock a.m. on November 11, 1918. Thus the impression of a work created with considerable dispatch, within a month's time in fact, is inferred. Moreover little more than one month later on December 19, Stravinsky signed a contract whereby Sirene, his publisher in this case, would issue 1,000 copies of the work's piano reduction.[32] This further advances the notion of an expeditious process, implying that the piano reduction must have been at least promised, if not already finished, soon after the ensemble score in order for negotiations regarding its release to have been accomplished so quickly. One must also consider that in the fall and winter of 1918, Stravinsky was by no means exclusively involved with the writing of *Ragtime*. Sketches for several other works are dated from this time in his notebooks, though the full extent of their development cannot be ascertained at present. Yet there are indications that this piano reduction—and here one must carefully note Stravinsky's interchangeable usage of the terms reduction and transcription—was indeed completed at least around the time of the Sirene contract, if not much earlier. Indeed, as reported in *Pictures and Documents,* Jean Hugo recalls that

> One day in our apartment in the Palais-Royal, Stravinsky, after having drunk an immeasurable amount, played a ragtime that he had just composed, for an audience of Picasso, Diaghilev, Massine, Auric, and Poulenc.[33]

Craft suggests that this performance probably occurred in December of 1918. In this regard, Stravinsky had invited Picasso to design "some continuous line drawings to grace the cover of this 'reduction.' " Cocteau confirms this exchange in a February 20, 1919, letter to the composer, reporting that "Yesterday I brought your *Ragtime* to Madame Gulon the engraver. The work will be started immediately. I also saw Picasso who will do the cover."[34] Yet five months later in a July 23, 1919, letter to Ansermet, Stravinsky requests that Ansermet ask Picasso if "My vignette for the Sirene *Ragtime* was completed yet" thus indicating a rather protracted affair.[35]

On the strength of this evidence alone, the history of *Ragtime's* composition consumed at least 10 months. However, additional source materials not mentioned by Stravinsky conclusively establish that the work

Plate 8. *Ragtime for Eleven Instruments*, first page of piano autograph

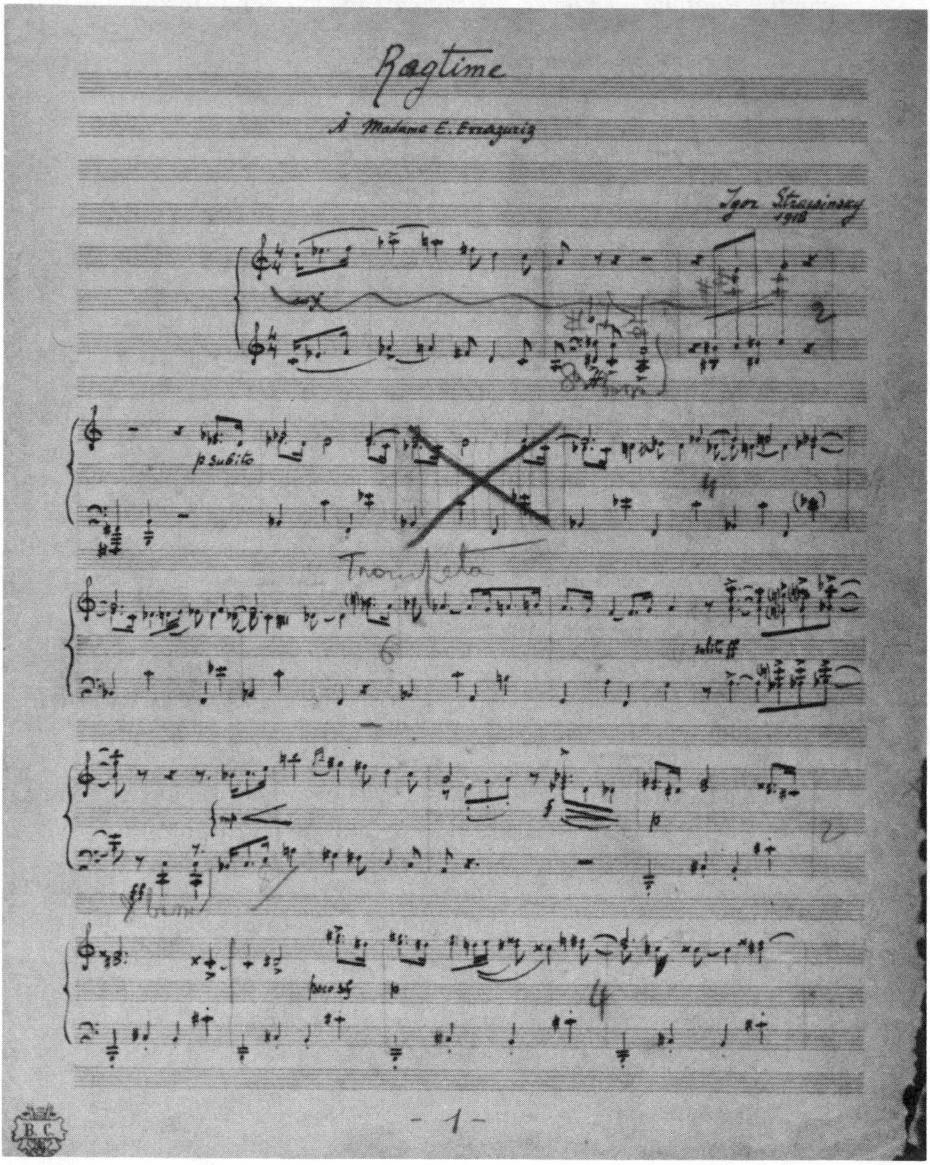

The Robert Owen Lehman Collection, on deposit in The Pierpont Morgan Library

Plate 9. *Ragtime for Eleven Instruments*, last page of piano
autograph

was not only begun long before the October 1918 date given, but to a rather substantial degree was actually completed. While these sources are currently unavailable, the well-documented accounts of Craft regarding these manuscript materials when gathered from scattered references, accrue in presenting a fairly clear chronology.

The summary sketch in the possession of the Stravinsky archives is dated March 21, 1918, that is already eight months before Stravinsky supposedly began the composition the following October. Other sketches for both the *Ragtime* and the still later *Piano-Rag-Music* are to be located in a sketchbook dating from earlier that same March. Craft also reports that the *Ragtime* was actually in a rather completed form as early as February 5, 1918, and as such was written "just before the *Piano-Rag-Music* was begun."[36] Elsewhere, Craft indicates that the very first ideas were entered in a sketchbook as early as November 27, 1917, thereby stretching the evolution of the work as far back as nearly a year before Stravinsky speaks of its conception. More importantly, with both the tracing of these sketches to late 1917, and a finished draft dating from the 1918 spring, it is clear that the actual composing of the *Ragtime* antedates Stravinsky's so-called first rag, the "Ragtime" of *Histoire*. The *Histoire* rag, being one of the later parts of that composition to be undertaken, according to Craft was at the earliest not completed until May of 1918.[37] Moreover, the fact that the *Piano-Rag-Music's* genesis is traceable to the previous February suggests that conceivably, the "Ragtime" of *Histoire* was not the first but perhaps even the last of Stravinsky's three ragtime efforts.

With the extended pre-October 1918 history of *Ragtime,* and because of what would have appeared to be the very late instrumentation of the work, one must consider the possibility of the piano exerting a profoundly formative influence on what was to become an ensemble rag. Indeed there is evidence to suggest that while Stravinsky openly spoke of writing the *Ragtime* at the cimbalom, the piano still remained the indispensable component in the work's development. Stravinsky himself, while praising the cimbalom's novel sound on one hand, also declares his intention in using it as being a desire to evoke the "whorehouse piano sonority" of what he perceived to be the essence of the ragtime culture. Also, in examining the March 5, 1918, draft of the score, Craft reveals that the piano, like the cimbalom, was originally assigned its own part in the ensemble version and only at some later point deleted.[38] Finally, on March 23, 1918, only two days after the completed draft was prepared, Stravinsky telegrammed Mme Errazuriz, the work's dedicatee, "you will be sent shortly a ragtime recently composed for you," suggesting that the work at one point was virtually finished in Stravinsky's opinion long before the Armistice of eight months later.[39]

A holograph is what is listed as the piano transcription of *Ragtime* is held by the Pierpont Morgan Library, thus enabling a relatively rare opportunity for study of a primary source. The importance of such an examination centers upon the fact that while the manuscript is thought to be the transcription of December 1918, though no such indication appears anywhere upon the manuscript itself, numerous telling signs such as deletions, additions, revisions, and other emendative markings suggest that this autograph may well surpass its transcriptional appellation. The first and last pages of the manuscript are offered in plates 8 and 9. These two reproductions are representative of the three-stave open scoring found throughout the eight autograph pages of the manuscript. While such an open scoring normally indicates an orchestral setting or short score, it should be noted that the use of three staves is quite common in Stravinsky's piano literature as well, including the transcription of this *Ragtime* and even the *Piano-Rag-Music*. In this manuscript, instrumental designations, such as the trompeta of measure 11 (see pl. 8) are written in pencil in the manner of suggestions rather than firmly made decisions. Bar lines are sketched in pencil also, hinting at Stravinsky's rather late contemplation of metric divisions as he attempted to retain a rhythmically improvisational sense within rag's metrically regular patterns. Though the manuscript is almost entirely in ink, other notes are added in pencil. For example, the third measure of plate 8 indicates the addition of several octave doublings, while in the next bar a few pitches neither appearing in the ensemble or transcription version are also added in pencil. These two measures, extracted from plate 8 are given in example 63.

Example   63.   *Ragtime   for   Eleven   Instruments*,   mm.   3-4
(transcription)

Further octave doublings are penciled in throughout the manuscript. In this regard, a comparison of the autograph with both the published piano transcription and the ensemble score is enlightening. First consider measures 26-29. The published transcription includes the bass note octaves E and B crossing bars 26 and 27, and similarly F and B flat across bars 28 and 29, thus accenting the stylistically weak to strong pulse patterns. The autograph confirms that these doublings were not included originally, and it is therefore quite likely that Stravinsky chose to add them later, as indicated by their appearance in pencil rather than ink, thus reinforcing these moments of the texture in a thoroughly pianistic and conventionally rag-styled fashion. Next, a comparison with the ensemble score reveals that these same notes are not doubled in the equivalent bars, though the cimbalom and contrabass do share the same concert pitch in the first of the two instances. Example 64 reproduces measures 26-29 of the piano transcription, indicating by circle those points in the autograph where Stravinsky's penciled additions were made. Example 65 reprints the corresponding bars of the ensemble version.

Example 64.   *Ragtime*, mm. 26-29

Used by kind permission of J&W Chester/Edition Wilhelm Hansen London Ltd.

Given the customary status accorded transcriptions or reductions, structural revisions would be unlikely. A deletion, however, struck in blue pencil as was often the composer's habit, is observed in measure six of plate 8. Stravinsky's decision to excise what he apparently deemed an unwarranted repetition seems to fall more within the drafting process of a work rather than the preparation of a transcription. More typically transcriptional is the addition of several performance indications, such as specific dynamic markings or the pencil staccatos in the bass of measures 21-22 which while appearing in the piano version are absent in the ensemble score.

Finally, plate 9 presents two further cases of interest: the closing chord has been restructured as evident by its penciling, so that its doublings match the corresponding chord in the published transcription. This seems to suggest an addition that is more appendicularly pianistic than anything else. More important is the inscription of the date "L'hiver,

Example 65. *Ragtime* (ensemble score)

1918'' which appears in ink, as does Stravinsky's signature. In attempting to determine as precisely as possible the date of this autograph, this seasonal designation in itself permits no more than an approximate time frame. Could this mean the winter of 1918, that is, January, February, or perhaps even March; or might this be interpreted as December of 1918, nearly a year later? The implications of either judgment arc pertinent. The earlier dating would suggest that the autograph was completed while Stravinsky was in the formative stages of writing *Ragtime,* while the possibility of the manuscript having been completed in December implies a post-Armistice transcription, and so prepared after the instrumention had already been settled.

Though it is impossible to make this determination without the benefit of examining the other primary sources, nevertheless the preponderance of observations adduced from both a chronological reconstruction of the events that surround the composition's development, as well as the examination of the autograph itself, strongly suggest that the manuscript originates from early rather then late 1918. After all, why would Stravinsky in late 1918 be laboring over matters of instrumentation, adding suggested metric patterns by penciling in bar lines, or altering the work's proportions by deleting a passage. Surely these are the emendations of a genuine composing score, or a rather intact draft such as the one that according to Craft is known to have been completed on February 5.

In light of these implications, the transcription of *Ragtime* assumes a notability seldom associated with such frequently maligned pianistic conversions. Indeed, in preparing this arrangement for piano solo, as Stravinsky himself often referred to it, it would appear that this early 1918 source was utilized as a virtually finished model, then at some later point, probably November or early December, the manuscript was only modified in an amazingly slight degree. Moreover, in gaining a sharper perception of Stravinsky's near dependency upon the keyboard as the *sine qua non* in his compositional process, this particular transcription becomes especially illuminating. Such a compositional method is reminiscent of Haydn's supposed manner of working, wherein he would regularly improvise at the keyboard, or as James Webster suggests, "fantasize and diddle around" in order to acquire his creative ideas.[40] Yet Stravinsky's reliance surpasses this initial stage of idea development. In the manuscript of *Ragtime,* clearly Stravinsky found it unnecessary to undertake anything but the smallest repartitions as he prepared the work for Sirene. Thus one might conclude that the work was in many ways fundamentally pianistic in the pre-instrumental phases of its evolution. In effect, the more recognized ensemble version of the composition was by Stravinsky's own physical hand a near completed piano piece long before the specific instrumental colors and the idioms of jazz scoring were finalized. Moreover, this procedure as it seems to have been adopted in this instance was not unusual. Craft reports that similar instrumental suggestions appear on the piano manuscript of the earlier discussed March from the *Three Easy Pieces* which was soon to be orchestrated.[41] Such thoughts are not offered towards the repudiation of the rightful place traditionally occupied by *Ragtime* as an authentic ensemble "jazz portraiture" as Stravinsky called it. There is no incontrovertability to sway one into believing that Stravinsky ever intended to release the work as a genuine piano piece, albeit his March 23 communiqué to Mme Errazuriz remains puzzling in this regard. Nonetheless, Stravinsky's irrefragable fingerprints are especially apparent in this opus and by this virtue his pianistic shaping of what would frequently evolve to be nonkeyboard works is again reinforced.

Between the completion of this transcription and Stravinsky's third and final rag composition, other projects were undertaken, including the revised orchestration of *The Firebird*. More importantly, in tracing Stravinsky's interests in ragtime as fostered by the piano, are the *Four Russian Songs,* written during late 1918 and the winter of 1919. This often neglected collection based upon Russian popular texts are in many ways, while distinctly retrospective, nevertheless surprisingly symptomatic of the composer's current enchantment with rag. A wonderfully refreshing blend results. The piano accompaniment is especially revealing in its adoption of certain chordal constructions whose textural disposition, discussed below, will be transferred unaltered into sections of the *Piano-Rag-Music*. Several relevant source materials indicate other connections to various keyboard related instruments, including a complete version of three of the four pieces in a setting which uses the cimbalom. There is a transcription for the Pleyela as well, the aforementioned instrument that was commanding much of Stravinsky's attention during this period and into the next decade.

During this same winter, Stravinsky chose to finish his *Piano-Rag-Music,* a work which he "had begun some time before with Arthur Rubinstein and his strong, agile, clever fingers in mind."[42] It was to be the first of two ultimately failed Stravinskyan endeavors (the second being *Three Movements from Petrouchka*) offered as an attempt to entice Rubinstein into playing more contemporary music.[43] Stravinsky's recollection of the circumstances inspiring the *Piano-Rag-Music* as expressed in his *Chroniques* warrants quotation.

> I was inspired by the same ideas, and my aim was the same, as in *Ragtime,* but in this case I stressed the percussion possibilities of the piano. What fascinated me most

of all in the work was that the different rhythmic episodes were dictated by the fingers themselves. My own fingers seemed to enjoy it so much that I began to practice the piece; not that I wanted to play it in public . . . but simply for my personal satisfaction. Fingers are not to be despised: they are great inspirers, and, in contact with a musical instrument, often give birth to subconscious ideas which might otherwise never come to life.[44]

The work is dated June 27, 1919. Stravinsky, eager to secure a publication contract as soon as possible, quickly pursued the matter in a letter to Ansermet dated July 23. Ansermet, it may be recalled, had earlier interceded for Stravinsky in attempting to win an American publication of the easy piano duets. Amidst a medley of topics to be found in this particular letter, as reprinted by Craft in the first of three epostilary volumes of Stravinsky's correspondence, Stravinsky interjects the cryptic instruction: "Show Kling my new piece for piano solo called *Piano-Rag-Music* which I recently composed for Art. Rubinstein."[45] Kling was then director of J & W Chester, who did in fact publish the work in 1920. The first performance seems to have taken place at the Conservatoire in Lausanne on November 8, 1919, with José Iturbi as the pianist. A copy of the printed program for that occasion (reproduced in *Pictures and Documents*) also lists Iturbi as having played the piano transcription of *Ragtime,* as well as joining the composer in a performance of both sets of easy duets. For whatever reason one chooses to speculate, it is curious to note that Stravinsky elected not to perform either of the rag pieces himself. In both instances, the pianistic technique demanded is so unorthodox, so idiosyncratically Stravinskyan, that it is difficult to imagine how anyone more than he could have been better prepared to present the very clearly specified interpretive directions that mark each score. His autobiographical comment, as quoted earlier, suggests that he indeed enjoyed practicing the *Piano-Rag-Music*; moreover, as already established, we know that he performed the transcribed *Ragtime* privately for an audience of Picasso, Poulenc, and others. Yet public performance seems to have disinterested him at this point. Perhaps because of this, and thus the necessity of entrusting performances to others, the score for the *Piano-Rag-Music* abounds with such exhortations as "brillante e secco," "excessivement court et fort," "attaquez chaque fois," as well as such directions as "répétez les sol b de la façon la plus liée possible (legato des doigts et ped)," and even a framed measure, reprinted in example 66, reminiscent of directions more commonly found in piano literature of a more current vintage. In this instance, the piano writing is particularly imitative of the style one associates with the piano rags Stravinsky no doubt employed, directly or otherwise, as models.

Example 66.   *Piano-Rag-Music*

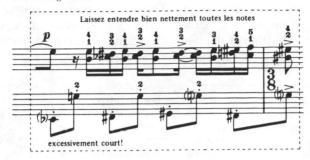

Such indicia disappear nearly altogether in Stravinsky's piano works of the next decade, a period during which he actively resumed the role of pianist himself, seldom allowing the performance rights of these works to pass beyond his personal control. This *satis verborum* posture, so evident in works such as the Piano Sonata and the *Serenade en La,* suggests that Stravinsky, as the foremost guardian of his own literature in the 1920s, apparently found it less obligatory to specify his interpretive guidance as extensively—an attitude which he was eventually to regret perhaps, since other performers unfamiliar with his playing interpreted the scores literally and so quite blandly, though of course this was not at all the composer's intent.

Thus the *Piano-Rag-Music* seems to have been played only by others in the years immediately following its premiere. For example, at the International Music Festival of Salzburg in 1922, the work was programmed, without either the composer's knowledge or sanction, as an exemplification of his current compositional style. According to Diaghilev's secretary Boris Kuchno, who notified Stravinsky of this unauthorized performance, the festival originally planned to include the transcription of *Histoire,* but since adequate rehearsals could not be arranged, Stravinsky's name was simply to be erased from the program. However, Kuchno and Poulenc so convincingly implored the festival committee to change its mind that the *Piano-Rag-Music* was substituted. Jean Wiener, a pianist with whom Stravinsky was on friendly terms, played the work much to the success of the composer's name. Yet Stravinsky's omission from the festival as an artistic consultant or invited participant seems to have disturbed him considerably, as an insincerely expressed congratulatory note to Wiener attests: "I am thrilled to know that you had such a great success with my *Rag-Music* and I am flattered by the passionate interest in me shown by the illustrious 'International Congress' of Salzburg."[46]

The chronology of the *Piano-Rag-Music's* development is important enough to recount in some depth. Though the primary source materials are currently unavailable, Craft's informed account in reporting the sketching and drafting of the work once again deserve a verbatim reporting since it is the most reliable information we have.

> Immediately after completing the *Ragtime* (February 5), Stravinsky began the *Piano-Rag-Music,* but after six pages of sketches he entered two notations for the opening "bell-motive" of the *Symphonies of Wind Instruments*. The *Piano-Rag-Music* was probably resumed in March, 1919, but again about half-way through the new draft, Stravinsky composed the first motive for the chorale eventually used in the *Symphonies*—and entered a figure marked for harmonium. These sketches probably date from May, 1919.[47]

Not only was the harmonium once considered in an instrumentation for the *Symphonies of Winds,* but also according to Craft, the earliest ideas for the 1922 *Octet,* also begun about this time, were sketched for the same keyboard instrument. More importantly, in comparing a sketch for the *Symphonies'* Chorale (ex. 67), as reproduced in *Pictures and Documents,* with a passage extracted from the completed *Piano-Rag-Music* ex. 68, a notable congruence arises.

Example 67.   Sketch for Chorale from *Symphonies of Winds*

Example 68.   *Piano-Rag-Music*

The linear outline of the *Symphonies'* motive as seen in the sketch differs only slightly from the version upon which Stravinsky ultimately settled. The unmistakable similarity between examples 67 and 68 suggest that Stravinsky's preoccupation in writing the *Piano-Rag-Music,* significantly, though perhaps indirectly, provoked some of the initial ideas to be developed more fully when he turned his attention to the *Symphonies.* Naturally some transference would be anticipated in approaching the completion of one work while simultaneously envisioning the basic materials for another.

Yet if there are some documented connections between these two compositions, there is also a clear bond between the *Piano-Rag-Music* and its predecessor, *Histoire.* One might reasonably expect at least a surface resemblance between *Histoire's* "Ragtime" and the later piano piece; however, other sections of *Histoire* share conspicuously similar ties with the *Piano-Rag-Music.* Perhaps the clearest instance is cited by White who suggests that the passage of the piano work, reprinted in example 69, recalls the excerpt of *Histoire's* "Little Concert," illustrated in example 70. The similarities are clear. Not only are the linear and rhythmic treatments alike, but the textural stratification of each also shares common properties.

Example 69.   *Piano-Rag-Music*

Used by kind permission of J&W Chester/Edition Wilhelm Hansen London Ltd.

Moreover, in light of the chronology given by Craft, it is quite conceivable, perhaps even likely, that the basic elements of the *Piano-Rag-Music* might actually have been in part an antecedent to *Histoire*; for while the sketches for this piano work were entered in Stravinsky's February 1918 notebook, the "Little Concert" was one of the final parts of *Histoire* completed, not being drafted in fact until the following August, and still undergoing revision as late as September 19.[48] Finally, while the exact chronological sequence of these events must for the time being at least remain conjectural, more germane is the unarguable fact that the development of *Ragtime,* the *Symphonies,* the *Four Russian Songs, Histoire,* and of course the *Piano-Rag-Music* itself, were evolving at approximately the same time. From the materials available, it would appear that to a measurable extent, all were influenced by Stravinsky's habit of drafting ideas at the keyboard.

The *Piano-Rag-Music* has fared as both the most provocative and most maligned of Stravinsky's three ragtime compositions. Frequently it has been judged as no more than a stylistic anomaly, a waggish deflection

Example 70.   *Histoire du Soldat*, "Little Concert"

Used by kind permission of J&W Chester/Edition Wilhelm Hansen London Ltd.

of energy that furnished only a brief respite before the larger projects of
Pulcinella and the *Symphonies* were to occupy engrossingly the composer's attention. In his 1930 *Stravinsky's Sacrifice to Apollo,* for example,
White censures the work as a product of errancy, asserting that "The
1919 *Piano-Rag-Music* is a disgracefully botched piece of work which
even if perpetrated in an unfortunate moment, ought never to have been
published." More graphically still: "It is hard to credit any serious composer with the inanity of such passages as bars 33 to 36 [and] 42 to 50.
. . .''[49] But White's obloquy is not to be dismissed lightly, for doubtlessly
it reflected a prevalent criticism voiced by those convinced that once
again the mercurial Stravinsky was somehow shunning a certain implicit
noblesse obligé propriety befitting any creative composer by persistently
dabbling in no better than cabaret music. Equally bewildering was the
brittle, even ferocious style of piano writing from a composer whose last
substantive piano solo, the Opus 7 *Etudes* of a decade before, was satu-
rated by the decadence of a lingering romanticism. Yet even the very
passages that White decries should not be dismissed as a mere aberration.

Measures 33 to 36, reproduced in example 71, exhibit a marked textural, intervallic, and rhythmic resemblance to the opening of the first of the *Four Russian Songs* written during the same winter and reprinted in example 72. Perhaps most obvious is the shared use of the compound minor ninth interval, employed in an identical rhythmic fashion and providing a similar ostinato for each work.

Example 71.   *Piano-Rag-Music*, mm. 33-42

Used by kind permission of J&W Chester/Edition Wilhelm Hansen London Ltd.

Example 72.   *Four Russian Songs*, No. 1

The octave displacement of the figure in the *Piano-Rag-Music* conforms to the conventional vamping accompaniment style one would normally expect in such a work. The asymmetrical groupings of the respective right hand passages are also analogous. Such repetitive patterns, both texturally and pianistically alike, permeate each composition. In this respect, especially correlative are the excerpts of examples 73 and 74 wherein the added relationship of an "unbarred" measure is explicit. Moreover, a motivic similarity, based upon the same intervallic cells discussed in the piano duets, is apparent, as circled in the respective passages.

Example 73. *Piano-Rag-Music*

Used by kind permission of J&W Chester/Edition Wilhelm Hansen London Ltd.

Example 74. *Four Russian Songs*

Despite such interior similarities, the surface of the composition was so uncompromisingly violent as to astound Rubinstein immediately upon his receipt of the manuscript.

> On my return to New York, at the desk of the Biltmore, a small, carefully packed item which had arrived from Europe awaited me. My heart was beating as I opened it carefully. I knew what it was: the composition Stravinsky had promised me. The title of it was *Piano Rag Music,* dedicated to Arthur Rubinstein. It was a meticulously and beautifully written autographed manuscript. He had even drawn some flowers around my name. With awe I put this precious sheet on the desk of my piano and began to read it. It took me four or five readings to understand the meaning of this music. It bore out Stravinsky's indication that it was going to be "the first real piano piece." In his sense, it was just that; but to me it sounded like an exercise for percussion and had nothing to do with any rag music, or with any other music in my sense. I must admit I was bitterly, bitterly disappointed. Good musicians to whom I showed it shared my opinion.[50]

In his later and more extensive biography of Stravinsky, White tempered his earlier objurgation by suggesting that in the *Piano-Rag-Music* "Stravinsky relaxed his discipline and allowed a sense of improvisation to dictate a work that is almost rhapsodic in form—a turbulent spate of music carrying all sorts of flotsam in its stream. The result is rather incoherent."[51]

In writing the *Piano-Rag-Music,* Stravinsky's aim unquestionably was the simulation of the strident comedic effects often identified with the barroom rag style. But at the same time, one suspects that Rubin-stein's and especially White's allegation of a resultant unintelligibility is a perceptual judgment, for incoherence never found a welcome asylum in Stravinsky's workshop. While a rhapsodic intent seems surely to have rested at the center of his intention, any notion of the work being genu-inely improvised is quickly dispelled since numerous primary source ma-terials have survived. Thus, some analytic means should exist by which to decode this refractory "flotsam" and so bring some measure of ac-countability in understanding more fully the work's internal structure. But before proceeding with such an analysis, it is essential to consider first the rather intriguing proposition Stravinsky struck for himself in un-dertaking this musical caricature.

We know that Stravinsky was wont to view each new composition as a fresh challenge, a problem to be studied methodically towards dis-covering the one correct solution. Understandably, he did not wish to foresake those taxonomical characteristics endemic to the highly stylized nature of the genre. Yet short of creating some pastiche whose pitch syntax was firmly rooted in the soil of tonality and whose structure was securely fastened to the clear sectionalization of ideas into rag's strains and breaks, what creative alternative might there be to explore? It was just the kind of compositional dilemma that Stravinsky seems always to have relished.

Regarding structure, only the most general semblance of a more or less typical rag form is to be noted in the work. This abstention from a repetition of broad, expectant patterns was, however, conducive to the achievement of the improvisational goal sought. Yet this purposeful resis-tance to the norm must not be interpreted as tantamount to a freely composed, amorphous work, as yet another biographer paroxysmally implies:

> The jazz elements are broken down and crushed to a pulp, then reassembled as if processed by some diabolical machine. In the turbulent sea of clashing rhythms, a nervous syncopated little theme appears from time to time, like a shoal emerging and quickly disappearing in the centre of a boiling whirlpool. . . .[52]

Once again, the implied undercurrent of this turbulent sea is that of an architectural void, an escapade in which Stravinsky takes momentary license to move about freely, perhaps even randomly. Yet despite the fanfaronade spontaneity of the work's overall sound, the notion that Stra-vinsky here, or for that matter anywhere, eshews the basic principles of a fundamental architectonics is very doubtful indeed. More than any other aspect of musical structure, Stravinsky was uncommonly outspoken concerning the intimately related architectural elements of shape, form, balance, pacing and so on: "I attempt to create certain kinds of architectural constructions. My objective is form. My improvisations inevitably evolve into formal constructions."[53] It is towards a morphological study of this seemingly improvised piano work that the following speculation is offered.

Example 75 offers a representative instance of Stravinsky's attempt to endue the *Piano-Rag-Music* with the surface traits synonomous with the popular style.

Example 75.   *Piano-Rag-Music*, mm. 15-19

Used by kind permission of J&W Chester/Edition Wilhelm Hansen London Ltd.

Rhythm and meter are used primarily to promote the syncopes and relentless accompanimental figures commonly associated with rag. While such stylized patterns lend immediate definition to localized rhythmic and metric events, they do not figure prominantly or pervasively enough to be credited as the principal structural pillars of the macroform. Their purpose is narrowly rhetorical rather than broadly functional. Obvious, too, is the use of a triad laden vocabulary, again infused, no doubt, as another contributor towards aping the rag formula of predictable harmonic progressions. Yet such traces are once again only momentarily coloristic and ultimately only remotely tonal; for no broadly construed hierarchical tonal scheme can be said to control the work's architectural coherence.

Other aspects of early as well as classic ragtime, as Berlin differentiates, are carried over to Stravinsky's adaptation. Some ethnomusicological research, for example, suggests a certain pentatonic influence in the melodies of early black composers of ragtime.[54] It is impossible to ascertain whether the rags with which Stravinsky was familiar exhibited such characteristics; yet a pentatonic affinity is apparent in such melodic fragments as that of the right-hand figure quoted earlier in example 73, as well as in the circled transitional motive of example 76.

Example 76. *Piano-Rag-Music*, mm. 14-15

Nor can the humor inherit in the cadential mimicry of a stock rag progression, illustrated in example 77, be missed. Not only is the shifting meter blatant, but the sudden and contextually incongruous closure in A flat, also serves to satirize the passage. But even in such a burlesquely partitive moment in the form, Stravinsky forges a structural elision by enharmonically respelling the cadential A flat triad as a transformed G# ostinato of the next passage.

Example 77. *Piano-Rag-Music*, mm. 22-30

Such observations should be viewed only as a representatitive ex-emplification of the unitive steps Stravinsky takes in bringing some degree of microformal cohesion to this work. But is there a more sweeping architectural flow? To begin, seven divisions, based upon the appearance of new or clearly divided materials, are suggested in delineating the macroformal organization of the work. Each is seemingly unrelated, thus producing an aurally distinct sectionalization.

Table 1.   *Piano-Rag-Music* Surface Organization

Large Divisions	Internal Organization*		
I. Mm. 1-9	Mm. 1-2 ⎤ 3 ⎟ 4 ⎟ 5-7 ⎟ 8-9 ⎦		
II. Mm. 10-14	Mm. 10-13 14		
III. Mm. 15-23	Mm. 15-16 17 18-19 ⎤ 20 ⎟ 21 ⎦		22-23 24
IV. Mm. 25-54	Mm. 25-28 29-32 ⎤ ⎡33-36 ⎥ ⎢37-41 ⎦ ⎣42-49		50 51-54
V. Mm. 55-82	Mm. 55-66 67-72 73-76 77-80 81-82		
VI. Measure 83 (unbarred)			
VII. Mm. 84-113	Mm. 84-87⎤ ⎡88 ⎟ ⎢89-92⎦ ⎣93 ⎤ 94 ⎟ 95 ⎦		96-98 ⎤ ⎡99 ⎟ ⎢100-101⎦ ⎡102 ⎣103-112 113

*Hyphenated measures indicate a formal unit based on some common structural element such as a rhythmic or linear motive. Bracketed measures specify a still closer (and more obvious) surface relationship such as a literal repetition.

The classifications of table 1 offer a summary of one plausible surface articulation as an initial step in probing whatever architectural coherence might exist. It does not, however, pretend any insight into the syntactical elements of the composition or the specific strength of relations among the more elemental musical units involved. Rhythm and meter, as well as certain tonal inferences, have already been determined to occupy a generally referential function in Stravinsky's retention of those traits most associable with the ragtime stereotype. Moreover, as outlined in table 1, this apparent deviation from the more or less traditional rag form seems to suggest that other architectural issues might be better pursued towards comprehending any sense of a macroformal design. In this regard, Stravinsky himself provides a clue in assessing his architectural concerns as a component of the compositional process. Matters of musical time, especially the pacing of temporal events held a special significance for him. The precedence of this issue regularly surfaces in his writings about music: "Music presupposes before all else a certain organization of time, a chronology. . . ."[55] Moreover he clearly distinguished music's "ontological and psychological time" frames (to use his own descriptions) and was particularly sensitive to the necessity of equilibrating these cardinal forces in achieving an architectural whole. In considering the pacing of events in the *Piano-Rag-Music,* this holds a special relevancy. Simply stated, why did Stravinsky, unconstrained by any conformance to the normal strains and breaks syndrome of ragtime, articulate the surface divisions diagrammed in table 1 at the precise junctures he freely chose? Is there an infrastructure that orders the work's architectonics in some traceable way?

In addressing such questions, a portion of the piece corresponding to division V of table 1 is first presented. Immediately apparent is a structural similarity between measures 67-72 as bracketed in example 78 and the work's opening measures, reproduced in example 79. A type of reprise is effected as may be ascertained by a quick comparison of the two examples.

Measures 65 and 66, that is, the two measures immediately prefacing the reprise, mark a dynamic and textural focus by crowning the accumulating propulsion which had been unfolding in measures 61-64. The insertion of the seventh chords as circled in measures 65-66 add another embellishing element to the textural enhancement of these two architecturally pivotal bars. Durationally, these two measures appear at a temporal point approximately two-thirds through the 18-measure passage. Next, consider that the full span of division V, as marked in table 1 encloses 28 measures whereupon division VI ensues. The aforementioned reprise of the work's opening after recapitulating several measures, ends

Example 78. *Piano-Rag-Music*, mm. 55-72

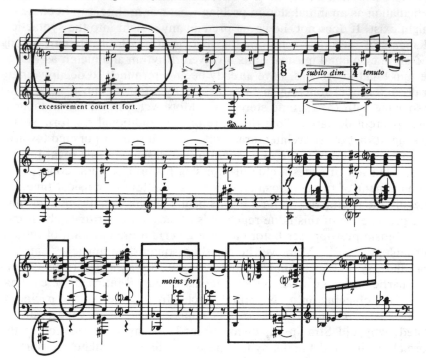

Used by kind permission of J&W Chester/Edition Wilhelm Hansen London Ltd.

Example 79. *Piano-Rag-Music*, mm. 1-4

Used by kind permission of J&W Chester/Edition Wilhelm Hansen London Ltd.

at bar 72, that is, the last measure reprinted in example 78. Once again, this measure similarly demarcates an approximate two-thirds juncture along the larger time line. Both of these durational phases of the event pacing are plotted in example 80.

   An examination of the larger divisions demonstrates the existence of the same pattern as an analogue in macroformal pacing. The first 83 measures of the piece are submitted as proof of a proportional regularity. Also, with measure 83 marking the largest gesture illustrated, the immediately adjacent division of measure 55 occurs again at about the two-thirds mark of the total duration. The pattern is regular. Each appearance of new surface material occurs in proportionately parallel recessive durations of approximately the same length. All of these larger divisions of the *Piano-Rag-Music* are summarized in example 81.

Example 80. Durational Pacing, mm. 55-83

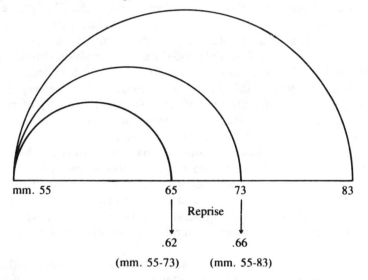

Example 81. Durational Pacing, mm. 1-83

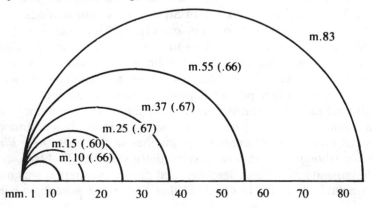

Example 81 does not represent the entire duration of the work. Because Stravinsky dispenses with bar lines for several passages beyond measure 83—presumably to reinforce the work's improvisatory flavor—the reconciliation of the number of total measures and the pertaining proportions must be computed on the basis of the work's invariable quarter note pulse, of which there totals 451 beats. With this as a chronographic means of evaluation, bar 83 in relation to division VII's bar 84 is somewhat disproportionate (.74), though bar 84 in relation to the 113 barred measures of the piece yields a more conforming ratio of .62.

This kind of systemic regularlity would seem to corroborate Stravinsky's expressed interest in the pacing of musical events. That the release of these events matches such a patterned dissemination within an "incoherent" piano rag, perhaps invites skepticism, as might the very concept of mathematical plotting. Certainly the durational analysis should not be misconstrued as an eristic attempt to demonstrate any Stravinskyan consciousness in engineering this particular architectural shape so prevalent in western art music. Yet Stravinsky often spoke specifically of musical form as a product of the "logical discussion of musical materials," and that music was "far closer to mathematics than literature . . . certainly something like mathematical thinking and mathematical relationships."[56] That such mathematical and compositional relationships were "festering in the unconscious" as he once expressed, suggests normally unquestioned aspects of Stravinsky's interior creative process that deserve exploration, but because of the slippery speculative realm in which such examinations must be conducted, have traditionally been regarded as ineffable.[57]

When the sum of these analytic suggestions are combined with Stravinsky's own attention to musical architecture's mathematical foundation, the possibility of a resultant eurythmy in lieu of some normative form seems justified. Whatever the stream of improvisatory surface events imparts, the *Piano-Rag-Music,* like all of Stravinsky's compositions, shows no signs of substructural erosion. For even in thrashing out a raucously fashioned piano rag, Stravinsky seems to have remained ever the vigilant protector of an architectural order. Nor is the specific structural schemata suggested here an exception in Stravinsky's overall catalogue of works, as will be seen with other piano compositions to be examined.

With the *Piano-Rag-Music,* Stravinsky's interest in the ragtime style reached a summit. Its utility had amounted to far more than an innocent flirtation, as evinced by its continuing influence in the 1919 *Three Pieces for Clarinet* (though this was at least partially sketched in 1918). To be sure, the intensity of interest demonstrated during this period was not to recur with such zeal. Yet to conclude that Stravinsky somehow simply outgrew what others saw as the puerility of these works is unquestionably both an historical and judgmental error. Stravinsky obviously approached each of his ragtime compositions with the same sedulousness as any of his more seriously perceived works. Finally, with the 1919 *Piano-Rag-Music,* Stravinsky returned to the composition of solo piano literature, a return that would inaugurate the most productive decade of piano writing in his career, and at the same time, provide an important literature with which to examine many of the most fundamental compositional concepts of his neoclassicism.

5

Works from France

When Stravinsky moved his family to Brittany in June 1920, there must have been some sense of deliverance in now placing behind him what had been an unforced, but nonetheless artistically incommodious period of exile. The isolation that naturally accompanied life in the remote villages of Claren and Morges had proven surprisingly conducive to a rather un-abated compositional flow, especially given the severe economic strictures that surrounded him. Yet it was inevitable that when the opportunity arose, Stravinsky's *vis vitae,* and perhaps even his still youthful compul-sion to be seen once again at the eye of some vigorously musical mecca, would finally prevail in prompting him to leave his "Alpine colleagues" as Diaghilev somewhat despiteously referred to them. So as the European world gradually regained its equilibrium in the postwar years, choices of a new homeland once more began to avail themselves, and Stravinsky was quick to relocate.

Stravinsky's wartime journeys to neighboring metropolitan centers seem always to have buoyed his spirit. Particularly, nowhere are his mem-oirs more vibrant than in relating his visits to Spain and Italy. Indeed, as early as 1911, as he was finishing the score of *Petrouchka* in Rome, the composer had already declared that this would be the chosen city of his eventual residence.[1] Though Rome rather than Paris continued to be his preferred future domicile throughout what he surely knew would be only a temporary Swiss sanctuary, his relocation to the Italian capital was never to be. Thus when suitable accommodations could not be found in Italy, Stravinsky amended his plans and departed first for Carantec where he spent the summer months of 1920, then to the Parisian suburb of Garches where he settled in September.

Pulcinella was the last work completed before embarking for France. In some ways this popular *commedia dell arte* ballet served as a repatriat-ing work, for it helped to ameliorate relations that had become increas-ingly strained between Stravinsky and Diaghilev, owing to the fact that the exiled composer had captured a success independent of Diaghilev's autarchy. The work was premiered by the *Ballet Russe* in Paris on May 15, only weeks before Stravinsky's departure from Switzerland. Though an examination of this *actions dansante* as Stravinsky preferred to call it, rests beyond this study, it should be noted that a good portion of Stravinsky's model was drawn from that keyboard music of Pergolesi; for example various trio sonatas and harpsichord lessons were used.[2] Thus there can be little question that this music, like the earlier models of his youth and of the ragtime period, was rehearsed at the piano and so again provided Stravinsky a closer contact with the actual music to be first assimilated, then refurbished in his own shaping conception of the work.

Stravinsky worked at two compositions during the summer at Carantec: the *Concertino for String Quartet* was the first completed; the *Symphonies of Winds* was also begun during the same season though as mentioned earlier, sketches in keyboard notation date from earlier years. The music that was eventually to serve as the closing section of this 1920 work was originally published as a short piano piece (discussed in chap. 7).

The years that followed these early months in what was to become a nearly two-decade inhabitancy in various French cities were filled with a myriad of both musical and nonmusical interests and outlets. As mentioned in chapter 4, little is known of Stravinsky's prolific transcriptions of his works for Pleyel, though surely this was a consuming task and one that Stravinsky clearly felt strongly about, enough so that he chose to rob time from composition in order to prepare these valuable documents. Also, after a period of relative domesticity during the years in Switzerland, a time that often found Stravinsky in the company of his children, his attachment to home and family was gradually abandoned in favor of cultivating new friends and personal relationships. It was during these early French years that Stravinsky met his second wife to be, Vera deBosset Sudeikinia (1888–1982). A few years later, Stravinsky's decision to pursue an active career as a pianist and conductor would make greater demands upon his time, as will be seen. All of these events were by one tangent or another related, and surely steered the direction of his compositional productivity. Thus it is not surprising to find the majority of his piano literature arising from the years in France (especially 1923–35) as his ardent interest in piano performance and piano composition became more inextricably bound than during any other period of his life.

The first piano work undertaken in France, however, was not a personal performance vehicle, for Stravinsky had not yet considered a career as a concert pianist. Rather, it is another work steeped in didactic principles and aimed towards the musical enlightenment of children, though in this case and unlike the earlier duets, not specifically intended for his own family. It has already been noted that some of the ideas for the 1921 *The Five Fingers* date from about the same time as the writing of the easy piano duets years earlier; however, all eight pieces of this new solo piano collection were completed during January and February while the composer still was residing in Garches.[3] The circumstances that led to the writing of these miniatures has, until recently, never been very clear. To be sure, Stravinsky did address the work in several of his writings, even signaling the intent of the composition in his *Chroniques*:

> . . . I wrote a group of little pieces for children, which were published under the title *Les Cinq Doigts*. In these eight pieces, which are very easy, the five fingers of the right hand, once on the keys, remain in the same place sometimes even for the whole piece, while the left hand, which is destined to accompany the melody, executes a pattern either harmonic or contrapuntal, of the utmost simplicity. I found it rather amusing, with these very much restricted means, to try to awaken in the child a taste for melodic design in its combination with a rudimentary accompaniment.[4]

It is rather unusual for Stravinsky not to have enunciated the external events that led him to undertaking any compositional project. In this case especially, why would the recently transplanted composer, fresh from such formidable works as *Pulcinella* and the *Symphonies,* now retrench, electing to write a set of elementary piano duets more in the character of the decidedly modest Swiss compositions for piano than his recent creative enterprises? It appears that the work may have been commissioned. Craft reports that a request was made from America (though any specific identity is not given) for such a collection and relayed to Stravinsky by Alfred Pochon of the Flonzaley Quartet, the ensemble for whom Stravinsky had recently dedicated the *Concertino*.[5] There seem to have been 10 pieces requested—5 for piano solo and 5 for piano and voice. The particulars of the commission were even more specific according to Craft:

> Stravinsky answered Pochon on November 15, 1920, saying that it was impossible to guarantee that the piano pieces would be based on Russian folklore, as requested, because that could not be done to order. Stravinsky added that he would prefer to compose for flute or violin, or two violins, which he had wanted to do for a long time.[6]

Soulima Stravinsky's recollection of a recording of the work made in 1925 for Brunswick by his father while on his first American tour is reported in Soulima's own edition of his father's short piano pieces: "I vividly remember the subtle choice of nuances and I particularly noted the timing used in his interpretation. No printed symbol can fully translate the poetic mood of this unique performance. . . ."[7] But indeed Soulima

does attempt to recreate his father's interpretation by adding several performance directions not present in any previous edition. For example, a
first ending and repeat indication are added to the seventh piece of the
collection, Vivo. According to Soulima, these "were added by the composer in his recorded performance." Equally interesting is a passage from
the Lento, sixth in order, wherein the editor adds a sustained D that
apparently was "suggested by the composer at a later time." Examples
82 and 83 reprint the traditional engraving as well as Soulima's version
respectively.

Example 82.   Lento

Example 83.   Lento (Soulima Stravinsky's edition)

The retained D of the right hand in example 83 makes musical sense
enough, and in fact appears in just such a fashion in the subsequent
orchestral version of these pieces in 1962 entitled *Eight Instrumental Miniatures*. However, as an improvement to the piano score, not only is its
extended duration of five measures a rather moot issue, for clearly
the sound quickly decays, but more importantly, it would seem to com-
promise the stated intent of the pedagogy by now demanding a rather
awkward fingering to be negotiated on the child's part. Such editorial
decisions by one so close to Stravinsky's music as his son, who remained
unquestionably the pre-eminent interpreter of his father's literature
throughout his own concertizing career, cannot be taken lightly. Yet even
within the narrow context of these little piano pieces, the obvious need
for a reliable critical edition of all the piano works (to say nothing of the

Stravinsky literature in toto) is emphasized. As information steadily becomes available in regard to sketches and the autographs of the piano literature, it becomes increasingly clear that not only is a complete *corrigenda* desirable, but insights regarding Stravinsky's interpretation of the printed page may also be gained through such manuscript studies.

These *Eight Easy Pieces on Five Notes,* as Stravinsky subtitled the work, bear titles that reveal little about the evocative moods each piece suggests. The Lento discussed above, for example, actually comes fairly close in spirit to the Russian ethos that seems to have been originally requested of Stravinsky. The fourth piece, Larghetto, embodies the style of a siciliano, not unlike the Serenata of the slightly earlier *Pulcinella*; and the final Pesante referred to by Stravinsky as the "Tijuanan Blues" in 1960 is unmistakably a tango parody.

As might have been anticipated, the pitch vocabulary of these pieces shares the same basic trichordal and tetrachordal cells seen so pervasively in the duets of 1915 and 1917, as exemplified here by an excerpt from the Allegretto, the third of the 1921 set. One also observes in example 84, the preciseness with which Stravinsky notates the continuance of a four-part texture by carefully writing the appropriate rests in the uppermost voice.

Example 84.   Allegretto, mm. 27-30

Indeed, the origins of this Allegretto are traceable to a 1917 sketchbook, a time during which the preponderant usage of such pitch cells is observed with regularity.[8] Moreover, the initial melodic gesture of the piece (ex. 85) is remarkably similar to the opening material of *Histoire's* "Little Concert," a work written in August of the following year (ex. 86). Once more then, the chronology of an idea best known in its instrumental guise but probably first forged at the keyboard is reinforced, and appears to apply here especially in light of *Histoire's* already documented kinship to the earlier easy duets that immediately preceded it.

In addition to these by now conventional pitch-class sets, other harmonic and linear patterns emerge. As an example, the use of full triads

Example 85.   Allegretto

Example 86.   *Histoire du Soldat*, "Little Concert"

typify the final piece of this octuple collection (ex. 87) and are referentially employed towards aping the tango model in a manner similar to the enlistment of tertian intervals in the earlier *Piano-Rag-Music*.

The juxtaposition of the sonorities in the first two measures of example 87 is characteristic of Stravinsky's pitting triads against one another at the distance of a tone or semitone throughout the piece. The idea is continued in the $^6/_4$ measure with a C♯ triad hovering above a D minor/major arpeggiated figure. When the roots of these four triads are compiled, an overall linear scheme linked by step is deducible, as seen in example 88.

The pattern is not only representative in the particular, but more importantly is symptomatic of a structural technique to be employed more widely in larger works of the 1920s and 1930s, as will be examined in tracing the formal design of the 1924 Piano Sonata.

Example 87.   Pesante, mm. 8-14

Example 88.   Linear reduction

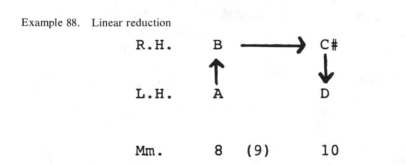

     The challenge that existed in creating compositionally expressive statements within the restricted environment of these pieces was acknowledged by Stravinsky, as mentioned earlier. The simplest materials undergo the same kind of transformation usually associated with more dramatic musical propositons. Consider the first five measures of the Lento (ex. 89).

     The insert of the D-E-F#-G-A pentachord is Stravinsky's own and appears throughout the set each time a hand shift is required. A study of the melody indicates the kind of subtle variation regularly employed by the composer in extending a simple motive. The left hand triadically structured ostinato is enlivened by the asymmetry of its rhythmic disposition, no newer than an ars nova talea but still a viable and recognizable staple

Example 89.   Lento

of the Stravinskyan repertory. But surely the most obvious interest lies in the conflict of the major/minor third, F-F#. Such a semitonal clash is of course by no means unprecedented in the Stravinsky literature; indeed, it goes right to the center of many of the early folkloristic works. But more and more the axial usage of these oppositive thirds would surface as perhaps the paramount component of the pitch collections found in so many of the neoclassic works. The constitution of these tertian intervals within the scale is outlined in example 90. The outer bracket indicating the ambitus when combined with the interior E and G cumulatively yield the tetrachordal cell C discussed in chapter 3. The lower crescents outline the various major/minor thirds that naturally result by the inclusion of both tertian forms. The numerals indicate the symmetry of the total pitch collection, and it is the abstract principle of symmetry, as mentioned earlier, that continued to intrigue the composer as he set about planning his musical architectures.

Example 90.   Tertian Resources

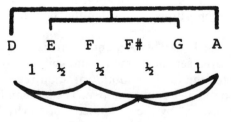

Such a pitch vocabulary as apparent in this instance is no doubt more aurally modal in effect; but nonetheless it is the essence of the fundamental D-F-F#-A structure that will soon be seen to provide the scaffolding for such impressive musical edifices as the Piano Concerto and the *Symphony of Psalms*. Furthermore, as the middle section of this ternary shaped piece begins, a new ostinato commences, here introducing the new pitch B flat; while in the right hand a melodic idea is initiated by another formerly unseen pitch, the repetitive C (see ex. 82). These new pitches of course are natural members of the five-note scale Stravinsky employs as the underpinning of this B section of the form. Thus it is the F-F# dyad that evolves as the crucial pivot in the complete pitch system of the piece (the G and A are invariant) (ex. 91).

Example 91.

```
A section (mm. 1-9)     D    E   ┃ F#  G    A ┃
                                  ┃            ┃
B section (mm. 9-13)              ┃ F   G    A ┃ Bᵇ  C
```

The idea of working within such a limited series of pitches, so tightly controlled and thereby purposefully taxing his powers of compositional imagination, surely gave rise to Stravinsky's statement in 1966 that such five note rows were not unlike "an idea repeated in the "Gigue" in my *Septet*," a work completed in 1953.[9] Such a tempting invitation has sent more than one analyst scurring upon a search to find specific similarities, though most attempts to construct a closely knit bond between the two disparate works leans dangerously towards contrivance. Yet certain pitch collections, and even more importantly, the subsequent manipulation of these materials do seem to be shared. The opening measures of the *Septet's* first movement (ex. 92) exhibits the same kind of five-note pattern, in this case pivoting on the C-C# axis of a pitch collection firmly anchored in A.

The very first measure employs exclusively, transpositionally equivalent pentachordal arrays that were observed in the Lento. Here, at the level of A-B-C#-D-E, there is a pivot at the major/minor third on C natural and a projection of the second pentachord C-D-E-F-G follows. The Gigue which concludes the three movement chamber work is more thoroughly serial than anything Stravinsky had written to that point; yet it is the logical extension of the same type of pitch control presaged in the earlier

Example 92. *Septet*, mm. 1-2 (two-piano version)

movements of that work, and for that matter, similar techniques appear in the *Cantata* of the year before. Yet if the pitch materials of such chronologically distant works as the 1921 *The Five Fingers* and the *Septet* are at least in someway analogous, an even stronger relationship exists through the specific controls to which these materials subscribed. Surely it is this fundamental concept of regulating a limited pitch series that Stravinsky had in mind when he suggested the existence of such a relationship. Ultimately, what may be safely concluded is that once again here, as in the case of the earlier duets, the significance of this children's collection should not be undervalued in tracing some of the more fundamental tenets of Stravinsky's compositional approach; for certainly these piano pieces should surpass such implicitly pejorative descriptions as merely "delightful."

Perhaps no greater quantum leap exists in all pianism than the compositional adjacency of *The Five Fingers* and Stravinsky's next major work undertaken in August of the same year in Anglet.

> There I began a task which enthralled me—a transcription for the piano which I called *Three Movements from Petrouchka*. I wanted with this to provide piano virtuosi with a piece having sufficient scope to enable them to add to their modern repertory and display their technique.[10]

But in the same year that Stravinsky so states, his remarks presented to a literary society at the L'Université des Annales on November 22 warn that the epithetic term transcription is liable to misconception. The pyrotechnical grandiloquence of this the most popular of Stravinsky's piano music is per the composer's own words ". . . one should not look upon this as a piano reduction, but better a piece written especially for the piano, or stated differently, piano music. I insist on this point. . . ."[11]

Transcriptional or not, *Three Movements from Petrouchka* exacts the most awesome pianistic demands. Stravinsky was quick to eliminate himself from the scroll of would-be executants, claiming that his left-hand technique was insufficient; nor did he shrink from dissuading those who in his opinion were perhaps also not equal to the task. Apparently, however, the composer at one point at least did contemplate performing the work himself, for as Craft reports, on the first page of his personal copy, Stravinsky wrote "on July 8, 1924, I began to learn to play it," even though the piece was written years earlier. Craft further indicates that Stravinsky's fingerings throughout the work are plentiful and that he rewrote several sections.[12] Moreover during the next year, Stravinsky wrote to Henri Prunières (editor of *La Revue Musicale*): "Last year I spoke to [Jean] Wiener myself, advising him not to play the *Three Movements from Petrouchka*: I find that his technique and strength are not equal to the score."[13] An honest enough appraisal one would assume; yet it was Weiner who had premiered the work in Paris on December 26, 1922.

Like the *Piano-Rag-Music* of two years earlier, Arthur Rubinstein was the intended recipient of this commissioned work. Rubinstein's reporting of the scenario that led to the work's inception is so revealing that his account, as given in his autobiographical *My Many Years,* warrants full quotation.

> [Stravinsky] asked me, "Did you play in your concerts my *Piano-Rag-Music*?" I was frank. "Dear Igor, I'm more than proud to own your manuscript but I'm still the pianist of the old era. Your piece is written for percussion rather than for my kind of piano." He did not like my answer. . . . "I shall play it and make it clear to you." He then banged it out about ten times, making me more and more antagonistic to the piece. . . . "The piano is nothing but a utility instrument and it sounds right only as percussion."
>
> I was infuriated. "You know well that the public at large does not understand and does not like your music. . . . But for some mysterious reason when I play your music on the piano, it becomes clearer to them and they begin to like it." I went to the piano and played part of *Petrouchka,* especially the music in Petrouchka's room. Stravinsky—it was so like him—immediately forgot all that had been said . . . and became quite professional: "How do you make your bass sound like that? Do you use your pedal in a special way?"
>
> "Yes of course; my foot catches rapidly the still vibrating bass notes, which allows me to change harmonies in the treble." And I added fatuously "your hated piano can do all sorts of things, my dear." Completely serene now, Igor declared enthusiastically, "I shall write for you a sonata made of the material of *Petrouchka*" I embraced him with emotion and joy.[14]

Just how accurate a reconstruction Rubinstein's account is, cannot be determined of course, but in fact the work as premiered by Wiener did carry the subtitle of Sonata.[15] Moreover, Stravinsky's extolment of the percussive virtues of the piano around the turn of the decade are documented in various corroborating references as well. In his memoirs, Rubinstein adds that he premiered the work at the Salle Gaveau, "making it sound as I heard it by the orchestra more than as a piano piece."[16]

Plate 10.   *Petrouchka*, pianola sketch of final page

   Rubinstein goes further in suggesting that not only was he the catalyst in the work's creation but that he acted as Stravinsky's compositional advisor in the actual writing of the piece.

> [Stravinsky] showed me page by page as he composed it. I sometimes dared to show him a trick or two to make it sound better with my specialty for using the pedals and by advising him to alleviate the texture by leaving out some secondary stuff from the orchestral score.[17]

   While it is reasonable to assume that Rubinstein may have assisted or advised Stravinsky in some way during the writing of the transcription that summer in Anglet, it should also be noted that many of the figurations in this piano arrangement are antedated by the pianola version of 1918, a version that is almost entirely forgotten. The Library of Congress Music Division holds several unbound sketch pages of this rare document. An examination of these sources suggests that Stravinsky may have relied fairly heavily upon the inherent capabilities of the mechanical piano in transforming the transcription from the ballet score to the eventual 1921 piano solo.[18]. For example, first consider the lower third of the pianola sketch reprinted in plate 10. Here Stravinsky formulates a new closing gesture to the fourth tableau, beginning with the idea marked "cadenza a*FFF*." This appears to presage the cadential material actually employed three years later in the piano solo as well as that of the 1947 orchestral version. This particular sketch, as well as the others in Washington, clearly confirm Stravinsky's contention that his pianola works were in fact not merely transcriptions of his original music, but rather authentic reconstitutions.
   As a second example, the music reprinted in plate 11 corresponds to the original ballet passage beginning at rehearsal 56 as marked in the sketch, indicating of course that Stravinsky worked from his orchestral score carefully. Even a cursory comparison of example 93, which offers

Example 93.   *Three Movements from Petrouchka*

Plate 11. *Petrouchka*, pianola sketch (rehearsal 56)

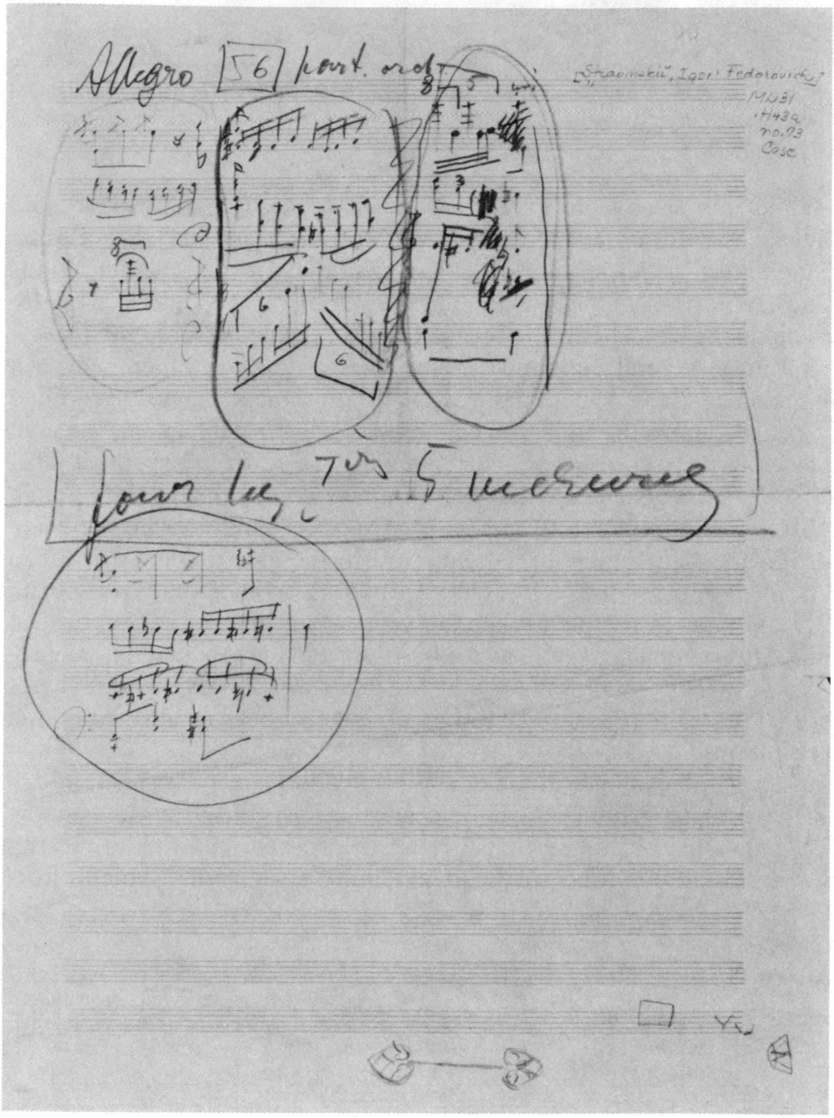

Library of Congress, Music Division

a section of the 1921 piano arrangement, with the plate suggests just how fully Stravinsky may have relied on the earlier pianola version in shaping the foudroyant figurations of this 1921 piano showcase.

Though *Petrouchka* occupied Stravinsky in Anglet, it was not the only project unfolding in his precompositional conscience. Indeed, Stravinsky traces the idea of *Mavra* to the spring of 1921 ("conceived in the Hotel Savoy, London"). This Russianized opera buffa was begun in August and completed in Biarritz in the spring of 1922. Many of the underlying harmonic and linear pillars of this opus duplicate several ideas of the earlier piano works. Even the textural disposition of the major and minor third alteration (C-E flat-E natural) in the piano reduction of Parasha's aria (ex. 94) is in its ostinato form similar to the earlier piano duets and *The Five Fingers*. Additionally, the upper orchestral lines both rhythmically and pianistically recall elements of the *Piano-Rag-Music*.

Example 94.   *Mavra* (piano reduction)

It is with the writing of the 1922/23 *Octet* that Stravinsky most closely previews the techniques to be seen in the neoclassic piano works that followed. This is especially so in its adoption of sonata procedures and contrapuntal fabric, both fundamental traits of the *Concerto for Piano and Winds,* the next work in sequence. Like *Histoire,* it is unlikely that one could conceive of a more instrumentally felicitous scoring than that ultimately chosen for the *Octet.* In recounting his initial thoughts about the instrumentation, a perplexing contrarity results from the two very different versions Stravinsky offers. In his *Chroniques,* the composer claims that it was only after having already completed the first movement that the instrumental path was made clear to him; yet years later, Stravinsky spins one of his somnolent dream visions in which a concert performed by the ultimately chosen ensemble of the *Octet* was revealed: "I awoke from the little concert in a state of great delight and anticipation and the next morning began to compose the *Octour* which I had no thought of the day before. . . ."[19] Yet despite this oneiromancy, there is substantial evidence to demonstrate the pianistic origins of this opus.

Sketches of the waltz variation, for example, date from as early as the spring of 1919 and are clearly scored for harmonium.[20] More revealing, at one early point, according to Craft, the work was intended for piano and wind ensemble with timpani, the very instrumentation selected for the Piano Concerto and begun the same year as the *Octet* was completed.[21]

Because of the more than tenuous bridge joining these two intersecting 1923 works, and before proceeding with a discussion of the Piano Concerto itself, Stravinsky's open endorsement about that time of an emerging contrapuntal devotion, especially as manifested within the province of wind and percussion rather than string colors, should be addressed. Reference has already been given to Stravinsky's assumption about this time of numerous expository essays outlining his own compositional *credenda*. In "Some Ideas About my *Octour*" first printed in the January 1924 *The Arts,* the author seizes the moment, defending what many perceived then as his recent and unexpected conversion to counterpoint as a compositional priority:

> Form in my music derives from counterpoint. I consider counterpoint as the only means through which the attention of the composer is concentrated on purely musical questions. Its elements also lend themselves perfectly to an architectural construction. This sort of music has no other aim than to be sufficient in itself. In general I consider that music is only able to solve musical problems; and nothing else, neither the literary or the picturesque, can be in music of any real interest. The play of musical elements is the thing.[22]

This rather reactionary view, which actually previews the later and infamous "music is powerless to express . . ." call to arms, was not to be a singular instance of such a philosophical stance. Later that same year, Stravinsky elsewhere offered: "Pure counterpoint provides me the basic material from which one forges powerful and effective musical form. Its place cannot be taken by refined harmony or opulent orchestration."[23] Moreover, returning to the *Octet,* Stravinsky elaborates a conjunction between the use of a wind ensemble with its intrinsic capability to "render a certain rigidity of the form I had in mind," and the employment of counterpoint, both of which make "more evident the musical architecture . . . the most important question in all of my recent musical compositions."[24]

The concept of an *orchestre d'harmonie,* as well as the use of the piano's birthright as a percussion instrument had been germinating for some time. The *Ragtime* of 1918, the *Symphonies of Winds,* even *Mavra* exhibit an attitudinal progression towards the crisp sound of the *Octet* and the Piano Concerto itself. Surely the final solution of employing a quartet of pianos within the sonic world of *Les Noces,* first performed in

1923, provides indubitable attestation to the composer's increasing repudiation of "string instruments, which are less cold and more vague," a common, even importunate saw about this time. Indeed, the opulence, even prodigality of his Parisian ballet triumphs—perhaps by 1923 an uneasy reminder of what Stravinsky now contended to be a remote and artistically obsolescent St. Petersburg—might well have been included as a target of the following caution, also offered around 1923:

> . . . This dangerous point of view concerning instrumentation, coupled with the unhealthy greed for orchestral opulence today, has corrupted the judgement of the public, and they, being impressed by the immediate effect of tone color, can no longer solve the problem of whether this is intrinsic in the music or simply padding. Orchestration has become a source of enjoyment independent of the music, and the time has surely come to put things in their proper places. [25]

In Stravinsky's mind, "to put things in their proper places" included the preterition of anything that smacked of orchestral pomposity. Moreover, the potentially sentimental use of strings now brought disfavor, for "the suppleness of the string instruments can lend itself to . . . works built on an emotive basis. My *Octour* is not an emotive work." [26]

Ironically, while the *Octet* was once destined to become a piano concerto, the 1923/24 *Concerto pour Piano suivi d'Orchestre d'Harmonie,* as it was originally titled, was not conceived as a keyboard work:

> . . . at the beginning of the composition I did not see that it would take the form of a concerto for piano and orchestra. Only gradually, while already composing, did I understand that the musical material could be used to most advantage in the piano, whose neat, clear sonority and polyphonic resources suited the dryness and neatness which I was seeking in the structure of the music I had composed. [27]

Ultimately, the instrumentation included a full complement of winds, brass, as well as timpani and contrabass, with stringent demands made upon the ensemble in the anything but accompanimental tutti. Yet it is the manner in which the piano contributes that perhaps more than any other element reveals a continuing direction towards Stravinsky's percussive concept of keyboard writing, first initiated in the *Piano-Rag-Music,* then advanced by his eventual use of the four pianos in *Les Noces.* Furthermore, in the Piano Concerto, the sheer technical equipment needed by the pianist is considerable as perhaps best epitomized in Joachim Kaiser's informed judgment that here "Stravinsky's piano writing is merciless. Anyone who can keep a clear head and sure fingers . . . has nothing to fear in the world of black and white keys." [28] Stravinsky himself, in a letter to his friend Ansermet, spoke of the work's "special technique." [29] Other correspondence with Ansermet traces the evolution of the work whose origins date from the summer of 1923 while Stravinsky was living in Biarritz:

> *July 29*—I am composing a piece for piano and many other instruments and the work is coming along well.
>
> *February 23, 1924*—Unfortunately I cannot write at length, being very busy with: the composition of the last part of my Concerto; the orchestration of the first part (the second is finished): and the piano reduction.
>
> *March 28*—Imagine that I must finish the last part of my Concerto, learn to play the whole piece on the piano, and perform gloriously at the premiere on May 15th.[30]

The work was in fact introduced at two private performances given the same day exactly a week before the official public premiere on May 22, 1924. In these two preview recitals, Jean Wiener played the second piano score, while Stravinsky of course played the solo part. The home of the Princesse Edmond de Polignac, a fervent disciple of Stravinsky's music for some time, served as the location. Interestingly, Stravinsky began a careful log of these events on the end page of the orchestral autograph, now held by the Library of Congress Music Division and reprinted here as plate 12. In examining the plate, one also observes Stravinsky's affixing of the press notice of the official premiere concert onto the cover—a concert that included the three St. Petersburg ballets. Finally, Stravinsky first begins to track this performances of the Concerto (second playing in Paris again, third in Copenhagen), then abandons this diary ("etc., etc., etc.") with a synoptic declaration that he performed the work over 40 times, and all over the world, a statement that may not have been entered until 1931 when Stravinsky edited the manuscript.[31]

A more thorough study of the complete autograph, from which plate 12 was drawn, provides additional insight concerning both compositional and pianistic aspects of the Concerto.[32] Generally, the full score holograph exhibits many pencil corrections often relating to matters of performance articulation and clarification: slurs, alterations in dynamics, staccato, and tenuto signs are added or changed. Inserts marked in red ink are also found throughout the manuscript. Stravinsky's signature and his redating of this 1924 document in 1931 suggest that these emendations are of the class usually associated with the preparation of the publication score. An even stronger corroboration is apparent in noting Stravinsky's N.B. in the first movement, surely meant for the eyes of the editor and engraver: "Les chiffres noirs sont ceux de la reprise," that is, the repeat marks that the composer here includes in the manuscript at the end of the exposition indicates not that the material was to be immediately repeated, but that the same music would serve as the recapitulation starting at rehearsal 27.

Plate 12. Piano Concerto, inside back cover notes of autograph orchestral score

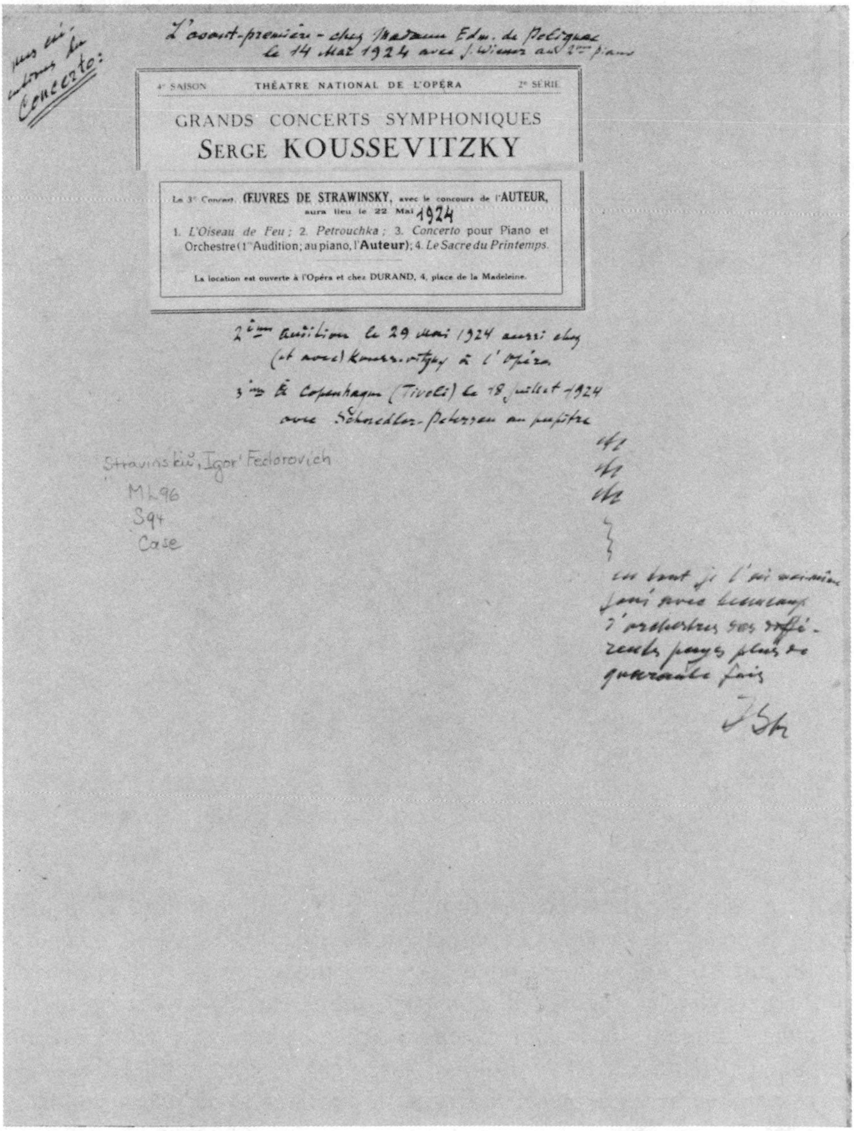
mes exécutions du Concerto:

L'avant-première chez Madame Edm. de Polignac le 14 Mai 1924 avec J. Wiener au 2nd piano

4e SAISON THÉATRE NATIONAL DE L'OPÉRA 2e SÉRIE

GRANDS CONCERTS SYMPHONIQUES

SERGE KOUSSEVITZKY

Le 3e Concert, ŒUVRES DE STRAWINSKY, avec le concours de l'AUTEUR, aura lieu le 22 Mai 1924

1. *L'Oiseau de Feu*; 2. *Petrouchka*; 3. *Concerto* pour Piano et Orchestre (1re Audition; au piano, l'**Auteur**); 4. *Le Sacre du Printemps.*

La location est ouverte à l'Opéra et chez DURAND, 4, place de la Madeleine.

2ème audition le 29 mai 1924 aussi chez (et avec) Koussevitzky à l'Opéra

3me à Copenhague (Tivoli) le 18 juillet 1924 avec Schnedler-Petersen au pupitre

en tout je l'ai exécuté avec beaucoup d'orchestres sous diff. pays plus de quarante fois

I Str

Library of Congress, Music Division

No doubt the original 1924 manuscript had served as the performing score for Koussevitzky, who conducted the premiere. Numerous reminders of metric shifts, for example, run the length of the score and

Example 95.   Piano Concerto (1950 score)

Plate 13.   Piano Concerto, (rehearsal 41)

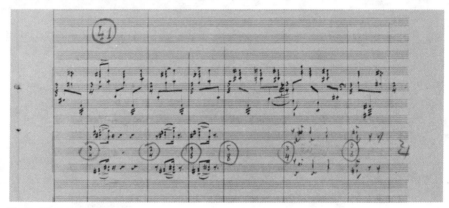

Library of Congress, Music Division

such conducting cues are consistently added in red and blue, a common
flag in so many of Stravinsky's conducting scores since at least *The Firebird*.[33] But Stravinsky must have taken up the score in 1931, now that
his "exclusivity" as he called it in performing the Piano Concerto was
no longer as important to him. Even so, the full orchestral score was not
published by Koussevitsky's *Edition Russe de Musique* until 1936.

As a specific example of the type of changes undertaken, compare
the passage commencing at rehearsal 41 of the opening largo/allegro
movement as printed in the revised 1950 Boosey & Hawkes version (ex.
95) with the corresponding section of the 1924 manuscript reprinted as
plate 13.[34]

The rehearsal number itself, as marked in the autograph, has been added in ink (actually red ink) as have circles signaling each measure's metric shift, a shifting that continues with each measure throughout the cadenza and producing the kind of vertigo feeling Stravinsky once spoke of in connection with this work. By the time of the published score's engraving in 1931, changes included the insertion of crescendi and slurs (compare the 2/4 and 3/8 bars after rehearsal 41) and the addition of the forte in the passage's final 3/4 measure. Also to be observed is the en-harmonic variance of the second chord in the right hand of the 5/8 mea-sure (B$^\sharp$ opposed to C natural), suggesting a more thoughtful attention to the broadly directional linearity of the cadenza, to be discussed below. Finally, the horns, as indicated in the last two bars of the plate, seem to have been a later addition; and by the 1950 revision, not only had the pitches themselves been altered but also redistributed to the first and second horns.

Throughout the manuscript, one of the most consistently reconsi-dered issues was the exact placement of slurs, both in the solo and or-chestral parts. Many erasures are evident; curiously they most often appear in the four horn parts, a choir of the ensemble which as already noted, drew the composer's scrutiny in several ways. The whole of the opening largo, scored for the horn quartet, underwent re-examination. For example, a slur originally connected the figure in measure four to the next bar, and similarly, the figure there is joined across that bar line to measure six. But the slurs erased in the manuscript, which having served as the performing score, may have been a deletion resulting from Stra-vinsky's first actually having heard his original concept then electing to alter the notation. While the determination of the exact time at which the alteration was made is impossible, four accents were subsequently added, thus producing a noticeably different sound based upon four separate attacks rather than one as summarized in example 96.

Example 96. Piano Concerto, mm. 4-5

Autograph (Original)

Autograph (Revised)

mm.   4   5

Nor is this specific kind of rethinking a singular instance. Similar slur deletions occur throughout the horn lines of the Concerto (mm. 8-12 of the first movement; two bars before rehearsal 5, though by 1950 the slurs had been reinstated; one bar before rehearsal 15; and in the second movement, two bars after rehearsal 51). Moreover, numerous dynamic levels for the horns were adjusted and both accents (such as sforzandi) and articulative signs (such as staccati) are also added, though none of the other orchestral choirs seem to have troubled Stravinsky so much.

An examination of the manuscript is also instructive in glimpsing at least some of Stravinsky's thoughts regarding certain aspects of the Concerto's pianism. With respect to fingering, during the fugato section of the third movement, Stravinsky marks a specific fingering pattern in the left hand of the second and third bars after rehearsal 81. Traditional execution would have dictated a more prescriptive handling than that which Stravinsky chose, as illustrated in example 97.

Example 97.   Piano Concerto, III.

```
Stravinsky's Execution:  1 2 3 4 | 1 2 3 4
Traditional Pattern:     3 1 2 3 | 4 1 2 3
```

It would appear that Stravinsky's preferred execution was inserted towards upholding the "etc. staccato" direction he had decreed at the outset of the fugato section at rehearsal 80, a section in which the piano plays a more accompanimental role. Yet the pattern is frequently performed with a legato touch clearly contradictory to the more metallic, percussive idea expressly requested by the composer/pianist.[35] Yet the designated fingering in this particular instance, as well as in several other similarly marked passages, does not appear in any published score of the composition, again stressing the genuine need for a critical edition that would incorporate such illuminating authorial suggestions.

In another instance once again observable through the source examination of erasures in the autograph, one notes that Stravinsky originally planned a series of left hand octaves in a passage beginning in measure 47 of the final allegro (ex. 98). But here the deletions, as circled in example 98, seem not to have been engendered by a concession to a limited pianistic technique. Actually, continuous octaves would have been more easily executed. Moreover, even though Stravinsky speaks of his weak left-hand technique, several other passages in the work employ scales of octaves demanding a level of proficiency much greater than that required in this particular case (for example the left hand octaves at two bars before rehearsal 7 in the first movement). More likely, this discriminating change to the alternation of octaves and single notes was employed towards creating a certain textural effect. Such refinements were not uncommon, especially as verifiable when studying Stravinsky's orchestral manuscripts where octave doublings seem always to have caused the composer some consternation.

Example 98.   Piano Concerto, III., 44-50

The demonstrable consistency with which Stravinsky rethought such issues in the piano part is furthered by examining the original two-piano autograph of the Piano Concerto also housed at the Library of Congress. For instance, a similar octave deletion is apparent at rehearsal 82 of the third movement. The intent in choosing to incorporate this textural rather than pianistic revision was surely the same as that outlined in example 98.

Example 99.   Piano Concerto, mm. 169-170

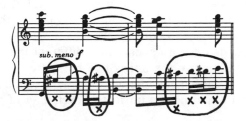

This two-piano holograph (ex. 99), preserved in Koussevitsky's Parisian vault until 1950, is perhaps even more valuable than the orchestral autograph as a primary source. The document appears to be the score from which Stravinsky (or Wiener) read at the two private performances on May 15. The first movement here is dated December 1923, that is, over four months after Stravinsky's July 29 letter to Ansermet that advised "the work is coming along well," and about three months before the movement was completed in its orchestral form dated March 3, 1924.

As noted earlier, some specific pianistic fingerings are marked in the orchestral autograph; but many more appear throughout the two-piano score, as might have been anticipated given the likelihood that this was the working score from which the composer learned the solo part. These fingerings, too, constitute rather strange patterns. What is most puzzling perhaps, is the fact that several of the fingering indications in the two-piano autograph were actually printed in the 1924 Koussevitsky publication which of course preceded the orchestral engraving by over a decade. The well-known violinist Albert Spalding is listed as the editor of this score, though his was only a titular role. Yet these same fingerings, for example those that appear in measures 77-86 of the first movement of the Spalding edition, were subsequently deleted in all later printings of the score (including the 1950 Boosey & Hawkes revision). Why these fingering suggestions were extracted is not known; but it is true that Stravinsky often registered his fingering preferences in the score as he actually wrote each passage. Whether or not it was the composer's desire to eliminate the fingerings in the later editions, now that he no longer played the work himself, raises yet another question. While these questions are presently at least unanswerable, they in no way mitigate the importance of Stravinsky's originally conceived thoughts to the well-informed pianist.

The middle movement of the Concerto also evinces some rethinking on the composer's part as the manuscript was being prepared. Perhaps the most surprising aspect of this largo is Stravinsky's inclusion of two rather supervenient passages bearing the rare direction "Cadenza poco rubato." Originally it seems, Stravinsky conceived of these two Chopinesque sections as solo cadenzas, the first occurring at rehearsal 52, the second at 58. But the orchestral doubling of the piano in the four measures following 58 upon which Stravinsky eventually decided seems to have been an afterthought since it appears in a different ink in the two piano score. Like the addition of the horns five bars after rehearsal 41 in the cadenza of the first movement, the addition here of music eventually to be scored for and requiring the intricate dovetailing of contrabass, timpani, tuba, trombone, and trumpets produces a rather unwieldy moment—one that is more often than not unsuccessfully negotiated in performance. One must remember, however, that in some ways, the Piano Concerto is an experimental work; for while Stravinsky had by 1924 written for wind ensemble on several previous occasions, he had not yet worked within the territory of a concerto environment where additional coordinative issues were involved. Even the piano writing is clumsy, especially in contrast to the adjacent movements, and so the overall ungraceful character of the movement is further abetted.

Finally, the two-piano manuscript reveals revisions in the closing movement. Most interesting are the tempo suggestions. This final allegro had originally been marked quarter note = 116. But by the time the orchestral manuscript was prepared a few months later, the movement had slowed to quarter = 112; and by the time it was printed by Koussevitsky, Stravinsky had further eased the tempo to quarter = 104, indeed a significant retarding of the first conceived pace. Likewise, the closing "Stringendo" at rehearsal 89 is calibrated at quarter = 144 in the Koussevitsky manuscript, but by the 1936 engraving of the orchestral score, the cadential drive was pulled back to quarter = 132.

While a more thorough inventory of the numerous and diverse vicissitudes apparent in these manuscript sources collectively provides a treasury of materials for the analyst, there is little to suggest that Stravinsky by this time at least labored over any of the Concerto's more structural aspects, such as pitch. One can only assume that whatever decisions were reached in this regard, occurred during earlier phases of sketching and so are likely to have been recorded at least partially, among the presently inaccessible 52 pages of summary sketches signed and dated Biarritz, April 13, 1924. Yet it is towards some understanding of the work's pitch system that what little analytic attention the Concerto has received previously has been directed. Apel's well-worn *Harvard Dictionary*, for example, goes so far as to illustrate Slonimsky's coined concept of pandiatonicism by including an excerpt of the Concerto in defining the term as "the absence of functional harmony [resulting] in a certain tonal staticity [*sic*], offset by a greater interest in counterpoint, rhythm, and chord spacing." Schenker even attempted to explain the work's pitch vocabulary according to his own structural principles, while more recent analysts have campaigned quite convincingly at times for octatonically derived pitch collections.[36] But whatever pitch camp one chooses to join, there is little doubt that Stravinsky now more than in any composition before thoroughly explores the potentialities of tertian intervals around a contextually centric pitch of A. Stravinsky himself referred to the work as his *Concerto en La.*[37] This is most definitely confirmed not only by the work's clear A pitch priority, but by the hierarchially functional E as a rather traditionally employed dominant. For example, in structurng the macroformal architecture of the first movement's more or less sonata-allegro form, a durationally accented E dominant preparation begins at rehearsal 23 and persists for 26 measures before the movement's reprise at rehearsal 27.

Additionally, it is the fluctuating tertian related C-C# to the priority A that looms perhaps even more significant in tracing Stravinsky's evolving codification of a pitch system during the early 1920s. Not only are these specific structural goals principal components of a tonal framework, but they also may be accommodated within an octatonic ordering with semitone, tone rotation. In this respect, the use of the split third as it is sometimes termed, has an evident identity with so many of Stravinsky's works in the 1920s and 1930s, most obviously perhaps with the pitch pillars of the *Symphony of Psalms*. The overlapping of these major and minor thirds is noted in example 100, the former by brackets, the latter by arches.

In suggesting these pitch conjugates, it should not be concluded that Stravinsky's boundaries of pitch exploration are restricted to this framework. While these priorities constitute the structural essence of the work, Stravinsky frequently advances other temporary centers by instituting operative directional tones towards establishing harmonic areas closely related to the movement's centric A. Consider that the final movement resolves around a C priority with excursions to traditionally relatable keys

Example 100.

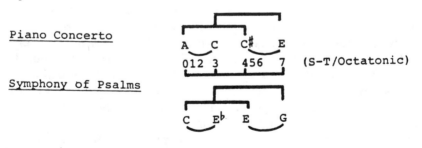

such as the one forming the basis of the passage shown in example 101. Both the A flat and F# converge upon the centric G. Two other observations are pertinent: the filling in of the octave in the second through third measures, here including the tertian intervals G-B flat- B, is a staple in the overall linearity of the work; second, the juxtaposition at the asterisked chord of the priority G with the leading tone, is also illustrative of a harmonic conflict characterizing the Concerto.

Example 101. Piano Concerto, III.

Each of the Concerto's three movements evokes a clear model. Several are apparent in the opening largo/allegro. The introductory section, which later serves as the movement's close as well, thus framing the limits of this sonata-allegro fashioned piece, is by Stravinsky's own admission, patterned after the dotted rhythm overture style of its eighteenth century model. Thereafter, the piano enterers whereupon a succession of stylistic references to baroque conventions, rag rhythms, and jazz-like cadenzas ensues. This is clearly the most relentless of the three movements, reflecting not only Stravinsky's own unwieldy pianistic approach, but perhaps also the mechanical influence of the pianola that seemed to be exerting a near spell over the composer at the moment. Many of the fundamental pitch aspects presented above are conveniently graspable within the first four bars of the introductory largo (ex. 102).

Example 102.

Again the tertian A-C-C$^{\sharp}$ conflict presents itself, as does a confound-
ing G natural placed below what functions as a leading G$^{\sharp}$. The cadence
in measure four at the level of F amounts to a traditional deceptive cadence. Finally, the fundamentally linear projection of the gesture presages
an overriding occupation with counterpoint throughout the Concerto, thus
continuing the path set in the *Octet*. Architecturally, the stream of musical
events as exhibited in these introductory measures is no less important
than Stravinsky's pitch choices, as may be determined from the above
reduction. For example, the conjunctly directed bass line arrives at its
destination one bar too soon, that is, before the treble G$^{\sharp}$ resolves, thus
creating a contiguity of functionally stable and unstable sonorities not
unlike the asterisked chord marked in example 101.

The contrapuntal fabric of this opening represents only a microcosm
of the highly extended linearity, the *grand ligne* as Boulanger would have
called it, that brings coherence to the entire movement. At a slightly
larger level, the first of several piano cadenzas beginning at measure 70
also reveals a similar prolongation by allowing a long descending right
hand figure to fill in the distance of an octave over a left hand counterpoint
that outlines the overall harmonic progression. The entire passage is directed towards the initiation of a new section at rehearsal 13.[38] A near
identical projection, though here in ascending form from A to A, forms
the background structure of another cadenza beginning at rehearsal 40
and culminating at rehearsal 45, the maestoso reprise of the opening largo.
In the following graph, a portion of the complete right hand line is sketched,
indicating how Stravinsky embellished what amounts to a simple ascending A major scale (ex. 103).

Example 103.   Piano Concerto, I., mm. 283-313

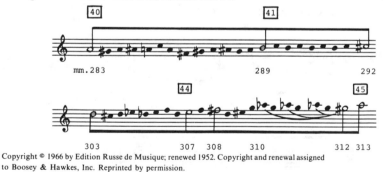

Similar patterns characterize the central movement marked largo
(originally larghissimo in 1924) such as the transitional piano cadenza at

measure 35. As recalled years later, Stravinsky claims to have mislaid part of the manuscript for this movement, and was unable to reconstruct the music originally conceived: "I do not know to what extent the published movement differs from the last one, but I am sure the two are very unlike."[39] Here one finds the most ornate piano writing to be seen in the composer's piano literature to this point. It shares virtually no common stylistic edge with its adjacent movements. Cast in a loosely structured tripartite design, surely Stravinsky intended this rather laborious sounding centerpiece to act as a counterweight to the incessant, propulsive energy of the first.

The concluding allegro is a neoclassic pasticcio, mixing cafe tunes, jazz rhythms, a fugato section—all within a toccata fashioned style. Each idea parades by the listener without concern for thematic unity, though the well-laid harmonic structure acts as an adequate architectural mainstay in bringing some macroformal coherence to the finale. As in the previous movement, here the priority pitch is again C, with not only a directed motion towards the lower third related A, but also to A flat as in the fugato beginning at rehearsal 80. Of course the enharmonic equivalency of G♯ and A flat provided a link that Stravinsky obviously found useful, as in the passage at rehearsal 86 wherein the G♯ is juxtaposed with the progenitor A, as cyclic allusions are now made to the first movement's introductory largo (ex. 104).[40]

Example 104. Piano Concerto, III., mm. 197-202

As is evident by his *Octet* apologia, Stravinsky was now being increasingly cajoled to analyze his compositions through various media channels such as interviews and periodical essays. "We are extremely eager to have an introduction and commentary by Stravinsky on his Piano Concerto for a demonstration at an audiographic exhibition in January

. . ." writes Stravinsky's New York pianola agent on November 27, 1928, to his counterpart in Paris.[41] Perhaps allured by a combination of financial and artistic interests, Stravinsky often complied with such requests. In the above instance, for example, Stravinsky did piece together some distinctly superficial replies to questions posed by his American agent. Regarding the second movement of the Concerto, Stravinsky comments: "I straight start with solemn and large song."[42] Nor was this to be the only occasion upon which Stravinsky would address this composition. In a 1928 written response to another inquiry, Stravinsky suggests that it was not until the writing of the toccata, presumably meaning the last movement, that the instrumentation was settled.

> The short crisp dance character of the Toccata, engendered by the percussion of the piano, led to the idea that a wind ensemble would suit the piano better than any other combination. In contrast to the percusiveness of the piano, the winds prolong the piano's sounds as well as provide the human element of respiration.[43]

A more substantive account of his ideas regarding various aspects of the Piano Concerto were offered in a statement appearing in the once popular American journal *The Etude*. Curiously, J. F. Cooke's "Chronological Progress in Musical Art," from which Stravinsky's comments are here excerpted, appeared in 1926, a few years earlier than the above citation. Cooke's reporting of the composer's comments must have resulted from an interview conducted during Stravinsky's American tour in 1925.

> In considering the possibilities of the pianoforte as a musical instrument in connection of my Concerto, I was confronted with the fact that the treatment of the instrument by the composers of the nineteenth century made no appeal to me whatever in the sense in which I desired to employ it. The composer has a definite obligation to his art which is destroyed if he is fettered by conventions. . . . If Schumann had held to the conventions of Scarlatti, there would have been no Schumann as we know him.
>   It is in orchestral employment that the piano appears to me as a wonderful percussion instrument. The piano has its own individuality and its own significance. Like all art, it is subject to a chronological development. In the past the piano has been treated at times as though it were a vocal instrument—that is it was made to sing, in fact it was cheated out of everything but its own very evident and individual character as a percussion instrument.
>   This concept of the piano seemed to be developed in my mind for a long period of time like a great tree. During the past year, it bore fruit in my Concerto. I have endeavored to restore the piano to its rightful place as a percussion instrument.[44]

But despite Stravinsky's *ex cathedra* attempt to indemnify himself through such a dialectic plea, the Concerto was frequently impugned, especially throughout the 1924–1929 quinquennium during which Stravinsky regularly performed the work. It seemed nearly equational that the more Stravinsky assumed the stance of an apologist, the more vitriolic the protestations grew. By the time of a 1929 performance in London, the critical reception expressed below had become nearly an expected reaction.

From the *Evening News*: "To the initiates, or propagandists, it is no doubt a miracle of beauty, better than the Matthew Passion. The plain man would call it a hoax."

From the *Sunday Times*: "The pleasure of seeing the composer of *Petrouchka* again was equalled only by the pain of hearing the composer of the piano concerto. It was sad to think that the one-time man of genius had degenerated into the manufacturer of this ugly and feeble commonplace."

And from the *New Age*: "Of the incredibility, lamentably feeble and dreary display made by M. Igor Stravinsky and his piano concerto, it is difficult to write adequately."[45]

The Piano Concerto marked the beginning of that period of Stravinsky's life during which he embarked upon a career as a pianist. It was not an entirely foreign role. There had been at least a few scattered public performances of the easy piano duets during the economically meager years in exile. Of course even earlier in St. Petersburg, Stravinsky appeared as both a soloist and as an accompanist. Finances surely played an important consideration in Stravinsky's decision to return to the concert stage in 1924. Craft reports that in a letter to Stravinsky's friend Werner Reinhart dated July 25, 1925, the composer states that he must perform a good bit each year in order to produce a living income.[46]

In both his *Chroniques* and the later conversations with Craft, Stravinsky often spoke of performance problems he experienced as a pianist, including his initial suffering from stage fright as he deemed it, and the "lack of what I call the performer's memory." Specifically regarding his return to piano performance with the Piano Concerto, Stravinsky recalled the by now commonly known incident wherein he momentarily forgot the opening piano solo of the second movement and had to be reminded of the initial notes by Koussevitsky. On another occasion "my memory froze because I suddenly noticed the reflection of my fingers in the glossy wood at the edge of the keyboard." There were at least two performances given while "I was moderately inebriated."[47] Moreover, even though Stravinsky charged these contretemps to his inexperience, by 1934, a time by which he was a veteran of the concert circuit, the composer/pianist was still somewhat insecure. Siohan reports that while he was conducting a performance of Stravinsky's 1929 *Capriccio* at the Salle Pleyel, Stravinsky suffered another memory slip during the cadenza and generally seemed to be always a rather anxious performer.[48]

Determining precisely from whence Stravinsky's interest in piano performance was sparked is difficult to say. Certainly what first appears to be the most direct source is documented by the composer himself:

> . . . I ought to say that the idea of playing my Concerto myself was suggested by Koussevitsky, who happened to be at Biarritz when I was finishing the composition. I hesitated at first, fearing that I should not have time to perfect my technique as a pianist, to practice enough, and to acquire the endurance necessary to execute a work demanding sustained effort. But as I am by nature always tempted by anything needing prolonged effort, and prone to persist in overcoming difficulties, and as, also, the prospect of creating my work for myself, and thus establishing the manner in which I wished it to be played, greatly attracted me, these influences combined to induce me to undertake it.
>
> I began, therefore, the loosening of my fingers by playing a lot of Czerny exercises, which was not only very useful but gave me keen musical pleasure. I have always admired Czerny, not only as a remarkable teacher but also as a thoroughbred musician.[49]

Not only did these Czerny etudes serve this limbering process, but they clearly played a part in shaping a good many pianistic passages of the Concerto, as may be seen in the measures that lead to the reprise of the first movement. Even more importantly, this pianistic technique seems to have been transferred to several instrumental figurations as well, as apparent in the knotty bassoon dialogue that accompanies the same recapitulative section (ex. 105).

In an even more extended manner, the spectral influence of Czerny is felt throughout the octaves, thirds, arpeggios, and scale passages of the final etude-like allegro, an excerpt of which is shown in example 106,

Example 105. Piano Concerto, I. 173-177

whereupon at rehearsal 80 the aforementioned instrumental fugato ensues above a continuous pianistic pattern.

Example 106.   Piano Concerto, III., 149-153

In addition to his reference to Czerny, it is known that in preparing for the May 1924 premiere of the composition, Stravinsky rather clandestinely received some piano lessons from Isidore Philipp whose own *Complete School of Technique for the Pianoforte* had been published years earlier.[50]

While there is no doubt that Koussevitsky's prominent presence about this time directly influenced Stravinsky's decision to perform his own Concerto, interestingly, Arthur Rubinstein, as he had done with the *Petrouchka* "Sonata," here claims that he was responsible in steering Stravinsky towards his new career as a performer:

> . . . "Igor," I said, "you play the piano abominably. . . . Why don't you write an easy concerto and play it in public? The whole world would flock to hear and see the greatest living composer." My suggestion did not fall on deaf ears. Besides being a genius, Stravinsky was a shrewd businessman. He took my advice and wrote in a few weeks his *Concerto for Piano and Wind Instruments*. Here I can proudly declare that I launched Stravinsky's career as a public performer.[51]

Whether or not Rubinstein here vaingloriously arrogates too much credit, the fact is he and Stravinsky had been frequent companions during the early 1920s and surely this friendship must have had its effects. Yet nowhere does Stravinsky himself directly acknowledge Rubinstein's ministrations in either the writing of *Petrouchka* or here in the case of the

Concerto. Rubinstein, however, mentions his influence on Stravinsky throughout his own memoirs. According to his recollection, Stravinsky often thanked Rubinstein for his counsel. In fact at a later point in his autobiographical account, Rubinstein rather reproachfully comments: "I lost sight of Stravinsky who had taken my advice too seriously and was now spending more time on concert tours than writing new music." Moreover, Rubinstein validates Stravinsky's earlier cited canonization of Carl Czerny, quoting Stravinsky as having said "My technique is much improved, and you know to whom I owe it. To Czerny, who was the greatest composer for the piano."[52] Such hyperbolic praise was of course part of Stravinsky's routinely inflated efforts to emphasize a particular point. Though this adulation is obviously excessive, Stravinsky's debt, not only to Czerny but to Bach and other such models, is traceable in most of his piano works. Indeed, with the Concerto, so promising were the prospects of future concerts that Stravinsky's enthusiasm for the piano redoubled. Another piano work was needed.

Though the three-movement 1924 Piano Sonata is a comparatively slight work, it is still no less valuable in widening our perception of Stravinsky's evolving style. This is especially so since by now Stravinsky's inseparable and pragmatic union with the piano nearly pre-empted all other musical activities. Suddenly the piano became for Stravinsky a utilitarian vehicle in gaining a more immediate and personal visibility. As Rubinstein had perceptively predicted, people simply wanted to see and hear the "world's greatest living composer." Begun in Biarritz soon after the Concerto's premiere, the Sonata was completed on October 21 in Nice where Stravinsky had relocated yet again in September.[53]

The work was published by Koussevitsky in 1925 with Stravinsky's inscription "Dediée a Madame la Princesse Edmond de Polignac." From the start, the Sonata seems to have been a less toilsome challenge than the more formidable Concerto, and so it was composed rather quickly. The outer movements are without a formal tempo title, respectively bearing the same metronomically prescribed quarter = 112. The middle movement carries no such suggested pulse but instead is marked adagietto. Once, Soulima programmed the Sonata adding his own titles: I, Comodo, III, Finale—apparently an innocuous enough supplement, for his father raised neither objection nor endorsement.[54]

Like the Concerto, and as he states in a September 17, 1924 letter to Ernest Oeberg a month before the Sonata was completed, Stravinsky initially wished to retain the exclusive performing rights for his new piano work.[55] But with the relatively expeditious publication of the score in early 1925 (as opposed to the protracted process of commercially releasing the Concerto) this of course was a moot request. Though the Sonata had been completed in the fall of 1924, it was not publicly performed until the next summer at the Donauseschingen Festival in July. During the eventful interim, Stravinsky had completed a highly successful winter tour of America, frequently performing his new Concerto. But such commitments conspired against the time needed for learning his new solo piano piece. The second officially recognized performance of the Sonata took place on September 8, 1925, at the I.S.C.M. Festival held in Venice. Perhaps the most memorable aspect of this concert is recounted by the composer himself:

> At the beginning of September 1925, with a suppurating abscess in my right forefinger, I left Nice to perform my piano Sonata in Venice. I had prayed in a little church near Nice, before an old and "miraculous" icon, but I expected that the concert would have to be canceled. My finger still was festering when I walked onto the stage at the Teatro La Fenice, and I addressed the audience, apologizing in advance for what would have to be a poor performance. I sat down, removed the little bandage, felt that the pain had suddenly stopped, and discovered that the finger was—miraculously, it seemed to me—healed.[56]

This wonderment, like so many Stravinskyan anecdotes, is amusing, yet in this specific instance reveals little about the performance itself. How might Stravinsky have performed the Sonata on that occasion or others contemporary with it? Fortunately, at least one audiographic artifact has survived and is accessible, thus permitting at least some limited insight about Stravinsky's execution and interpretive ideas.

The first movement of the work was issued in the Duo-Art AudioGraphic series (#D231). Actually the complete Sonata was recorded by Aeolian probably around 1925 or 1926. But the second and third movements were never released in the same series though a production must have been contemplated since sequential numbers in the recording series were reserved. Duo-Art was the American branch of the British owned Aeolian Company.[57] The roll for the first movement was merely one part of an annotated, grandly entitled plan "The World's Music; a new Aeolian Library of illustrated and descriptive Duo-Art and Pianola Rolls." The series was edited by Perry A. Scholes with a listener's introduction by Edwin Evans. In the prefatory material of the actual roll, Stravinsky's picture appears along with his signed validation "This roll is a correct reproduction of my performance." Evans introductory remarks (all of which are of course reprinted on the piano roll itself, as was the case with the earlier described *The Firebird*) include a brief description of neoclassicism, with a pictorial illustration of neoclassicism by Phyllis

Whiteman entitled "Unemotional Counterpoint," followed by an equally general account of Stravinsky's life leading to the writing of the Sonata. Both of these short narratives are here reprinted.

NEOCLASSICISM

In 1920 the Diaghileff Russian Ballet produced (in Paris and London) *Pulcinella*—to music by Pergolesi (1710–1736), which was entrusted to Stravinsky for adaptation. As the task proceeded the Stravinsky partner in this strange association gained the ascendant, until the later numbers were more characteristic of the Russian than the Neapolitan composer.

But the incidental renewal of contact with a classical idiom was to have profound consequences for Stravinsky himself. Four works followed which in various ways reflected this new tendancy: an Octet for Wind Instruments (1923) a Pianoforte Concerto (1924), the Piano Sonata (1925), and a Piano Serenade (1926) all written in idioms possessing historical sanction, but treated much as the composer had treated Pergolesi.

Nor does the influence of *Pulcinella* stop there. The neo-classicism it inaugurated is echoed in France by certain of the younger composers, once grouped together as "Les Six," in Germany by recent works of Paul Hindemith, in Italy by Rieti and occasionally by Casella.

There is a corresponding tendency in England, which, however, arose from other causes. It is represented by such works as Holst's *Fugal Overture* or Vaugh Williams' *Concerto Academico,* which have little in common with Stravinsky. But whatever its origins or methods, neo-classicism is a potent factor in current music.

THE FIRST MOVEMENT OF
STRAVINSKY'S PIANOFORTE SONATA

No composer of modern times has been the subject of more violent controversy than Igor Stravinsky, and only one other, Arnold Schonberg, wields an influence to be compared with his.

Stravinsky was born in Russia in 1882, but has lived since 1910 in France or Switzerland. It was the production in that year of the ballet *The Fire Bird,* that first made him famous. Then followed *Petrushka,* in 1911, and *The Rite of Spring,* in 1913, both works of remarkable originality.

His Opera, *The Nightingale,* produced in 1914, was afterwards converted into a Symphonic Poem which was made the basis of another Ballet. All these have been frequently performed by the Diaghileff Ballet. *The Marriage (Les Noces),* composed in 1917, was not produced until 1923 in Paris, and three years later in London.

Meanwhile the Composer's style and method, which had evolved so rapidly in the composition of his first three Ballets, underwent another startling change. He turned his attention from the masses of sound in *The Rite of Spring* to a more subtle exploitation of timbres, and of their mutual reactions, in which he discerned a new form of polyphony (or weaving together of simultaneous melodies), and the works of this period were even more hotly contested than their predecessors had been.

Evans continues by declaring that Stravinsky's Sonata provides a "release from the coma of romantic excess" and informs us that Stravinsky himself "desires that the piece should be played without emotional inflection."[58]

Stravinsky's performance as recorded on this piano roll is, as might have been anticipated, extremely brittle. Even in the "legatissimo" marked opening measures, the pianistic touch is far from being anything even remotely smooth. The left hand arpeggiated section of the Sonata upon which nearly the entire movement is constructed obviously demands constant shifting of hand positions. But Stravinsky's hand shifts are amazingly uneven, thus promoting a discontinuity that compromises the overall linear direction of the work. For the most part, a single tempo is preserved with very little internal nuance. Even the marked pauses clearly designated in the passage shown in example 107 are virtually disregarded. From the aural evidence of this performance it would seem that these pauses were included more as a visual delineation than anything else.

Example 107.   Sonata, I., mm. 122-124

The recording generally corroborates the representative opinion often expressed of Stravinsky's piano playing as being exceedingly secco, though at times in this roll at least, the pedal is occasionally pressed into service, often blurring sections. In the end, one is left with the impression that if this roll truly depicts Stravinsky's playing in the middle 1920s, he could not have been judged a very consistent pianist. Moreover, as the guardian/ performer of his own piano works at that time, critics of the music surely had the platform to castigate Stravinsky doubly. Prokofiev after hearing Stravinsky play the composition, wrote to Nicolas Miaskovsky: "Stravinsky has written a dreadful sonata, which he plays himself with a certain chic. The music is Bach but with pockmarks." Curiously, the letter is dated August 4, 1925, meaning that Prokofiev heard the piece prior to the Venetian Teatro La Fenice performance.[59] In respect to Prokofiev's opinion of Stravinsky's piano playing, it seems not to have been the only time upon which Prokofiev offered certain negative insinuations.[60] Nor can such a reprehension be simply dismissed as the natural residue of an enmity that divided the two competing composer/pianists. The objections, often somewhat whimsically expressed, were international. After a 1925 New York performance of the Sonata (which in itself indicates the rather swift dissemination of the work) Lawrence Gilman quipped, "Some men succumb to the Grape, some to the dreadful heart of woman. Stravinsky has succumbed to the eighteenth century."[61] Schoenberg, who attended the Venice performance of the Sonata, clearly, and perhaps somewhat ethnocentrically, targeted the last of his 1925/1926 *Drei Satiren* for "des kleine Modernsky." Finally from London, Eric Walter White's original reproof of the work, as included in his aforementioned 1930 *Stravinsky's Sacrifice to Apollo,* signals further contemporary evidence that globally, Stravinsky's adaptation of models could not hope to win the accolades of any but those few who chose to look beyond the laminated surface of what many perceived as facilely manneristic music. White commented: "As for the Piano Sonata, the second movement contains the most ill-sounding clashes between two opposing lines of consecutive thirds, and the third movement a passage of chromatic sentimentality that can only be compared to some of the worst Victorian hymn tunes . . . the sooner Stravinsky writes a second Piano Sonata the better."[62] White, whose critical views had changed by the time of his more extensive biography of Stravinsky decades later, represents many who at first found it perhaps fashionable to resist any form of Stravinsky's neoclassicism, but with the advantage of some distance, eventually came to see the merits of Stravinsky's adaptative techniques.

Stravinsky detailed much of the precompositional ideation of the Sonata in his *Chroniques*. It is well known that the term sonata was used in its denotative *sonare* sense, rather than as an implicative structural procedure. Thus Stravinsky spoke of his resolve not to restrict himself to any narrowly conceived form. Yet by his own admission, he did study several "sonatas of the classical masters," especially those of Beethoven in whom Stravinsky recognized "the indisputable monarch" of the piano. Most momentously: "Some for example compose music *for* the piano; others compose *piano music*. Beethoven is clearly in the second category."[63]

The central movement of the Sonata, the adagietto, most clearly exhibits the influence of Beethoven, both in its third related key of A flat compared to the first movement's priority C, and especially in the ornate, melismatic writing style—"Beethoven *frise*" as Stravinsky labeled it.[64] Even the two octave partition of the first movement's doubled line (see ex. 108) is strongly reminiscent of the opening gesture of the "Appassionata." Other specific parallels have often been suggested between one or another of Beethoven's sonatas and analogous passages of the Stravinsky work.

But if one chooses to credit Beethoven as a specific inspiration in the shaping of the Sonata, then likewise the more fundamental linear comception of the composition is traceable to Bach, especially in the final movement. Indeed, even the two-part imitative character of the opening measures are as referable to the E minor two-voice Fugue of the first book of *The Well-Tempered Clavier,* as are the first movement's introductory measures to Beethoven's Opus 57. Here such a conjecture is less tenuous, for Stravinsky specifically recalled that during the writing of this movement, "Bach's two-part *Inventions* were somewhere in the remote back of my mind."[65]

Remote or not, the most prominent structural feature of the work is the invention-like linearity of the outer movements. Such a fundamentally contrapuntal framework clearly brings a cohesion to what Boulanger once described as the architectonic character of the Sonata, and an exemplary instance of the *grand ligne* as she described such a concept.[66] Moreover, the linearly structured techniques that had begun to characterize the *Octet,* Piano Concerto and are here developed still further, were not merely a fleeting reflection of the models from which the music sprang, but were to be assimilated into most of Stravinsky's compositional output long after the immediacy of his interest in piano music passed. As seems to have been the pattern to this point, the piano music served as an exordium for a blossoming technique. In this particular Sonata (as well as the next work to be written, the *Serenade*) the seeds of *Apollo, Persephone,* and even later works were taking root. It is as Artur Lourie states in his 1925 article "La Sonate pour Piano de Stravinsky," the composer's "l'animation de la ligne" that perhaps best characterizes not only this work but all of his future compositional endeavors.[67]

A brief examination of a few sections of the first movement serves to illustrate various linear and architectural features of both content and process as it pertains to Lourie's concept. To begin, consider the opening thematic material (ex. 108).

Several aspects of the pitch organization are important, if not entirely new. The emphasis here, as in the Piano Concerto, centers around the manipulation of thirds. Especially apparent is the use of the equidistantly spaced minor third. There is a decidedly diminished triad flavor to this initial gesture, and indeed two forms of this sonority are employed as outlined below. When these two symmetrically based chords are com-

Example 108.   Sonata, I., mm. 1-6

bined, the resultant pitch union is that of the octatonic scale (tone, semitone rotation)—a stable collection throughout the movement. Moreover, the octatonicism of the opening seems to function only as one contributing component to the broader linear gesture that descends to the first principal cadence on the priority C at measure six (ex. 109).

Example 109.

    Within the complete thematic territory, only two pitches fall beyond these octatonic boundaries: both are structurally functional in other crucial ways. The E natural provides the split third alteration above C, which as seen in the Concerto is basic to Stravinsky's pitch usage; and the G, clearly employed here in a traditional dominant capacity. Thus the familiar line within a line concept as diagrammed is explored as a fundamental structural premise.[68]

    Two further occurences of a linearly expressed, octatonically generated gesture are offered. Example 110 amounts to a contrapuntal variation of the movement's initial material. Here the same tone, semitone collection is apparent and may be plotted above the cadential priority A of measure 40. Also, measure 40 itself, in establishing A as a priority (and thereby a third relationship to the overall movement's centric C is created) recalls the type of harmonic conflict seen earlier in various passages of the Piano Concerto wherein the leading tone triad is juxtaposed with its expected resolution chord. In this instance the contravention occurs twice in the measure, with the opposing sonorities exchanging textural positions (as indicated by the arrows in ex. 110). Also the presence of the diminished triad as the progenitor of the gesture is circled.

Example 110.   Sonata, I., mm. 40-44

Finally, the movement's closing passage provides still another clear illustration of the symmetrically constructed, equidistant use of minor thirds as a nuclear pitch set. Beginning in measure 151 and extending through measure 158 (the juncture where ex. 111 begins), Stravinsky had recapitulated the opening eleven measures of the movement literally. Now, the final projection towards C begins on B in the right hand and E flat in the left and continues in an arpeggiated gesture that employs two forms of the familiar diminished sonority. The resultant octatonic collection (identical to the transposition of the opening measures) is apparent: C-D- E flat- F-F#-A flat- A-B. Once again, as originally, it is only the E-G tertian interval pitches of the final two measures that escape the symmetrical system, and in this instance of course, they function as the mode definers of the major chord finalis. Finally, as illustrated in example 111, the simplicity of the fundamental contrapuntal progression is clear.

Example 111.   Sonata, I., mm. 156-160

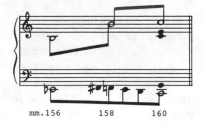

mm.156   158   160

Example 107 was first entered in relation to certain aspects of the composer's recorded performance of the first movement. Reconsider now the same passage from a structural vantage. The triplet arpeggiation of the left hand persists throughout these measures, as it has done throughout most of the movement, employing as its pitch content only the split-third D#-F# and E flat (D#)-G. The right hand dyads of measures 120-122 seem to function not as static blocks of sound but as a simple two-voice line that converges on the major third E flat-G, third beat of the 3/4 measure. Furthermore, the lower voice of the right hand serves a dual function; when it is combined with the left hand triplets, a familiar stepwise progression from a B triad to a C triad is accomplished. This fundamentally contrapuntal motion is reduced in example 112. Finally, as shown in the example, the implied counterpoint continues in measure 125, the bar that leads to the reprise, and the C-E flat third is once again split, resolving to the C-E interval of measure 126.

Example 112.   Sonata, I., mm. 124-126

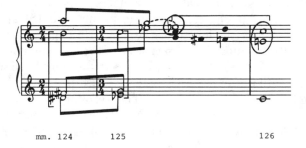

mm. 124   125   126

The linearity of the final movement is equally widespread. The priority pitch E is related of course by third to the first movement's centric C.

Perhaps the most immediately conspicuous contrapuntal feature of this movement is the strong reliance upon the augmentation of the original thematic material at various important junctures. As a representative instance, consider example 113. The material seen in the treble actually amounts to the movement's theme (which originally appeared as a solo left hand subject) and is here posited against its own augmented form.[69] In other ways this concluding movement is similar to its counterpart in the Piano Concerto. Neither movement subscribes to any strict formal procedure and both end with a cyclic allusion to the material of their respective first movement openings.

Example 113.   Sonata, III., mm. 19-24

The florid style of piano writing of the second movement, which here greatly expands the cadenza flourishes of the Concerto's second movement, is perhaps the most surprising textural characteristic of the Sonata and previews a style to be pursued in the 1929 *Capriccio* and the still later larghetto concertante of the 1940 *Symphony in C*. Complete with its A flat key signature, this movement is like the third, related by third to the initial movement's centric C. Internally, this adagietto reveals its own tertian macroformal structure with the middle section of its ternary format cast in C. Again, a similarity between this scheme and that of the Concerto's second movement is clear.

But structurally, it is Stravinsky's control of pacing in the unrestricted "by any predetermined form" first movement that is perhaps most enlightening in efforts to grasp the composer's evolving concept of musical architecture during this decade. As a discussion of event pacing was presented in conjunction with the *Piano-Rag-Music,* here also a durational analysis of the first movement is offered. Indeed, as Stravinsky had eschewed the acceptable tenets of a typical rag form in the 1919 work, the orthodoxy of sonata-allegro is here, if certainly not abolished altogether, at least transmuted according to what appears to be a rather systematic, proportionately regulated scheme. The following observations pertain to the graphic summary illustrated in example 114. There totals 160 measures in the movement. At the midpoint of this macroform, measure 81, the opening thematic material appears, suggesting the onset of a recapitulative passage, though here starting on the octatonic collection based upon B rather than the priority C. Moreover, within the first 80 measures, an internal symmetry accrues; for within this first half of the movement, three sections are clearly delineated: (1) mm. 1-31, divided by the cadence on the third related E; (2) mm. 32-50, a transitional passage leading to new thematic material at measure 51, and; (3) mm. 51-81, whereupon the passage mentioned above ensues. Thus these internal proportions are nearly durationally symmetrical within themselves; that is, mm. 1-31 total 31 bars, mm. 32-50 total 19 measures, and mm. 51-81 equal a sum of 30 measures, in effect a tripartite pacing that includes nearly identical outer sections while the central transitional passage is shorter by a third. Finally, each of these three divisions, as indicated in the graph, exhibits its own interior bipartite sectioning.

Conversely, the second half of the macroform, mm. 81-160, is comprised of two large internal divisions (mm. 81-125, and 126-160) within which each may be further partitioned into three sections. The bipartite division of mm. 81-160 is suggested on the strength of the distinctly recapitulative material beginning at measure 126 (amounting to a reprise of measure 13 and following). When the two recapitulative sections (mm. 81 and 126) are compared in proportional terms, the first is in the durational relation of .63 to the second. Several other similar proportions are apparent. For example, in the first 80 measures, the initiation of the second theme material at measure 51 begins at .63 of the entire 80-measure section.

The examination of Stravinsky's architectonic intricacy as a systemic aspect of his overall style is an area of inquiry that has as yet never been pursued earnestly. In the above case, similarities between the pacing of musical events in the *Piano-Rag-Music* and the Sonata may be noted.[70] But more importantly, the same fundamental precepts of symmetry that appear in these disparate works obtain to later and more familiar compositions in the same way that many of the pitch constructs first witnessed in the piano duets were developed in subsequent pieces.

With both architecture and pitch content in mind, more far reaching connections may be bridged between the Sonata and a work previously

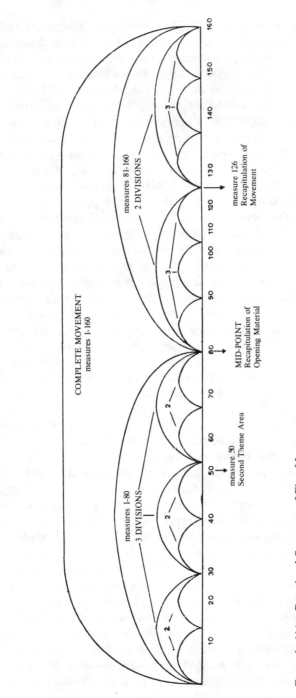

Example 114. Durational Summary of First Movement

mentioned, the 1940 *Symphony in C*. The textural correspondence of each work's second movement has been noted. But the structural similarities of each work's respective first movement runs much deeper. As Edward Cone points out in his classic essay "The Uses of Convention: Stravinsky and His Models," the *Symphony in C* is based on the model of a sonata form, especially as it relates to Beethoven.[71] In itself, this suggests a parallel with the Piano Sonata of 14 years earlier. Also, as the Sonata was Stravinsky's first true attempt at writing for a solo instrument in his own transformative treatment of sonata form, so too the *Symphony* was really his first purely orchestral work to employ symphonically the same structural principles. The very basis of the Sonata's harmonic homogeneity as noted, revolves around the use of a third relationship, C-E flat, as well as its transpositions. Furthermore, the significance of the pitch B, often functioning in lieu of a G, has already been implied in several instances: 1) at measure 81 where it acts as an incipit for the recapitulative material; 2) in example 111 where it progressed towards the priority C; and 3) in the final cadential gesture where it acts as an octatonic anchor for the arpeggiated diminished seventh sonority. Finally, the Sonata relied upon the progression, in traditional root movement terms, of I-II-III. For example, in recalling the architectural partitions outlined in the graph of example 114, measure 13, which represents the first important structural juncture, begins on C (I), moves to measure 22 where a similar gesture begins on D (II), and finally arrives at a clear resolution on E (III) in measure 31. All of these linear/harmonic pillars that collectively comprise the Sonatas's substratum are replicated in the later *Symphony in C*. In fact, Cone's analysis includes such revealing remarks as, "there is a tendancy of B to act as a dominant rather than as a leading tone . . ." and "the consequent struggle between E and C is evident throughout . . ." and finally, "what we hear then, suggests the stepwise shift of I-II-III as an alternative . . . of an ostensibly functional I-II-V."[72]

Yet an even stronger relationship founded upon structural similarities is at work here. Throughout his remarks on the architectural aspects of the *Symphony*, Cone pursues Stravinsky's employment of structural symmetry and the proportionate pacing of significant musical events as a central means by which the composer transforms the conventions of traditional sonata design. As one example of his discussion of internal divisions, Cone speaks of "parallel balance" and "a completely symmetrical layout" of the *Symphony's* subdivided second theme.[73] One observes that the similarity between his division here and those earlier outlined for the Sonata's first 80 measures are so close that both fail to form a perfectly symmetrical arch by the same number of measures—one. More broadly, both compositions clearly rely upon the same fundamental principles of balance, which as Cone so aptly concludes, enables and enhances Stravinsky's "articulated division of a uniform temporal flow."[74]

If the Sonata can be said to forecast in the manner just outlined, later works of Stravinsky's productivity, then it assumes its place along side so many other piano works discussed so far that seem to have acted in a similar precursive capacity. Naturally when parallels are forced, extrapolation can quickly turn into a convenient nostrum. Clearly the *Symphony in C* is as distinctive as any of Stravinsky's compositions; but distinctiveness in Stravinsky was never a preclusive characteristic. Patterns and models are almost always retrievable in examining his music, to such an extent in fact, that discovering some authentically *sui generis* element in most any of his compositions would seem more of a contrivance than not being able to trace the music's ancestral line of descent.

Even before the Sonata was premiered in July, 1925, Stravinsky had begun his third succesive piano opus, the *Serenade en La*. At first, it may seem somewhat strange that Stravinsky would have immediately undertaken yet another keyboard work, especially given the fact that the Sonata had not yet been publicly performed. But as often is the case, Stravinsky's acutely pragmatic approach to composition offers the explanation. As mentioned earlier, Stravinsky had spent several months touring America during the 1925 winter. The Piano Concerto of course often served as a centerpiece for these concerts; but the Sonata, despite Stravinsky's hope as expressed to Ansermet, was not yet prepared for inclusion on any public recital. Apparently the thought of still another piano work arose almost serendipitously during the course of Stravinsky's negotiations with a gramophone company in America. In his *Chroniques*, Stravinsky retells the events leading to the *Serenade's* genesis.

In America I had arranged with a gramophone firm to make records of some of my music. This suggested the idea that I should compose something whose length should be determined by the capacity of the record. I should in that way avoid all the trouble of cutting and adapting. And that is how my *Serenade en La* pour Piano came to be written. I had started it as early as April, beginning with the last portion, and now at Nice resumed its composition. The four movements constituting the piece are united under the title Serenade, in imitation of the *Nachtmusik* of the eighteenth century, which was usually commissioned by patron princes for various festive occasions, and included, as did the suites, an indeterminate number of pieces.

Whereas these compositions were written for ensembles of instruments of greater or less importance, I wanted to condense mine into a small number of movements for one polyphonic instrument. In these pieces I represented some of the most typical moments of this kind of musical fête. I began with a solemn entry, a sort of hymn; this I followed by a solo of ceremonial homage paid by the artist to the guests; the third part, rhythmical and sustained, took the place of the various kinds of dance music intercalated in accordance with the manner of the serenades and suites of the period; and I ended with a sort of epilogue which was tantamount to an ornate signature with numerous carefully inscribed flourishes. I had a definite purpose in calling my composition *Serenade en La*. The title does not refer to its tonality, but to the fact that I had made all the music revolve about an axis of sound which happened to be the La.[75]

Stravinsky returned to Paris in March whereupon a prearranged European tour obligated him to appearances first in Barcelona and later in Rome. Yet by May 9, one movement of the *Serenade* was already completed.[76] This cadenza finala became the ornate signature to which Stravinsky refers. Though not finished until five months later on October 9, the romanza was placed second in order in the Koussevitsky publication of 1926. The hymne, originally entitled "Hymne a l'Introduction" is dated August 3.[77] The rondoletto was probably completed in late August or early September since Stravinsky indicates that the *Serenade* was finished before he started for Vienna and the I.S.C.M. festival where as mentioned earlier, he performed his new sonata on September 8.

As might be surmised on the basis of this recently written sonata's delayed premiere, Stravinsky's travels, and in this case specifically the first American tour of 1925, were to conspire against Stravinsky composing with the same undivided attention he had enjoyed while working in prerevolutionary St. Petersburg or during the wartime seclusion in the Alps. Indeed, with the resumption of his piano playing, Stravinsky's career from this point forward was to become a matter of precariously balancing his many musicianly roles. With the *Serenade,* while Stravinsky declared his intent to compose this piano work specifically with a gramophone disc in mind, the four movement composition was not actually commissioned, nor was it recorded until July 1934 for Columbia, that is nearly a decade after the work was first publicly performed on November 25, 1925, in Frankfurt-am-Main.[78] But not only did the escalating demands of Stravinsky's concert schedule seemingly contribute to the abeyance of his original recording plan, but indeed the very form of the *Serenade* itself apparently fell victim to the itinerancy of the composer/pianist. In a September 23, 1925, letter to Ernest Oeberg of the Edition Russe de Musique, Stravinsky indicates that "in all probability there will be six parts" to the *Serenade*. In publishing this revealing letter, Craft rightly suggests that the last two planned movements were not completed because of concert interruptions.[79]

If, as seems to have been the scenario, Stravinsky planned each movement to fit exactly one side of a ten inch disc, then of course an even number of movements would have been appropriate. There is no indication that Stravinsky ever began a fifth movement which naturally would have then brought a sixth. As to source materials, there do not seem to be any sketches beyond the four published movements, though some important, and indeed puzzling, manuscript notations recently reported by Craft are valuable. For example, the title itself, about which Stravinsky raises the discrimination between "axis" and "tonality" seems to have undergone some rethinking. Originally the composition was simply entitled *Serenata,* as in the tenor solo section of *Pulcinella.* Moreover, the cardinally designative "en La" was only added in pencil to the cover page of the manuscript.[80]

The 1926 printed score included a multitude of misprints, many of which continue to plague current performances since no subsequently revised critical edition based upon the examination of Stravinsky's source materials has been prepared. Craft lists these errata in his discussion of "The Chronology of the *Serenade en La.*" Many of the errors are simply the oversights of careless engraving, a hindrance that continues to blemish the reliability of the score.[81] Various indications and dynamics are missing altogether or misplaced. Notes that should be tied are not, and several chromatic alterations are incorrect. As an example, Craft indicates that the first measure of the cadenza finala should actually be marked *mf,* and the second bar, subito piano, whereas the Koussevitsky printing has only the legato direction as shown in example 115. Still referring to example 115, one observes that the last left hand note of measure two, an F natural, continues its diatonic descent to E on the first pulse of measure three. When the same figure returns in bar 75, the F natural reappears as expected (ex. 116).

Example 115.   Cadenza Finala

However in this case, the final sonority of measure 75 becomes the first chord of bar 76, except that now an F$^\sharp$ is indicated. Actually the autograph reveals that in the measure 75 reprise of bar two, there should indeed be an F$^\sharp$ rather than the printed F natural on the final pulse of

Example 116. Cadenza Finala, mm. 75-78

mm.   75   76   77   78

measure 75, and understandably so, in the interest of preserving the elided sonority across the two octave register displacement. Finally, measure 77 reiterates the left hand F natural on the last pulse. The paranthetical natural sign serves as a reminder, and in this case the F natural is of course appropriate since, as had held for measure two, here again the line descends as part of the six-four chord inversions. Thus it would appear that while Stravinsky's sense of musical and orthographic logic was unfailing, none but the most perceptive performers today would probably be mindful of this small but nonetheless telling interior detail.

Just how vexatious Stravinsky found the rather extensive negligence in the preparation of his scores is demonstrated in a letter to Gavril Päichadze, Koussevitsky's editor in 1925, dated April 10, 1926. Hitherto unpublished, the letter is reprinted in plate 14. The translation follows.

> . . . two words only now to thank you for your nice letter. I have much to talk with you about, but I don't have the time now. . . . At present I am urgently notifying you about a *mistake* found by me in received copies of newly published Serenade—on page 16, fourth measure from the end in the right hand stands a natural before tied G. This is wrong. This natural belongs not to G but to F as a sign of warning, and therefore not compulsory. I ask that you cover this sign with ink. I hope that many copies have not gone out and we will be able to help this in time. . . . It is good that only one thousand copies were published.[82]

What to others probably appeared as a comparatively inconsequential variance obviously did not elude Stravinsky's concern, especially as his annoyance is expressed with such apparent urgency. In fact the natural sign was abolished in the 1947 Boosey & Hawkes engraving, though the precautionary F natural was not incorporated, as may be seen in Example 117.

However, in the most recent publication of the score by Boosey & Hawkes, Soulima Stravinsky again serving as editor, sheds an important new light on certain fundamental performance considerations. To begin,

Plate 14. Letter from Stravinsky to Gavril Païchadze

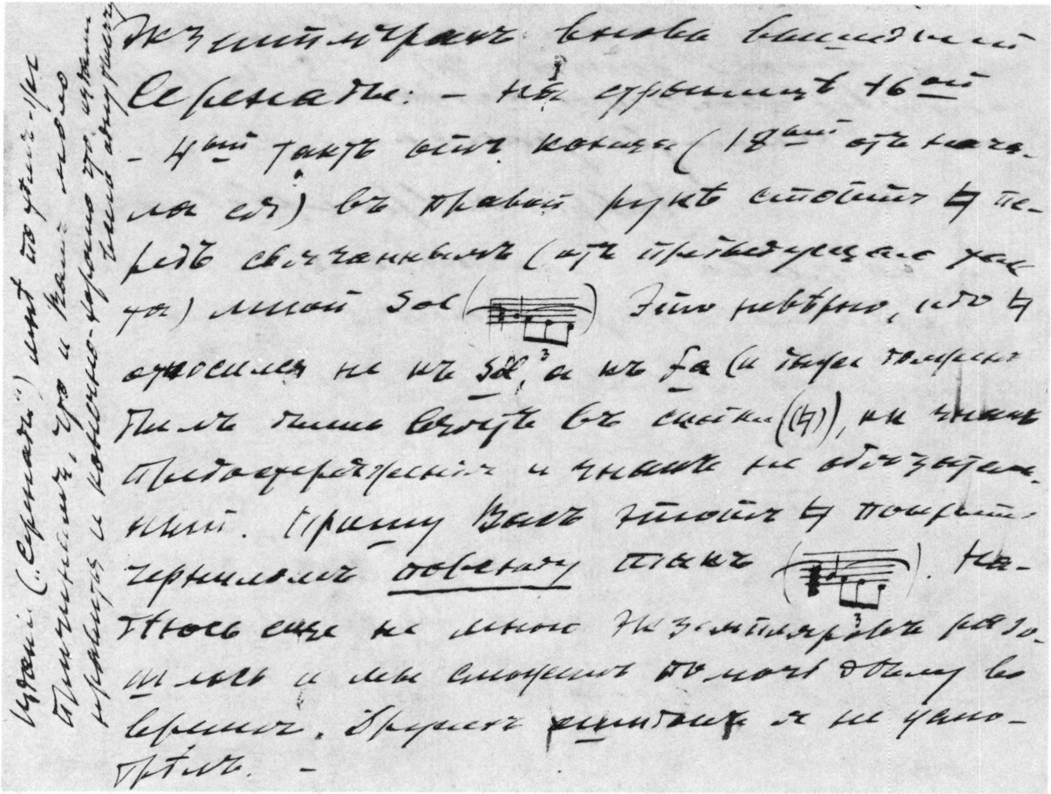

Van Katwijk Collection of Letters,
Southern Methodist University, Music Division

Example 117.   Rondoletto, mm. 124-127

Example 118.   Rondoletto (Soulima Stravinsky edition)

*Depress without striking

compare Soulima's notation of the same measures (ex. 118) as those addressed in the Païchadze document (ex. 117).

This score was issued in 1978 and does include the precautionary F natural as well as the G♯. Since Soulima knew his father's works well, it is very likely that he had access to Stravinsky's personal score and may have learned of his father's wish in this manner. But beyond the variance, one observes other differences in Stravinsky's 1926 printing and the 1978 edited score of his son. For example, Soulima adds a few performance directions (poco rit., molto dim,). Also, the pause that Stravinsky marks in bar 125 is renotated as a different note value and corresponding rest in Soulima's version, thereby emphasizing the desired silence at this cadential juncture. But curiously, in Stravinsky's own gramophone recording of the work in 1934 (and reissued years later in the United States by Seraphim) the composer/pianist completely ignores this pause here, and at all other analogously marked passages in the work, as in fact he had done in the piano roll of the Sonata discussed earlier.[83]

Since as Soulima states in his preface to the score, he had "the unique privilege of learning all Stravinsky's piano music under his guidance and direction, and maintained a longtime professional contact with him," Soulima felt that he "had an imperative obligation to transmit this precious tradition to future pianists and musicians."[84] Thus the license that he takes in adding an abundance of dynamic markings to the sparsely combed original score may in some ways be justified. Yet the fact that Stravinsky in those few aural testaments that survive chose not to incorporate much nuance or color remains enigmatic. Tempo discrepancies are equally confusing. Those marked in the early Edition Russe score are almost entirely at a suggested slower pace than those Stravinsky follows in his recording. Soulima usually chooses a tempo somewhere in between the two. Nor are these differences insignificant. In the cadenza finala for example, the original marking is quarter = 84. Soulima quickens it to quarter = 92 (marking the movement "Andantino" while Stravinsky's 1934 recording moves at a rate of quarter = 96.

Other conflicts also exist in comparing the Koussevitsky 1926 score with Soulima's, and those with the 1934 recording. For example, while Soulima incorporated the precautionary F natural referred to in example 118, he does not include the *mf* or subito piano indications Craft mentions in the first bars of the cadenza finala earlier addressed. Nor does Soulima's edition include the important F# that should have been printed in measure 75. Finally, Soulima marks the opening of this final movement with the direction "Sempre poco pedal," doubtlessly because this is as he remembers his father's interpretation. Yet again, the 1934 recording is at odds with this seemingly reasonable suggestion, for Stravinsky's performance is amazingly dry throughout, even detached, though he himself marked the opening "legato." Indeed, Walter Piston remembers that during Stravinsky's occupation of the Charles Eliot Norton Professorship at Harvard in 1939–1940, Stravinsky declared that the *Serenade* "was to be played absolutely without pedal, and he proceeded to do so."[85] Thus the would-be performer is again the hapless victim of such perplexities. Until such a time when all source materials are available and can be incorporated along with Soulima's recollections, Stravinsky's recordings, as well as others who remember Stravinsky's performances and sentiments, the situation is unlikely to be clarified satisfactorily. Moreover, such discrepancies are especially unfortunate here, for the *Serenade,* unlike its pianistic predecessors, is less percussive, less straightforward in many ways, and clearly makes greater musical demands upon the performer. There are of course the inevitable attempts to relate the musical ideas of the composition to specific pianistic models. Several commentators beginning with Casella have chosen to draw a parallel between the opening of the *Serenade's* hymne and Chopin's *Ballade in F Major,* Opus 38—a tenuous relationship at best—for there is no evidence to suggest that Chopin occupied Stravinsky's thoughts at this point.

According to Craft, a B flat was originally included in the key signature of the hymne. Moreover, the absolutely essential sixteenth notes of the opening gestures were apparently at one time not really so essential, for Stravinsky first wrote the passage without them, penciling them in later. Indeed without these added sixteenths, the movement does quickly take on more of the appearance of a hymn. The rondoletto, too, was prepared in pencil (the other movements mostly in ink) and is closest in spirit to some of the polyphonic writing of the Concerto and Sonata. Though the final version of the cadenza finala employs continuous eighth-note notation, apparently Stravinsky had earlier conceived the movement in sixteenth-note motion and had used a key signature of one flat here also—a very strange indication given the harmonic configurations of the movement.[86]

For the most part, the writing is awkward. The arpeggiated figures that launch the passage at measure 52 of the hymne and continue throughout, do not comform to any traditional pattern, while the right hand must accommodate some particularly unwieldy chordal writing. Perhaps the most novel use of the keyboard (though precedents in piano literature exist) is the sounding of the centric pitch A at the end of the first three movements whereby one of the doubled pitches is depressed silently as Stravinsky indicated by his explanatory footnote "Appuiez cette touche sans faire entendre le LA" (see ex. 118 for such an instance).

While the *Serenade* is a more mellifluous work than the two piano works of a few years earlier, it is further distinguished by its critical appearance near the exact center of Stravinsky's overall compositional productivity. In many ways it serves as a crucible that signals Stravinsky's concern about certain compositional issues in respect to pitch centricity. All those effusions about manipulating intervals, pitch axes, gravity, convergence, polarity, and of course paramountly in this case, the "en La" added apellation itself, now overtly recognizes a growing awareness, and maybe even a fundamental need to crystallize the linear/harmonic syntax that had been formulating in the works since the early Swiss years. Years later in his *Poetics of Music,* Stravinsky specifically addresses many of the basic structural principles that find their earlier application especially in the neoclassic piano works. With the concept of a centricity of certain pitches in these keyboard works in mind, Stravinsky's message as expressed in his Norton lectures is immediately relatable to the "musical topography" as he calls it, of the *Serenade*:

> . . . our chief concern is not so much what is known as tonality as what one might term the polar attraction of sound, of an interval, or even a complex of tones. The sounding tone constitutes in a way the essential axis of music. . . .
>
> In view of the fact that our poles of attraction are no longer within the closed system which was the diatonic system, we can bring the poles together without being compelled to conform to the exigencies of tonality. . . .
>
> Composing, for me, is putting into an order a certain number of these sounds according to certain interval relationships. This activity leads to a search for the center upon which the series of sounds involved in my undertaking should converge. Thus if a center is given, I shall have to find a combination that converges upon it.[87]

More recently, amongst the many tributes that followed Stravinsky's death, Arthur Berger goes so far as to suggest that the *Serenade* "reveals much more substantially than anything Stravinsky wrote before it in what sense he was developing his 'constructive values' in a direction that bears broad kinship to serial procedures."[88] Obviously the polemics of such a discussion have far reaching implications, and Berger himself is quick to point out that the *Serenade* was written, by coincidence or otherwise, the same year that Schoenberg gave full exposition to his dodecaphonic method in the *Piano Suite,* Opus 25.

In examining pitch control in Stravinsky's *Serenade,* first consider the opening measures of the Hymne (ex. 119).

Example 119.   Hymne, mm. 1-7

The insistence of the A as the pitch that frames the overall gesture in both hands is immediately apparent. But equally distinct is the F major triad environment in which this centric A often finds itself. Indeed a pure A triad does not appear until measure six. Thus within the vertical dimension of the opening gesture, an F-A major third axis evolves as a central issue. Moreover, the directional B flat, whether it be viewed as a phrygian inflection or not, clearly functions as a reinforcing agent in establishing the A as a pitch priority. However, the B natural, seen as an adjacency to the left hand B flat throughout, is equally directional in that it finds its resolution to the C octave of measure five, the first such appearance to this point in the passage. Two linear movements result: the right hand descent from A to E; and the A-C-A progression of the left hand (ex. 120).

Example 120.

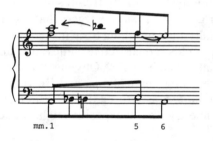

Taken together, the structurally important pitches of the gesture as graphed are the A-C-E triadic pitches; but also the F must be considered because of its vertical importance as indicated above. Moreover if the opening bar of the next passage is added, that is, measure seven of example 119, the importance of the pitch D as the left-hand octave analogous to measure one's octave A becomes clear. The similarity of measure seven with measure one is of course obvious and indeed the right hand pitch content is essentially the same, though less dense—perhaps because of the overall lower textural register. Thus the D is really the only new element; yet it is a significantly integrative pitch, symmetrically uniting the slightly varied gesture of measure seven with the pitch collection of the previous six measures. For if the D is now added to the structurally important pitches shown above, the symmetrical array radiates from the axial A as shown in example 121.

The alteration of major and minor thirds (numerically expressed by the sum of semitones in ex. 121) is regular, and it is this intervallic rotation rather than any residual tonal or modal inferences that seems to be at the architectural center. In this way, Berger's preserial notion gains support, for Stravinsky's early tone rows do in fact deal specifically with such

Example 121.

A <   3 — C — 4 — E
           \   \ 7
            > A   (C#-E, measure 14)
           /   / 7
      4 — F — 3 — D
              (m.7)

tertian rotations. Also as indicated in example 121, the gesture eventually returns to the centric A, though this time with a C♯ rather than C natural sounding as the modal identifier in this cadential sonority. Moreover, following an interpolation of the material first seen in the very opening measures, this same A major sonority initiates a new passage which, though stressing treble fourths, actually amounts to an uninterrupted stepwise progression of triads in the left hand ascending to G, functioning as the fifth of what evolves as a passage built upon the diatonic C pitch collection. In this sense, the split third A-C-C♯ priority again is clear, as it was in the previous two piano works. Measures 14-22 are illustrated in example 122.

Example 122.

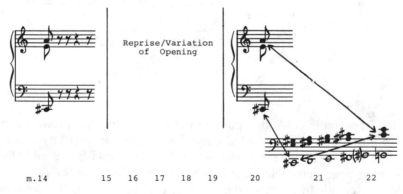

Reprise/Variation
of Opening

m.14   15   16   17   18   19   20   21   22

The idea of employing such stepwise progressions, rather than the more hierarchially oriented fifth related root movements was addressed in the sonata. But here the notion is expanded to include an overlapping of the seventh scale degree, both raised and lowered, sounding simultaneously with the polar sonority and not unlike moments encountered in the earlier *The Five Fingers*. This is especially apparent in the cadential gestures of the first three movements. All three of these closing passages exhibit the sympathetically engendered La as discussed earlier (ex. 123).

Example 123.   Hymne, Romanza, Rondoletto (cadences)

In example 123A, first pulse of the first bar, the A-E prolonged pitches are positioned against the left hand D (a familiar trichord by now). More importantly, the lowest D is sustained while the G-B are added on the second large pulse while the low A is articulated, thereby producing the lower seventh triad within the outer A pitches. Indeed, the conscientious pianist when attentive to Stravinsky's carefully notated direction (and assuming the pianist has a rather large hand) will insure, by means of a hand shift, that the dotted half D on pulse one continues to resonate throughout the measure so that the harmonic conflict is allowed to speak.

Example 123B displays both the diminished and major triads of the seventh degree, respectively built above G# and G natural. The G# resolves to the A as expected, though not before the diminished triad has sounded against the centric dotted half A of the middle stave. After silently depressing the octave A, it is a G major triad that is employed, perhaps a distant reminder of the romanza's central section that had begun around G in measure eight.

Finally, the closing measures of the rondoletto (ex. 123C) illustrate a similar instance wherein both forms of the seventh appear after the earlier discussed pause, and are sustained until the octave is depressed. Once again the notation is precise, demanding that the pianist carefully shift positions so that the desinigrative effect is clearly executed.

Apparently Stravinsky did not find the composition of the *Serenade* very taxing, or at least so he claims in his *Chroniques*.

> As soon as my *Serenade* was finished I felt the necessity for undertaking something big. I had in mind an opera or an oratorio on some universally familiar subject. . . .
>
> With my thoughts full of this project, I started for Venice where I had been invited to play my Sonata.[89]

Example 124.   *Oedipus Rex*, rehearsal 8-11 (piano reduction)

Actually the romanza was not completed until a month after the Sonata's Venetian performance. Thus the intersection of the *Serenade* and what would eventually come to be the composer's 1926/1927 Sophoclean opera-oratorio, *Oedipus Rex*, may be traced. As in previous instances, the natural transference of ideas that would normally occur between adjacently written works is once again apparent in *Oedipus* and the *Serenade*. Allusions have been made to the relationship of each work's respective opening.[90] But the similarities are more extensive. Consider the orchestral music of *Oedipus* from rehearsal number 8 to 11, given in the piano reduction (ex. 124).

This section is among the very first notations and dates from early January 1926, though Stravinsky had already approached Cocteau seeking his collaboration as early as October 1925.[91] While several months separate the completion of the *Serenade* and the music illustrated above, it seems clear that Stravinsky still found several of the fundamental textural ideas of the *Serenade* useful, as may be determined by comparing example 124 with example 125, an excerpt of the Hymne.

Example 125.   Hymne, mm. 43-55

Several similarities emerge. The scale ascent beginning at rehearsal number 8 of *Oedipus* (A#-B#-C#-D#-E, an octatonically structured segment) is analoguous to the linear rise of the hymne beginning at the 6/8

change of measure 47 (F#-G#-A-B-C). Even more linearly oriented is the *Oedipus* passage beginning at one bar before rehearsal number 10 where the stepwise rise of triads in the left hand of the piano reduction (A-B-C-D-E-F#-G#-A) produces a complete melodic minor ascent reminiscent of a similar, albeit abbreviated rise in measures 20-22 of the hymne as discussed earlier. Also, apparent is the natural pianistic look of this orchestral reduction, actually closely approaching the piano figurations of the Hymne. This is particularly just so in comparing the textural dispositions of both passages; for example, in the statically shifting sonorities at rehearsal number 9 in example 124 and measures 43-46 of example 125. Indeed, even the alternating C#-B# dyad of *Oedipus* is similar to the same verticalized pitches that repeat throughout the regularly changing 6/8 and 9/8 meters of the *Serenade's* passage. Moreover, one observes a further pianistic correspondence between the chordal movement at four bars after 9 and the section beginning at measure 52 of the Hymne, a similarity that is further sealed by each passage's use of a hemiola. (Also to be noted in measures 52-55 is the linear descent of the peak pitches in the left hand, G-F-E-D.)

If as one biographer contends, *Oedipus Rex* may be taken as the first pinnacle of Stravinsky's neoclassical maturity, then what of the three piano works that immediately preceded this 1927 plateau? To be sure, the "still-life" action of *Oedipus,* as the composer referred to it, marks a conception somewhat apart from the Concerto and Sonata, though not so distant from the *Serenade*. But more significantly, especially in terms of the more fundamental building blocks of composition, it becomes apparent that the piano works of 1923 to 1925 prepared the route leading to this culminative opera-oratorio.

The pitch system of the work, as one example, seems to rise from a central minor third emphasis such as the C#-E underlying dyad of the bass line seen at rehearsal number 9 in example 124, as well as the tertian structure right hand chords that follow. Often the extension of these thirds, as seen in the following graph (and here presenting a portion of the choral section at three bars before rehearsal number 10 in *Oedipus*) forms a distinctly octatonic collection, not unlike those discussed earlier in both the Concerto and Piano Sonata.

Even the larger harmonic scheme of the work with its frequently third related polarities, perhaps even its "search for D Major," as Mellers hypothesizes, from the opening "Caedid nos pestis" in B flat minor to the closing "Vale Oedipus" in G minor, simply continues the same macroformal patterns of organization that had been developing steadily and that eventually attained its most systematic realization in the *Serenade*.[92] Moreover the *Serenade* seems not only to presage *Oedipus* specifically,

Example 126. *Oedipus*

but in its less percussive, more pianistically dégagé style, it suggests a turn towards the writing of the comissioned ballets of the latter half of the decade, *Apollon Musagète* and *Le Baiser de la Fée*.

Of course Stravinsky more than ever continued to travel as a pianist during the interim that separates the *Serenade* from his next piano opus, the 1929 *Capriccio* for piano and orchestra. Moreover he not only added regularly to his legacy of recorded transcriptions for the mechanical piano during these years, but now he undertook, though with some reserve, his first gramophone recordings (including of course the *Serenade* as discussed previously). This added activity, when considered along with the commissioned ballets and his regular touring, surely accounts for what would seem to be the sudden demise of interest in writing new piano works. But the piano continued to interest Stravinsky in other ways; for example, its use in *Oedipus* and its once planned use in the ensemble for the 1927 *Apollo,* though the keyboard was eventually sacrificed there in favor of the homogeneous string scoring.[93] Also, with *Le Baiser de la Fée,* Stravinsky's reliance upon the short piano pieces of Tchaikovsky points towards a direct indebtedness to keyboard writing as his afflatus. The actual adaptation of Tchaikovsky's music into this 1928 ballet was now as it had been in his youth, not only an act of homage to one of his enduring models, but also as Lawrence Morton observes, "an act of criticism at its most rigorous."[94]

Engrossed as he was with the piano works of Tchaikovsky, is it any wonder that Stravinsky's next opus, the *Capriccio* (whose orchestra now reinstates a full complement of strings) exhibits a continued sympathy for the spirit that pervades *Le Baiser*? Tantamount to his second piano concerto, the *Capriccio's* preliminary thoughts are traceable to late December of 1928. In comparison to the more propulsive, even frenetic Piano Concerto, this is a freer work, substantially different in complexion, as its title suggests. Steeped in a more thoroughly nineteenth-century pianistic idiom than anything since his earliest works, the *Capriccio's* inception was addressed by Stravinsky towards the end of his autobiographical commentary.

> I worked at my *Capriccio* all summer and finished it at the end of September. I played it for the first time on December 6 at a Paris Symphony Orchestra concert, Ansermet conducting. I had so often been asked in the course of the last few years to play my *Concerto* that I thought that it was time to give the public another work for piano and orchestra. That is why I wrote another concerto, which I called *Capriccio,* that name seeming to indicate best the character of the music. I had in mind the definition of a capriccio given by Praetorius, the celebrated musical authority of the eighteenth century. He regarded it as a synonym for the *fantasia,* which was a free form made up of *fugato* instrumental passages. This form enabled me to develop my music by the juxtaposition of episodes of various kinds which follow one another and by their very nature give the piece that aspect of caprice from which it takes its name.[95]

Given that the *Capriccio* was the only composition completed in 1929, one might assume that it was a project that consumed a good slice of Stravinsky's creative time. But by the late 1920s, Stravinsky's compositional periods of activity had become increasingly intermittent. Engagements were now so frequent that after having begun the *Capriccio* on December 24, 1928, the composition was apparently temporarily abandoned throughout the winter and spring of 1929. Most of the writing resulted from a concentrated period of work during the following summer. While the essence of the three-movement composition was finished by the end of September, the instrumentation, as was so often the case in Stravinsky's register of works, was not completed until November.[96]

The work was received well. Of the premiere, Leon Edel reported ". . . when the last chords had sounded, the genial Igor was the recipient of a marked and vociferous ovation."[97] As with the Piano Concerto, Stravinsky performed the work frequently at first, and by 1931 the *Capriccio* had been programmed more than 20 times. Stravinsky recorded the work for French Columbia the following year. A few years later the *Capriccio* would mark another milestone, for it is with this work that Stravinsky introduced his son Soulima to the public in November of 1933 in Barcelona. By the early 1930s Soulima had already launched a career as a

pianist. His father specifically recalled a performance in 1933 with Soulima as the soloist while Stravinsky conducted. It was at this concert in
Venice that Stravinsky met Alban Berg whose manner, Stravinsky remembered, "seemed slightly condescending."[98]

It is curious that the second movement, marked andante rapsodico,
is dated September 13 though the concluding cadenza of the same movement was already fully drafted by July 25. More importantly, the sketch
for this passage, which was to become the music of rehearsal number 48
to 51, and is beautifully reprinted on page 292 of *Pictures and Documents,*
provides a rare opportunity to examine one aspect of Stravinsky's actual
writing process. Several points become clear in examining this sketch:
first, the sketch is in fact an amazingly finished document. Very few
alterations were necessitated in preparing the final printed version, a portion of which is reprinted as example 127.

Example 127.   *Capriccio*, II.

By the time they reached the written stage of the sketch that Craft
discusses, surely Stravinsky's initial thoughts had already experienced
several prenotational trials. Indeed, the sketch discloses well-formulated

thoughts rather than a collection of roughly scribbled ideas. While matters of pitch seem to have been virtually finalized by the time of this sketch, other issues were yet to be settled. Several rhythmic and metric decisions are not yet indicated. For example the placement of bar lines and the insertion of the 5/8 and 4/8 meters at measures 79 and 81 respectively, both suggest that these were secondary considerations in Stravinsky's estimate, easily amendable once the basic gestures were captured in some notational way. Likewise, the heavily marked performance indications of the printed score, rubato, accelerando, dolce, sempre marcato e piano, were yet to be added, and all of these doubtlessly had been specified to enhance the rapsodico feeling. But interestingly, Stravinsky here, as he had previously done in the Piano Concerto, did notate some specific piano fingerings that unfortunately do not survive in present editions. At measure 50 in example 127 for example, Stravinsky marked the fingering to be used in alternating hands.

Even at this rather fully worked out sketching stage, Stravinsky makes no distinction between material to be eventually orchestrated and that to be assigned to the piano, a fair indication of just how organically conceived the music is. For instance the first bar of example 127 (which is essentially recapped in the last measure of the same example) indicates an underlying support of strings before the cadenza begins. Example 128 provides a transcription of that measure of the sketch as well as the preceding bar.

Example 128.   *Capriccio*, Andante Rapsodico (transcription)

Not only do the left-hand octaves of the transcription (ultimately given to the ripieno lower strings) make good pianistic sense, but the preceding measure also employs a series of rising chords, though while densely structured in terms of traditional piano writing, were not at all uncommon in Stravinsky's piano music (the specific spacing of these chords have special implications to be explored in chap. 7). Moreover, Stravinsky gives no clue here that this measure will eventually be divided between strings, trumpets, and flutes, nor is there any sign that this orchestral material will end just at the bar line and that the piano will then assume the idea expressed in the upper stave. Such clearly identifiable symptoms continue to suggest just how interrelated the influential use of the piano was in Stravinsky's compositional process.

Stravinsky himself mentioned that while composing the *Capriccio* his thoughts were "dominated by that prince of music, Carl Maria von Weber, whose genius lent itself to this manner."[99] There is no question that Weber was the prototype upon whom Stravinsky modeled the demanding pianistic technique of the *Capriccio*. Stravinsky remembered that after a performance of *Der Freischütz* "I acquainted myself with all of Weber's music," going on to admit that Weber's piano music—the sonatas, the *Konzertstück,* etc., "may have exercised a spell over me at the time I composed my *Capriccio.*"[100] The fact that Stravinsky again created a work founded upon a specific model was by now an expectancy, but that his point of departure, especially in terms of the pianism itself should be such musical persiflage as Weber's Opus 79 *Konzertstück,* is curious indeed. The pianistic style of the *Capriccio* is utterly foreign to the Piano Concerto though Stravinsky continued to perform both. However the fundamental keyboard technique of each was in fact so very different that Stravinsky refused to play the works on the same program: "To play both the *Concerto en La* and the *Capriccio* in the same concert would require too many rehearsals . . . while the difficulty of the change of technique involved in such different pieces is enormous."[101] The sheer physical energy needed to perform the *Capriccio* is quite substantial. The wide arsenal of techniques required to match the full spectrum of nineteenth century virtuosic writing affords some indication of Stravinsky's pianistic versatility. Double note figures employed in a *moto perpetuo* fashion are frequent; and while the endurance needed to execute such passages as those at rehearsal number 86 is in itself demanding, one must also remember that pianistically such passages continue to be recognizably awkward and no doubt were tailored for Stravinsky's hand.

While composing the *Symphony of Psalms,* Stravinsky continued to perform the *Capriccio* widely, in Berlin, Leipzig, Bucharest, Prague, and Winterthur. While his interest in the performance of his own works continued, there were soon to be more collaborative efforts with his son Soulima. More importantly, through the intercession of Willie Strecker, the director of B. Schott's publication firm, Stravinsky made the acquaintance of Samuel Dushkin, the violinist principally responsible in motivating the composer to write several piano and violin works in the early 1930s. The acquaintance warmed to more than a working association, and Stravinsky recounts the friendship with genuine affection in the closing pages of his *Chroniques,* as does Dushkin in his own recollective essay "Working with Stravinsky."[102] Dushkin's contributions were more than merely advisory: they were truly integral to the actual string writing of these new works. Stravinsky, for example, adds "Partie de Violin avec le collaboration de Samuel Dushkin," to both the 1931 Violin Concerto and the 1932 *Duo Concertante.*

The piano, besides its solo and concerto capacities, had been used by Stravinsky as an orchestral instrument in such well-known works as *The Firebird, Petrouchka, Les Noces, Oedipus Rex,* and *Symphony of Psalms.* Now the piano took on another new role, that of a chamber music instrument. While Stravinsky continued to perform the piano literature of the 1920s, his association with Dushkin opened a whole new arena of opportunities. While the *Duo Concertante* is a major opus, other pieces had to be added in order for a complete violin and piano program of Stravinsky's works to be available for touring. Several transcriptions of the composer's earlier and most popular works were thus prepared. Dushkin himself addressed the earnestness with which Stravinsky approached what could have been a perfunctory task, as he described Stravinsky's returning to "the essence" of the original music in order to "rewrite or recreate the music in the spirit of the new instrument." And further,

> My role was to extract from the original score of former works we were transcribing, a violin part which I thought appropriate for the violin as a virtuoso instrument and characteristic of his musical intentions. After I had written out the violin part, we would meet, and Stravinsky then wrote the piano part which very often resulted in something different from the original composition, Stravinsky sometimes also altered details of the violin parts which I had extracted. I believe I am not exaggerating when I say that Stravinsky has thus given us a series of short pieces for violin and piano which, although they are transcriptions, have the flavor and authenticity of original works.[103]

These transcriptions included a rewriting of sections of *Pulcinella,* resulting in the 1933 *Suite Italienne,* a work whose piano writing is nearly as demanding as many of the piano works of a decade earlier. But the idea of transcribing music for violin and piano should not mistakenly be linked only to Dushkin, as is often the case. Stravinsky had already prepared several such arrangements years earlier, and though they were published by Koussevitsky and Schott in the 1920s, they were quickly replaced by the early 1930 transcriptions with Dushkin. In these earlier versions, it was the hand of the Polish violinist Paul Kochanski (1887–1934) who, like Dushkin, later, seems to have served as Stravinsky's advisor. Not only was the first transcription of *Pulcinella* released in 1925 as a *Suite for Violin and Piano* (and dedicated to Kochanski), but also sections of

Plate 15. "Prelude et Ronde des Princesses," violin and piano transcription (Paul Kochanski/Stravinsky)

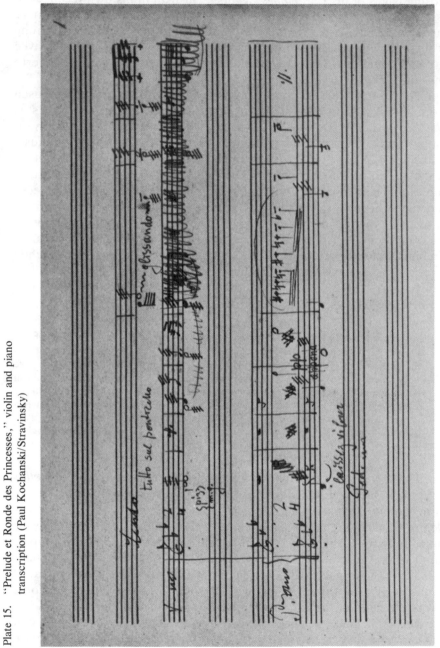

The Firebird, such as the "Berceuse," later arranged with Dushkin, were actually prepared in 1929 with Kochanski.

For reasons that are not clear, Stravinsky chose not to mention this earlier association, though Kochanski surely was more than a dedicatee in preparing these versions. The well-known violinist was a friend of Szymanowski and in fact had served as that composer's "Dushkin," collaborating with Szymanowski on several violin works such as the 1915 *Mitz* and the first Concerto of a year later. Thus it is reasonable to assume that since Kochanski fulfilled this role with that composer, Stravinsky may have relied similarly upon Kochanski, at least in an editorial manner during his original violin transcription preparations. One notes for example that on the original manuscript of the 1926 transcribed "Prelude et Ronde des Princesses," held by the Pierpont Morgan Library, the notation (in pencil) "edited and fingered by Paul Kochanski" appears. Also, as seen in plate 15, Stravinsky seems to have worked at the transcription in stages, as evidenced by the pen and pencil differences, thus suggesting that indeed the transcriptional projects even then were thoughtfully prepared and that perhaps Stravinsky relied upon Kochanski as the work evolved, seeking his advice in much the same manner as he did later with Dushkin.

As interesting as these piano and violin arrangements are, they do not reflect Stravinsky's continuing interest in piano writing to the extent displayed in the 1931/1932 *Duo Concertante.* The piano half of this chamber duo is as fresh, and most of the time as formidable, as any work from the piano literature of the previous decade. Again, Stravinsky's motivation in writing the work seems to have arisen out of a very practical sense. He found that it would be easier to arrange chamber concerts rather than orchestral programs in which he could participate. Thus the piano writing, intended for his own performance as always, reflects his unidiomatic approach to the keyboard. Much of the writing is reminiscent of the *Capriccio,* especially in many of the repeated note ideas of the *Duo's* opening cantilene movement (ex. 124). More importantly, such effects are often

Example 129.   *Duo Concertante,* Cantilene

expanded into figurations that appear closer to the style of piano reductions than authentic pianism.

Moreover, Stravinsky's unusually large hand surely is evident in certain finger extensions as in the cantilene's cadence, shown in example 130.

Example 130.   Cantilene

Copyright 1933 by Edition Russe de Musique; renewed 1960. Copyright © and renewal assigned to Boosey & Hawkes, Inc. Reprinted by permission.

Here, his desire to sustain precisely the fingered notes necessitates an extremely large extension of the left hand's fifth finger for the A. Such specificity surely suggests Stravinsky's punctillious concern with the exactness of textural ideas. While such fingerings are more commonly found in the *Duo* than in the published piano works, Craft reports that while other fingerings were not included, Stravinsky often marked such fingerings as he composed, clearly demonstrating that he was equally concerned with the performance of the score.[104]

Stravinsky and Dushkin toured the United States in 1935. In the time between the composition of the *Duo* in 1931/1932 and this American tour (Stravinsky's second), the composer completed two short religious choruses (*Credo,* 1932, *Ave Maria,* 1934) as well as the Ida Rubenstien commissioned melodrama, *Persephone* (1933/1934), a work that once again includes a significant piano part in the orchestra and reflects much of the piano writing style of the *Duo.*[105]

But before *Persephone,* and in fact even prior to the first notations for the *Duo,* entered on December 27, 1931, Stravinsky had already completed a large sonata-allegro styled movement for two pianos. Stravinsky makes no mention of this composition in his *Chroniques,* but instead proceeds directly from his remembrances surrounding the 1931 Violin Concerto to his detailing of the *Duo.* In all probability this omission stems from the fact that this two-piano work was incomplete at the time Stravinsky was finishing his autobiography. Still, the fact that Stravinsky had not only begun, but actually completed what was to become the initial movement of the substantial *Concerto for Two Solo Pianos* during the autumn of 1931 is rather astounding; this was a period during which Stravinsky was also involved with the premiere of the Violin Concerto on

October 23 and subsequent performances in November and December in Frankfurt-am-Main, London, Cologne, Hanover, and Paris.[106] Thus the con moto movement of the *Two Piano Concerto* was composed swiftly.[107] Surely this indicates the deftness with which he worked in a medium that was familiar to him since he had composed many of his orchestral works in a two-piano format orginally.

The relationship of the *Two Piano Concerto*'s first movement to the piano writing in the cantilene of the *Duo,* given the chronology, becomes apparent, especially in the repeated note figurations of the con moto. But perhaps more important than such specific parallels is the fact that both works are rooted in Stravinsky's continuing pragmatisim. As the *Duo* would help in enabling chamber music recitals, so, too, the *Two Piano Concerto* had a practical appeal.

> I needed a solo work for myself and my son, and I wished to incorporate the orchestra and do away with it. The *Concerto* was intended as a vehicle for concert tours in orchestraless cities.[108]

Soulima was 21 at the time the first movement was drafted, and had not yet begun appearing with his father in the pianist and conductor partnership soon to be cultivated. Even so, Soulima remembers that such collaborations were on the horizon and already he knew his father's music so well that he was entrusted with the piano reductions of the *Symphony of Psalms* and later with *Persephone.* Moreover, Soulima indicates that it was he who suggested the idea of a two-piano work to his father, remembering specifically that the idea arose during a motor trip in 1931 and that his father was so elated that he began work on the first movement shortly after moving to Voreppe.[109] The other three movements were completed in 1935, and when the published score was released in 1936 by Schott, the following inscription appeared.

> Ce concerto a été execute par moi et mon fils Sviatoslav Soulima-Stravinsky pour le première fois a l'Université des Annales à Paris en la Salle Gaveau, 13 21 Novembre 1935.

But Soulima warns that this prefatory note was not to be taken as a formal dedication. Still, memorialized in print or not, the work is a direct result of the father-son relationship and illustrates the familial closeness shared at the time. Moreover, when Stravinsky resumed work on the *Two Piano Concerto* in 1934 after having completed *Persephone,* Soulima seems to have become intimately involved in the actual process of ascertaining what pianistic effects would work best. His father remembers, "I asked the Pleyel Company to build me a double piano in the form of a small box of two tightly-wedged triangles. I then completed the *Concerto* in my Pleyel studio, test-hearing it measure by measure with my son Soulima at the other keyboard."[110]

The work was premiered by Soulima and his father as stated above, then repeated later the same day as well as on November 22. Soulima played the piano I part, and even in later years when Stravinsky performed the work with other pianists, he always played piano II. As had become customary during the 1920s, Stravinsky continued to introduce each of his new works with some prefatory remarks. In this case, a brief lecture subsequently reprinted as "Quelques Confidences Sur la Musique" in the *Journal de l'université des Annales* (December, 1935) was presented.[111] Upon that occasion, Soulima also performed *Trois Movements de Petoruchka* and Stravinsky's precurtain lecture included a rather elucidative commentary as to why that work should not be considered a transcription. In addressing the *Two Piano Concerto,* Stravinsky discussed his concept of the term concerto and his application to this his newest work. Summarily, he emphasized the concertante equality of the two pianos as each contributed to the thoroughly contrapuntal fabric of the composition. He advised his audience that the second movement, notturno, was not to be interpreted in the style of a Field or Chopin, but rather like the cassations associated normally with eighteenth-century "after-dinner music" as Stravinsky later referred to it. As for the concluding two movements, interestingly, Stravinsky refers to the third as the last, "a prelude and fugue preceded by four variations." though in the published score the variations are listed as a separate third movement and the prelude and fugue as the fourth. Finally, Stravinsky closed this address with several ideas that were to be expanded further a few years later in his lectures at Harvard. "Nothing is more difficult than speaking about music," he declares, then proceeds to raise the matters of analysis, aesthetics, logic, mathematics, and emotion, indeed a veritable menu of items that were to occupy him in his discussion of musical poetics.

The premiere, as well as many subsequent performances, did not fare well critically. In commenting that the *Concerto* "baffled its first audiences," perhaps Craft has provided the most astute estimate of the work's effect, as he provides a few reactions to these early performances: "Admirable technically, but without the slightest inwardness"; and as Prokofiev declared, "It is difficult to follow, with lots of notes jumping on each other, but the piece is interesting. . . ."[112] Yet despite whatever lukewarm reception such a densely chromatic, uncompromising work was bound to evoke (for it is surely one of Stravinsky's most complex creations), the *Concerto* was very marketable, providing audiences with the grand spectacle of not one, but two Stravinskys simultaneously on stage.

While Stravinsky continued to perform the Piano Concerto and *Capriccio* on his regular tours, Soulima and he now presented the new *Two Piano Concerto* in Europe and during the South American tour of 1936. Moreover during Stravinsky's subsequent immigration to America, an immigration that was unaccompanied by Soulima, he performed the work with several American pianists. Among these, Stravinsky fondly remembered the well-known pianist and pedagogue, Adele Marcus of the Julliard School in his *Dialogues*.

Stravinsky performed the work with Marcus nine times in 1940, six of these performances taking place in a period of less than three weeks. Her recollections of this intense period of collaboration provide a revealing insight into Stravinsky's approach to performance at this stage of his early American residence, often verifying earlier assumptions, other times suggesting hitherto unimagined ideas.[113] Marcus recalls that Stravinsky would always begin his practice sessions with Philipp exercises in order to "stimulate his blood and his brain," a ritual traceable to the early 1920s when he briefly studied with Philipp. Stravinsky sat very high at the piano and was very conscientious about the precision of the many articulative directions now marking his scores. An examination of even a few pages of the first movement exhibits an amazingly wide repertory of such guidelines: poco *sf* ma *p,* sempre détaché, cantabile, tenuto, various weights of accents, marciale, senza pedale, marcato, marcatissimo, martele, etc., all quite specific in comparison to the piano scores of a decade earlier. Professor Marcus further remembers that despite—or maybe because of—the pervasive specificity of these performance suggestions, Stravinsky declared that the music was to be played "ohne espressione," no doubt still betraying his misgivings about the excessive liberties exercised by some interpreters. Moreover he seems to have preferred slower tempi, thus facilitating the accuracy of the marked articulations, though curiously most of Stravinsky's earlier recordings and piano rolls of the keyboard literature, as mentioned earlier, are faster than the metronomic indications printed. He was especially attentive to matters of rhythmic fidelity, did not wish to rehearse very much, and was nervous about performing, a sentiment that has been echoed by others.

But perhaps most bizarre, Marcus recalls that before a performance, Stravinsky would apply some concoctive paste to the pads of his fingers that would quickly dry and act as a weighting agent. It is known for example, that Stravinsky seemed to be preoccupied with the element of key touch and weight peculiar to any one piano. On several earlier occasions, Stravinsky's concern over this variable surfaced through such requests as "Ask Steinway to reserve a large concert instrument with a light fingering and a bright (not velvety) sound"; or his expressed inclination to use such other European models as the Pleyel because of its "lightness and strength."[114] Thus it would appear that Stravinsky's mysterious adhesive substance was an attempt to counterbalance artificially the resistance of the piano's keys with which he found fault.

Stravinsky stated that the *Concerto* was "written for the love of pure art" and indeed it is one of the few noncommissioned works of the period. The approach is symphonic, so grand are the proportions, so varied the texture and so unified the whole. Stravinsky himself suggested that the work could have been orchestrated. Others, too, have addressed the symbiotic roles each piano serves in creating a contrapuntally hewn synthesis.[115] Example 131, excerpted from the first movement, is representative of the polyphony as suggested by the stemming of notes from one piano to the other.

Example 131.   *Two Piano Concerto*, I., mm. 16-18

Perhaps most obvious (and therefore of course most often cited) is the rather strictly fashioned counterpoint of the Preludio e Fuga, what with its concluding and explicit Lo stesso tempo della Fuga nell' inversione emulation of opus 110 ("I am very fond of my fugue, and especially of the after-fugue or fugue consequent. . . ."). Nor did Stravinsky attempt to conceal his perusal of Beethoven's fugues, or his study of the variation technique of both Beethoven and Brahms, though such an examination seems only to have been undertaken after the first movement was completed. But the similarities to Beethoven's overall structural control are far greater and can be sensed immediately now, as they were by Andre Schaeffner at one of the earliest performances of the work: "The most remarkable part of the whole work is its sense of form; one thinks of the last sonatas of Beethoven, with their elisions, their phrases suspended in mid-air or as if enclosed in parentheses, the thread breaking off, then joining again, without ever being lost."[116]

The "Voreppe" movement had been described in the l'Université des Annales disquisition as a sonata-allegro, and by virtue of its delineation of harmonic areas and central development section (mm. 92-169) such an analysis might apply. But perhaps more important are the dual polarities

Example 132.   Con moto, mm. 1-11

of the centric E priority and the B flat harmonic area clearly established in measure 92 by virtue of piano II's ostinato. One also notes a similar polar opposition by the tritone relationship G-D flat (measure 36) and returning to G of the notturno. Moreover, while the tritone related arrangement seems to have embued the first movement's macroformal architecture with the most distant and thereby unmistakably poignant harmonically oriented opposition, an identical subdivision of the E-E octave in the opening passage (mm. 1-11), especially as emphasized by the highly attended B flat of measures four and five, replicates this macroformal dual polarity within a linearly descending, microformal level. The projection of this array is summarized in example 132.

Such a linear approach brings coherence to all other divisions at the middle and microformal levels of the movement. Moreover, after the reannunciation of the opening theme in piano II at measure 11, whose basic pitch collection includes the tetrachordal cell E-G-B-D, a B flat next evolves as the most significant pitch (see, for example, the repeated B flat of piano I as illustrated earlier in ex. 131) in this passage. The tritone related B flat has already been shown to be significant as a cornerstone in the movement's architectural construction. When added to the basic four note cell, the octatonic array E-G-B flat - B-D results, by now a recognizable tertian segment in Stravinsky's literature. Coincidentally perhaps, one observes that the fundamental polarities of each of the four movements in order, I.-E, II.-G, III.-B flat, IV.-D, follows a similar tertian scheme. While this may first seem to be unlikely since the first movement is divided from the final three by the interruption of several years, still, there seems to be a certain inter-movement reticulum, especially regarding the interval content of the fundamental pitch cells.

In tracing this aspect of the *Concerto's* structure, the notion of an interval vector will be useful and may be summarized as follows. Since there are six possible interval classes (abbreviated as ic), that is semitone, tone, minor third, major third, perfect fourth, and tritone (this idea of course enfolds the basic concept of complement equivalency, that is, a major sixth = minor third, and so on), it is possible to view a cell's interval chemistry by arranging the number of incidences each ic appears in the cell's overall vector. These are arranged smallest to largest, left to right. For example, the first movement's opening thematic cell in measures one and two of piano II (refer to ex. 132) is E-G-B-D, as mentioned earlier, and yields the vector 012120, that is, no semitone or tritones as indicated by the zero entry, one whole step, one major third, and two minor thirds and perfect fourths. Example 133 illustrates this analysis.

Example 133.

As a second example, consider the clearly delineated cell of measure 2, piano I (again, see ex. 132) whose four notes D-E-G-A yield the vector 021030. One may recognize this familiar cell as a fundamental resource in earlier works as discussed in chapter 3 (*Petrouchka,* the easy piano duets, *Renard,* and others). Finally, if all the notes of both pianos in these opening two measures are taken as a collection (D-E-G-A-B), the resultant vector is 032140.

Even with these three basic units alone, the relationship of intervallic cells between collections of notes that appear to be different at the surface but in fact share an identical interval valency can be demonstrated easily. Consider first the important sempre détaché figure of piano I at measure six. It begins with the set of four notes C-E-G-A, and while this vertical tetrachord appears unrelated to the movement's opening linear cell (E-G-B-D) it is actually only a transposition. Thus the interval vector 012120 is shared. Other instances of this particular vector occur regularly in both a linear and vertical context and at many transpositional levels (for example, the very next vertical change of piano I in measure seven to the pitches C-D-F-A also yields the 012120 vector).

Often such appearances are articulated at structurally significant junctures. Consider next, measures 55-57 as reprinted in example 134.

This passage is analogous to that just discussed in measures six to nine by virtue of the shared melodic motive that here appears in the treble of piano II (A-B-A-G), whereas it originally was seen in the left hand of

Example 134.   Con moto, mm. 55-57

piano II (C-D-C-B). Perhaps most aurally obvious is the difference in the textural environment that surrounds this commonly held motive. Again, however, the interval vector provides a less evident but nonetheless substructurally unifying layer. First, when the notes of piano I's arpeggiated figure are condensed, the tetrachord C-F-G-A results. The vector for this set of pitches is 021030, that is, the same as earlier in the work's opening measures. Thus while the first appearance of the conjunct melodic motive in measures six through eight was accompanied by the vector 012120, here the other vector from the initial measures of the movement is now employed.

But other vector parallels are apparent. Continuing with the same passage, consider the initial sonority on the first pulse of measure 55 that launches the gesture D-F-A-A flat, and the cadence chord of F-A flat-A-C in measure 57. The invariant pitches F-A flat-A (again by now a characteristic intervallic cell) are extended a minor third in each case; that is, D-F in the first instance, and A-C in the second. Moreover, when the pitches are combined as a pentachord D-F-A flat-A-C, an octatonic rotation results. Finally, the structural pitches of the self-contained gesture at a microformal level are seen to be parallel with the structural pitches mentioned earlier (E-G-B flat-B-D) which form the basic pitch content for the work's macroformal construction. These relationships are schematically expressed in example 135.

Example 135.

mm. 55-57	d - f - a - a - c	Interval Vector 113221
mm. 1 - 6	e - g - b - b - d	113221

But as suggested earlier, even more significant inter-movement relationships can be demonstrated through the use of these interval vectors.
It is known that the thematic material upon which the third movement,
quattro variazioni, is based originated in material drawn from the fourth
movement, preludio e fuga, a movement that was actually written before
the variations then later paced last in order, no doubt for greater drama.
Clearly Stravinsky's treatment of this material in these variations has
received the most analytic attention, especially through such an illuminating and by now classic essay as Robert Nelson's.[117] Perhaps most
revealing throughout these variations is Stravinsky's rather novel use of
octave displacement, fragmentation, and interval exchange, all of which
anticipate later variation sets as well as the composer's eventual conversion to certain serial techniques. Nelson's analysis deals with matters of
thematic manipulation and identifies the cellular material drawn from the
preludio e fuga (an identification that Stravinsky himself had pointed out),
thus demonstrating the kinship of these two movements. According to
Nelson, the pitch material used for the variations comes from "the subject
of the fourth movement fugue . . . and the melodic fragment in measures
6-8 of the Preludio."[118] These two seminal motives are reproduced in
example 136.

Example 136.   Preludio

In arriving at the thematic material derived from measures six through
eight, the pitch content moves from the half note E in piano II (circled
in ex. 136) to the treble of piano I. This being the case, the incipit of the
fugue subject itself can be constructed similarly by examining the initial
measures of the preludio (ex. 137).

The construction of the double theme is interesting. In the first instance, if the vertical pitches of measures one through three of example

Example 137. Preludio, mm. 1-4

137 are combined, the tetrachord E-G-B-D results, that is of course, the same cell as the principal motive of the first movement, and naturally the shared vector 012120 is also apparent. Furthermore, if the first tetrachordal pitch members of the fugal subject itself (D-E-B-C#) are expressed in vector terms, 122010, it will be seen that another important parallel may be drawn with the first movement, viz., the four-note figure of piano I's bass in measures six through nine (A-B-C-D) which was discussed in its transposed form in example 134 (F-G-A flat-B flat) share the identical 122010 chemistry. Finally, if the second section of this double theme, E-G-A-C-D, that is, measures six through eight of the preludio, is reduced to the vector 032140, it is seen to correspond to the identical vector of the pitch collection of measures one and two of the first movement, D-E-G-A-B. Thus a relationship between the various structurally significant components of the respective openings of the *Concerto's* boundary movements may be appreciated, and by association, the variation movement as well.

Craft's claim that the *Concerto* is "Stravinsky's most powerful creation of the 1930s" is probably not far from the mark. Its appearance midway in a decade bordered by the *Symphony of Psalms* and the *Symphony in C* marks another critical juncture in the composer's evolution. Moreover its effect was immediately felt in the last few works to be written in Europe. Connections are clear with the 1936 *Jeu de Cartes,* especially in the shaping of the ballet's set of variations, as well as with the 1937/1938 "Dumbarton Oaks" Concerto, which first existed in a finished two-piano version as early as January 1938, months before its instrumentation.[119]

More importantly, the *Concerto* laid the groundwork for many of the techniques to be incorporated into Stravinsky's American works just ahead. The broad intervallic relatedness of its movements only suggested above is indicative of the cyclicism Tangeman addressed in the *Symphony in C*.[120] Indeed, Stravinsky himself spoke with his friend Ingolf Dahl about the "close relationship" of the *Concerto* to the 1945 *Symphony in Three Movements*.[121] In this regard, unquestionably the medium of two pianos provided yet another instance of Stravinsky's comfortable reliance upon the piano as a vehicle for testing new ideas, now drafted in larger proportions than ever before. Also, certain techniques of interval manipulation to be explored more systematically and more pervasively in the works of the early 1950s are here unmistakable. As a specific example, the look of the two piano version of the 1952/1953 *Septet,* with its variations and adoption of at least a limited pitch series, is closely allied with the *Concerto,* and also amazingly similar in its textural disposition.

Stravinsky held the *Two Piano Concerto* in especially high regard, going so far as to christen it "my favorite among my purely instrumental pieces."[122] It was to be the last of the piano works written during the productive period 1923–1935. By the time Stravinsky would again write a piano piece, it would be an ocean away both in geopgraphic distance and in musical intent. By 1940, Stravinsky was settled in Hollywood and now turned his attention to works of a more musically modest but assuredly gainful nature.

6

The American Piano Works

New York, September 30, 1939. When he stepped down from the S.S. Manhattan that autumn day, Stravinsky entered upon what was originally to have been an American sojourn, but ultimately proved to be a permanent residence. As the distinquished recipient of the Norton Poetry Chair at Harvard, Stravinsky had journeyed to Cambridge to present six public lectures, the first to be delivered on October 18. He also held composition class twice weekly with several of the university students. During these sessions, the piano was routinely used by the composer in offering his criticisms and demonstrating ideas for the class. Seated at the keyboard, Stravinsky's suggestions seem to have taken various forms: often he would play sections of one or another of his own recently completed orchestral works as models; at other times Stravinsky would assist one of the students by participating in a realization of the young composer's score, even playing some of the parts himself.[1]

The ambiance of the Harvard lectureship could not have gone undigested by Stravinsky, who was, after all, at the center of what one observer recalled as a series of "social soirées."[2] In some ways the notoriety the composer drew during his appointment was similar to the public attention accorded him upon his arrival in France nearly two decades earlier. Moreover, the amenities of the Harvard post, especially when coupled with his growing distress over a darkening European political scene, surely beckoned Stravinsky to consider immediately the wisdom of remaining in America beyond the 1939–40 academic year. Consequently, Vera de Bosset arrived in New York, in January 1940, and married Stravinsky on March 9. Once the duties of his Harvard University appointment were completed in May, a move was made to California where Stravinsky's often frail health could benefit from the salubrious climate.

The composer's acclimatization to America, and specifically to Hollywood, seems to have been accomplished without particular strain. Indeed, the utter contrast between Stravinsky's wartime refuge in

Switzerland and the cornucopia of compositional opportunities now available in America's film hub was surely all but intoxicating for the newly arrived resident. The idealogy of capitalism came easily for Stravinsky. But the many offers with which he was approached (including legitimate as well as some rather unethical commissions) were all considered carefully. Ultimately the numerous film scores that he began then later aborted or rearranged towards a different purpose, played a comparatively small part in Stravinsky's American years.

Two of the earliest American works are associated with the piano. The *Tango* of 1940 quickly reflects Stravinsky's susceptibility to the infectious dance spirit of the 1940s. Of course tangos had won favor with the composer years before in both *Histoire* and *The Five Fingers*. But here it appears to be Stravinsky's intention to be swiftly swept into the mainstream of the music then in vogue. Having just completed the *Symphony in C* in August, and while awaiting its November 7 premiere in Chicago, Stravinsky diverted his attention to this amusing stylization.

The work is listed as an authentic piano solo and indeed it was so published in 1941. Like so many of Stravinsky's efforts, it was drafted at the keyboard in a more or less complete pianistic layout. But that it was originally or even primarily designed to be a piano solo only, would be a false assumption. As a piano work the *Tango* is as pianistic as the 1919 transcription of the *Ragtime for Eleven Instruments,* which is to say that it is not particularly idiomatic. Quite likely, the *Tango,* like the *Ragtime* transcription, was from the start the equivalent of a short score that with minor alterations could also double as a piano piece. The texture at times is extremely murky, with densely chromatic internal lines often assigned to the pianist's right hand. The complexity of the polyphony is often lost amidst the pervasively thick sound. All of these factors hint that from the beginning, the *Tango* was destined to appear in more congenial arrangements.

In his short biography of Stravinsky, Frank Onnen postulates that the *Tango* originally existed in a two-piano version.[3] While this seems to be an unfounded assertion, a duo piano arrangement authorized by Stravinsky does in fact survive among the Stravinsky holdings at the Library of Congress. Prepared by Victor Babin, the manuscript includes extensive corrections in red pencil by Stravinsky, especially corrections in rhythmic divisions and registral placement. There are also two rather detailed letters to Babin which include musical examples and enumerate both the attractive as well as unacceptable aspects of the arranger's version.

Other commonly known arrangements were either prepared by Stravinsky himself, or as in the above instance, fully sanctioned. The two most well-known are: 1) a mixed ensemble version scored by Felix

Guenther and first played by Benny Goodman in July 1941; 2) Stravinsky's own instrumentation in 1953 for winds, brass, and strings, Also, Stravinsky and Dushkin prepared a violin and piano version in 1940 though it remains unpublished. While all of these arrangements are of relative inconsequence, they do suggest Stravinsky's early American willingness to exploit as fully as possible any remunerative avenue that still fell within his own, and perhaps expanding, limits of artistic propriety. Even now, one must remember, Stravinsky was hardly a wealthy man, and any perceived profiteering instinct would surely be understandable given the wholly meager profits he had previously won as a direct result of his European compositions.

In tracing the chronology of the *Tango,* Craft comments, "On October 14 [Stravinsky] finished a Tango for voice (without words) and piano."[4] The existence of this "cabaret vocalise" as Craft later dubbed it, has been known for some time, though the possibility that it preceded the piano solo version, whose exact dating remains unknown, is new. Among the folios of the aforementioned Babin two-piano arrangement, a single page of this piano and voice manuscript is preserved, and is here reprinted as plate 16.[5] The manuscript's marginalia, still written in his native Russian, reveals that Stravinsky had once intended to underlay words rather than have this version stand as a vocalise. But at that moment, it would seem, he had not yet found a text that was deemed appropriate. Perhaps his failure to identify a suitable text led to his decision to abandon the version as he turned his attention to other more substantive projects. The superscribed commentary, including the two inserted chords, suggests that the composer weighed the options in rescoring certain textural and rhythmic dispositions based upon what may have been the already completed piano solo, thereby implying that the piano version must have been composed in September or early October. Generally, the manuscript exhibits a near total concordance with the piano solo, though a closer comparison yields some melodic variance in the linear contours.

The musical message of this slightly modified tripartite work is naturally very lightweight. Its parody stems from the manipulation of the dance's endemic metric/rhythmic patterns that are preserved, yet cleverly distorted through exaggeration as well as by linear and harmonic clashes at structurally prominent moments. The Stravinskyan penchant for chromatic conflicts that temporarily obscure the tonal center (and here the music surely aims at a concerted warping of tonality rather than anything so elaborative as a surrogate polarity) overlay the metric regularity with its internal and constantly stylized syncopations. Example 138 exhibits this fluctuation between D minor and major through the arpeggiated left hand triads, vertically articulated cadences (see boxes in ex. 138), and

Plate 16. *Tango*, piano and voice sketch

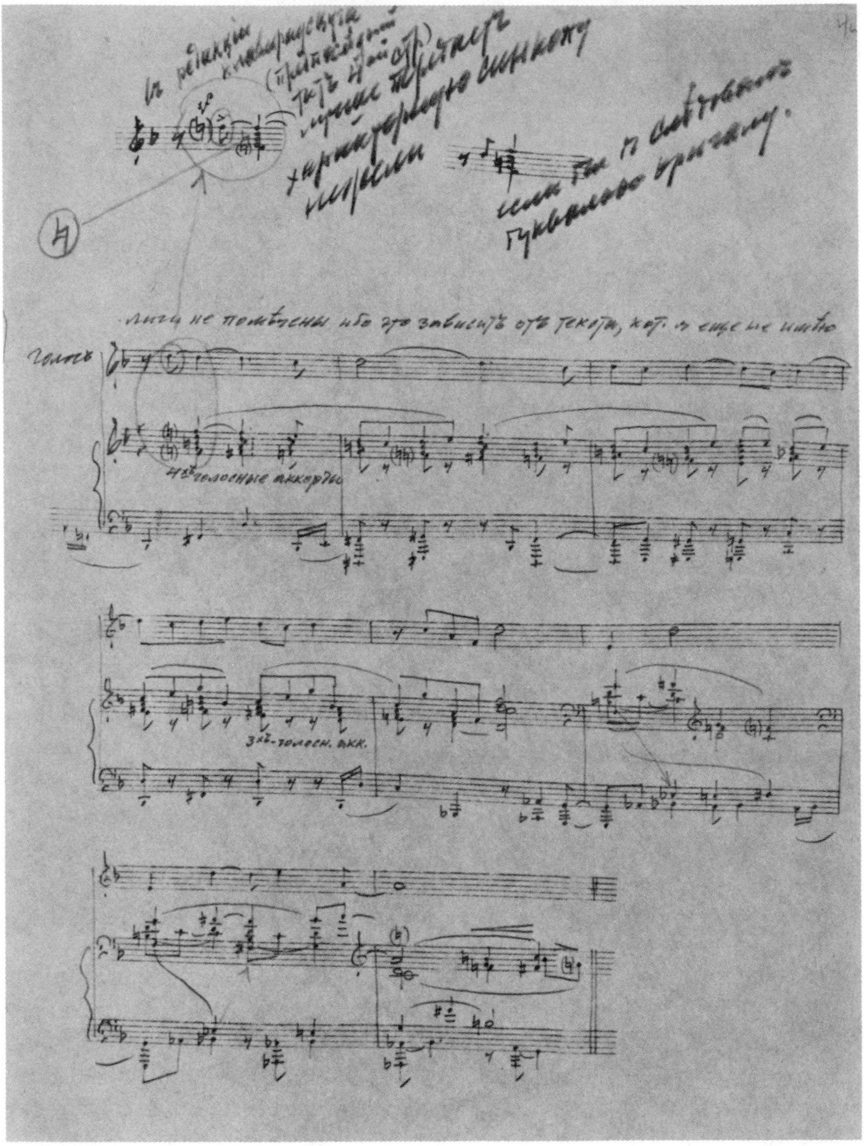

Library of Congress, Music Division

often the modally defining F-F$^{\#}$ pitches that occur simultaneously as seen in the bracketed chords on the second and third pulse of measure 25.

Example 138. *Tango*, mm. 23-25

If the *Tango* is to be viewed kindly as one of Stravinsky's more innocuously faddish escapades, then surely the 1942 *Circus Polka* flings us into the realm of sheer musical lunacy. Actually this once immensely popular work, performed more than 400 times, began in a fully drafted piano version, though it has now come to be classified as a transcription. But in fact, it is neither more nor less a transcription in spirit than the *Tango* or *Ragtime,* for it is only the chronology of publication that determines into which descriptive category one may pigeonhole this commercially inspired twaddle. Apparently Stravinsky was enticed by the notion of writing the *Circus Polka* on November 12, 1941, as he was finishing his *Danses Concertantes,* a work commissioned by the Werner Jansen orchestra that occupied Stravinsky during a good part of 1941.[6] George Balanchine wanted a short ballet for a troupe that eventually would include 50 elephants and 50 girls, to be performed by the famed Ringling Brothers Circus. It was, as Stravinsky openly confessed, a "journeyman job," and one of the "commissions I was forced to accept because the war in Europe had so drastically reduced the income from my compositions."[7]

The work was begun as early as December, and by February 5, 1942, the piano version was completed. Only a few sketch pages survive, attesting to the quickness with which this pachydermal pastiche (concluding with the well-known, blatant quotation of Schubert's *March Militaire*) was composed. A band version arranged by David Raksin was used at the premiere in New York, April 9, 1942. Stravinsky's orchestral scoring of the work followed in October. The composer's claim that this orchestral version was the original is no doubt an error, though the original piano version (published almost immediately) was from the start unquestionably aimed towards quick gain in as many dresses as possible.[8]

In considering the mercinariness of these two early Hollywood works (as well as the *Danses Concertantes* that separates them), surely one is struck by the most superficial elements of each work's attempted parody. The mimicry exhibited is certainly less thoughtful, less structured in terms of transforming the idea into something bearing a Stravinsky imprint. Unlike the earlier ragtime pieces, for example, wherein the identifiable components of the style served merely as a departure, a challenge, here Stravinsky appears to be less committed to any such introspective reshaping of the equally recognizable tango and polka conventions. For sure, they remain musically inexpiable and the nugatory creations of a composer caught up in the frippery surrounding him. Pianistically, these surely were not works to join the piano compositions of the 1920s or the *Two Piano Concerto* as vehicles for personal performance. Their ties to the piano are parenthetical even though they began at the keyboard and are still frequently performed in their piano versions as prime specimens of Stravinsky's satirical humor. Writing piano music, especially now that his concertizing as a pianist moderated while his conducting career continued to flourish, was naturally less of a priority and certainly no longer the necessity it once had been. Moreover the works that immediately followed (*Four Norwegian Moods,* 1942; *Ode,* 1943, *Babel Scherzo à la Russe, Scènes de Ballet,* and *Elegy,* all from 1944) clearly exhibit Stravinsky's ready acceptance of his new American life by composing for big bands, Broadway, and films (as they were originally planned).

Even the origins of Stravinsky's next piano opus, the *Sonata for Two Pianos* begun in 1943 then finished in 1944 after he completed the Billy Rose commissioned *Scènes de Ballet,* are traceable to a film project. Craft states that the first of the *Sonata's* three movements "was adapted from an orchestral piece conceived for a film," though the film itself is not identified.[9] The orchestral work of which Craft speaks was completed on August 12, 1943. It was never published. Interestingly, the first of 54 pages of sketches for the *Two Piano Sonata* are also dated August 12. Through a brief comparison of the two works as founded upon Craft's description of the original orchestral piece, an insight is gained into some aspects of Stravinsky's compositional process. Craft reports:

> The music for this opus for orchestra begins at [rehersal] 17 in the *Sonata* and is nearly identical with that work for eleven measures, continuing with eight measures that occur in the piano piece, but transposed, at sixteen measures from the end of the first movement.[10]

Example 139 reprints measures 17-24 of the *Sonata,* a juncture commonly taken as the work's second thematic area. One notices the meticulously differentiated articulative levels in both pianos—differences that surely were pronounced in the original orchestral scoring.

Example 139.   *Two Piano Sonata*, I., 17-24

Several points emerge, the most obvious of course being that Stravinsky elected to permit the originally conceived opening orchestral material now to stand second in order of thematic presentation. Nor was it unusual for Stravinsky to begin a piece with ideas other than those eventually chosen to initiate the composition. Such re-orderings suggest the fundamentally organic essence of the compositional, constructive blocks with which the composer felt free to build a work's overall architecture.[11]

The left-hand cell (F-G-B) circled in example 140, is of course relatable to what finally would serve as the *Sonata's* first theme (piano I, right hand, as circled).

Yet remembering the re-ordering of Stravinsky's original materials, one may conclude that the F-G-B cell of the second theme is not a derivative, as is often suggested; to the contrary, the entire first section of the *Sonata* is a consequence of Stravinsky's having largely expanded this seminal trichord. Moreover, the fact that Stravinsky initially extended the orchestral idea by continuing with a passage that now appears in the

Example 140. *Two Piano Sonata*, I.

Sonata "sixteen measures from the end of the first movement," further
indicates the compatibility of the work's individual units.

The relatedness of the passage beginning at measure 17 with the later
composed opening measure is further demonstrable through a brief comparison constructed upon the equivalency of interval vectors, as were
used in the analysis of the *Two Piano Concerto* (ex. 141).[12]

Example 141. *Two Piano Sonata*, interval vectors

				Vector
m. 17	Piano I	R.H.	b-c-d-e-g	122230
m. 17	Piano I	L.H.	f-g-b	010101
m.17/18	Piano II	Both	b-c-d-e-g	122230
m. 1	Piano I	Both	g-a-b♭-c-e	123121
m. 1	Piano I	R.H.	b♭-c-e	010101
m. 1	Piano II	Both	f-g-a-c-e	122230

Even the transitional material that joins the fifth related F centric
opening idea with the C centric measure 17 theme conforms to by now
familiar pitch formations (ex. 142).

Example 142. *Two Piano Sonata*, I., mm. 14-16

The three measures of piano I illustrated in Example 142 exhibit in effect a sonority that functions as a traditional dominant (G-B-D) with the intercalative leading tone F$^\sharp$, obviously an old but still useful tetrachordal pitch set in Stravinsky's estimation. Further, if the repeated G of measure 17 is added to the final left-hand gesture of piano II, the pentachord F-G-A flat-B flat-D accrues, providing the same interval vector as the only unpaired one in example 141 (measure one of piano I): 123121, and thereby coalescing the opening section with the originally conceived material of measure 17.

Stravinsky once declared that the "Sonata began as a piece for one performer, but was redesigned for two pianos when I saw that four hands were required to voice the four lines clearly."[13] But there seems to be nothing to corroborate this. It is more likely that when Stravinsky decided to withhold the orchestral score (which itself was doubtlessly drafted at one of the two pianos in his California study), he soon saw the advantages of scoring for two instruments rather than one. Nor does there appear to be any reliable documentation to substantiate Drushkin's supposition that the work was conceived for Stravinsky and Soulima as yet another father and son performance venture.[14] Soulima, surely the most likely candidate to have joined his father in performing this work, had remained in Europe during the war years. The ocean separating father and son obviously prohibited any further duo piano collaborations, while at the same time a growing contingent of American pianists was now performing Stravinsky's piano works more regularly.

This very modest composition (half as long as the titanic *Two Piano Concerto*) was publicly premiered on August 2, 1944, at Edgewood College of the Dominican Sisters, Madison, Wisconsin—an acutely different location from Hollywood or the Ringling Brothers Circus. The explanation rests in the fact that the *Sonata* was performed there by Stravinsky's long-time advocate Nadia Boulanger, whose student, a Sister Edward, was a member of the resident convent.[15] Stravinsky himself recalled only having played the *Sonata* once with Boulanger as his partner.

In many ways the *Sonata* appeared unexpectedly. It is strikingly dissimilar to the other works written during the early California years. Like the *Two Piano Concerto* of nearly a decade before, it is by Stravinsky's measure another pure art work, as he called it, meaning noncommissioned, though in fact it was salvaged from a composition that apparently grew from pragmatic soil. But in a more musical sense, the *Sonata* is more honest than the slickly styled neighborhood of compositions in which it was born. The overall transparency of its texture, the simplicity of its diatonically constructed melodies and the frequently retrospective moments of a distant folkloristic element, all contribute to the incunabular distinctness of this often neglected work. Drushkin, among others, here rightfully detects "a clear Russian suggestion," while Berger is more to the point in perceiving the "burly peasant-like themes that insinuate themselves into the otherwise classical texture of the *Sonata,* which could very well bear the rubric *Russe.* . . ."[16]

It is known that Stravinsky's library in California included many of the folk song anthologies upon which he relied so extensively in earlier years. Indeed the folk elements of the *Two Piano Sonata* may be so explained; for the melodic fount that provides many of the thematic materials for all three movements of the composition are directly traceable to a single anthology owned by Stravinsky. It is a collection of *protiazhnye* (lyrical songs) compiled by M. Bernard. Stravinsky's friend Lawrence Morton identified both the second theme of the *Sonata's* first movement and the trio from the third movement as being based upon two of the Bernard melodies.[17] More recently, Richard Taruskin has traced virtually every theme of the *Sonata* to the same Bernard collection published by Jurgenson during the late nineteenth century.[18] The second theme of the first movement mentioned by Morton (and remembering that Stravinsky originally conceived this as the first theme) is in fact the ninth in order of Bernard's collection (ex. 143).

A comparison of this source with its eventual disposition as seen in example 139 clearly demonstrates how Stravinsky manipulated the basic melodic cells. For example the A-C-E rising triad of the folk song's measure two, when compared with measure two of example 139, reveals that Stravinsky altered the melodic shape by first displacing the concluding E, then extending the gesture by a single rhythmic variation before resuming the melodic contour of the original source (notice the descending pentachord D-C-B-A-G in both examples). Such quotations, or more properly, paraphrases, permeate the *Sonata* as discussed below. Surely their usage stems from Stravinsky's unashamedly nostalgic feelings about his homeland as yet another war was being waged—a "recherche du temps perdu" sentiment as Vlad aptly describes it.

Though one might have presumed that the material originating from the orchestral opus would have been used initially by Stravinsky in composing the *Sonata* (and remembering that the first sketches date from mid-August), it was in fact the third movement, marked allegretto, that was completed first in September. The published first movement, moderato, followed in October, and the middle, theme and variations, was written during January and February of 1944.[19] The opening moderato's sonata form reverses the expositional key areas of F and C in its brief recapitulation, followed by an even briefer eight-measure codetta. Rhythmically, the music is very simple, as is the overall textural fabric. In comparison

Example 143.   Pensi Russkago Naroda, #9, M. Bernard

to the *Two Piano Concerto,* here the range over which both pianos travel is far more restricted. Moreover there is virtually no contrapuntal migration of voices from one keyboard to the other. Pianistically, the work sheds all of the virtuoso display so central to the 1935 *Concerto* whose purpose was of course quite different. The closing allegretto bears what at first might be seen as a rather curious key signature of two flats, especially in that Stravinsky immediately cancels several of the affected pitches in the opening moments of this simple tripartite movement. Here again, however, the fact that the melodic idea is based upon a precompositional source offers the explanation. The implication is G minor, to be balanced by the 24-measure poco piu mosso around G major, though this central section is certainly not firmly planted in the traditional sense of a key.

In attempting to perceive Stravinsky's pitch system, what in fact

surfaces is the employment of simple tertian sonorities, regularly embellished by a single additional pitch, and in many ways relatable to the
Bernard source. Yet these nontertian members of the pitch vocabulary
should not be construed merely as added tones—an expression that does
not accurately address the true significance of these pitches as integral
components of two elemental tetrachords fundamental to the movement's
language. The prevalent diatonicism of the *Sonata* owes not only to the
presence of these tetrachords but equally to the conspicuous absence of
the thickly weaved chromatic counterpoint that marked the earlier *Two
Piano Concerto.*

These two basic tetrachords are closely related, as the similarity in
their interval vectors shows (ex. 144). The only divergence occurs in that
the first tetrachord, designated as *A,* contains two major seconds, while
the tetrachord labeled *B* contains one major and minor second each.

Example 144.   Tetrachords

Tetrachord B = 111120

Tetrachord A = 021120

Instances of these two cells, both linearly and vertically expressed,
most frequently appear at structurally crucial junctures: cadences, tran-
sitions, and in the opening gesture of new sections. Examples 145 and 146
respectively display the initial measures of the allegretto and the middle
section of the movement marked poco più mosso (measure 20).

Example 145.   Allegretto

Example 146.   III., mm. 20-22

In accomplishing the transition returning to the allegretto's opening statement, these same cells migrate from one keyboard to the other and amazingly, except for a few pitches that clearly act in a linearly coadunative capacity, this entire structural elision is founded upon the manipulation of these same two archetypal tetrachords (ex. 147).

Example 147.   III., mm. 38-41

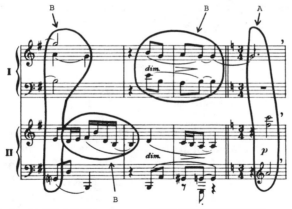

Yet here again the language of the basic melodic materials of the allegretto's opening theme (ex. 145) and the theme of the trio (ex. 146) are traceable to the Bernard collection as reprinted in examples 148 and 149.

Example 148.   From the Bernard Collection

Also, the final chord of the movement, C-D-E-G, retains the same pattern—a pattern tantamount to the same usage of unordered sets of pitches. Moreover the incipit of the second movement's *dux,* as Burkhart sees it, provides yet another instance of the *B* tetrachord.[20] Even the finalis of the 16-measure theme illustrates the second of the two familiar tetrachordal collections. Both the opening and ending measures are reprinted as example 150.

The theme of this often dissected set of four variations moves from the realm of an unordered pitch set vocabulary into the more rigorously dictated boundaries of a genuine series orbit. The subsequent application of this ordered pitch technique (which amounts to a 29-note row) to the variations is so pervasive, and for the most part so immediately apprehensible, that doubtlessly Stravinsky was moving with characteristic de-

Example 149.   From the Bernard Collection

Example 150.   *Two Piano Sonata*, II., mm. 1 and 16

m.1

m.16

Tetrachord A = 021120   Tetrachord B = 111120

liberateness in the direction of the *Cantata, Septet,* and other such works
of the early 1950s.[21] But even as it does so, the 29-note theme of this
variation set is inextricably bound to yet another Bernard source. Compare the entire theme of this second movement (ex. 151) with #46, *Ne
poi, ne poi* (ex. 152) of the anthology. The two differ only in octave
displaced shifts and at one point a rhythmic variation.

The similarity of Stravinsky's and Schoenberg's progression from an
unordered to a tightly regulative pitch set language is categorical, though
indeed their interior treatment of serially derived ideas is starkly incom-
mensurable. But whatever the merits of such historical parallels may

Example 151. *Two Piano Sonata*, II., Opening Theme

Example 152. *Ne poi, ne poi* #46, Bernard Collection

bring, Stravinsky's conversion to the serial cause, unquestionably nur-
tured a few years hence through Craft's welcomed proselytizations, could
not have been as precipitous as some would argue.[22] As perhaps most
eloquently summarized by Milton Babbitt in his "Remarks on the Recent
Stravinsky," "a composer who has throughout all of his creative life been
consumed by the temporal, and—therefore—order, in music, by the constructive possibilities and significances of the interval, might well be
strongly attracted to the first widely employed musical system that incorporates temporality into the very foundation of its operations."[23] Stravinsky's concept of variational techniques, like any of his compositional
procedures, was a constantly evolving one, and as early as the *Octet,* a
path is taken that travels through the octave displacements, rhythmic
disguises, and contrapuntal intricacies of both the *Two Piano Concerto*

and the folk song laden *Two Piano Sonata*—important piano works that herald the passage to Stravinsky's final compositional period.

Bordered on one side by the *Symphony in C*, and on the other by the 1945 *Symphony in Three Movements*, the *Two Piano Sonata* has too frequently and undeservedly been dismissed as an incidental neoclassical gasp. Alexandre Tansman, Stravinsky's biographer and close friend during these early Hollywood years, perhaps best summarizes the jaded opinion in which this the last of Stravinsky's two piano works is viewed.

> . . . the very simplicity of its principle and of its structure gives it the appearance of an unimportant work. And yet, its substance is rich and its structure arresting. But we have so taken the habit of confusing volume with content, and brilliancy with richness, that simplicity often impresses us as a lack of inventiveness or as a sign of poverty.[24]

While Stravinsky never published another two piano work as such, the piano did continue to fulfill his compositional needs in a variety of ways: first, in the *Scherzo à la Russe,* initially envisioned as a two-piano piece and in fact performed as such with Boulanger; and second, in the *Symphony in Three Movements* where the piano assumes an important concertante role.

The latter work was begun as early as April 1942, interrupted by several other compositions mentioned earlier, and finally completed in August 1945. Stravinsky himself suggested that from the start what came to be his second symphonic work in America, actually began as a piano concerto. Here again Tansman testified that as early as 1942, he listened to Stravinsky play sections of the work and "throughout it was then intended to be a symphonic work with a concertante part for the piano."[25] Yet curiously, Craft observes that "none of the early sketches contain any piano part at all," and that Stravinsky "did not decide on the piano obbligato role until he embarked on the full score." But it is again very likely that many of the instrumental figures eventually rescored for piano actually were first shaped by Stravinsky's pianism. For example the passage beginning at rehersal 39 "was originally scored for bassoons" according to Craft, then only later assigned to the keyboard. But as illustrated in example 153, in his final conception, the piano part provides a typical specimen of Stravinsky's pianistic writing style and one that is plainly reminiscent of ideas in the earlier *Capriccio,* a work that often employs the piano in a similar concertante fashion.

Even the opening passage, a section noticeably unrelated to the body of the first movement, shares a similarity with the *Capriccio* (ex. 154) in both its pianistic and orchestral figurations. The glissando in measure one ascending from the G to the registrally higher A flat in the piano (and

Example 153. *Symphony in Three Movements*, rehearsal 39

duplicated in intent by the strings and winds) (ex. 155) is texturally relatable to the opening idea of its 1929 predecessor. (Even structurally both works are analogous in that these initial impulsions frame their respective movements.)

Example 154. *Capriccio*, mm. 1-3

Example 155. *Symphony in Three Movements*

Finally, textural aspects common to many of the piano works of the 1920s also reappear here as part of the obbligato line. Example 156, with its alternating octave, single note scale descent recalls Stravinsky's earlier decision to excise the uninterrupted series of octaves he had first composed in various passages of the 1923/24 Piano Concerto. Example 157 reprints a passage that Stravinsky supposedly first conceived without the piano since some later and according to Craft "more fully scored sketches" bear the composer's notation "new, with piano."[26] But the specific textural spacing of the orchestral sonorities seen in both winds and the divisi strings throughout this passage again are traceable to Stravinsky's unorthodox pianistic chords, such as those seen in the 1925 *Serenade* wherein a chord third is doubled and positioned a sixth below the full triad (see asterisked chords in ex. 157). The fact that such a pianistic disposition is clear, reflects not so much a decision to add something new, as to incorporate what Stravinsky surely first played at the keyboard then orchestrated.

Example 156. *Symphony in Three Movements*

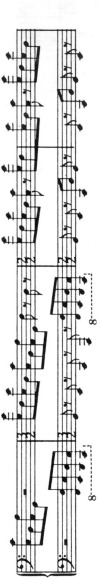

Example 157. *Symphony in Three Movements*

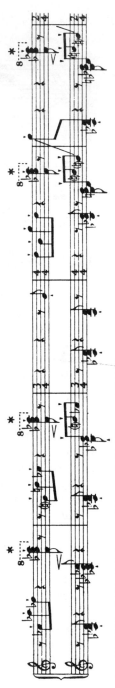

The use of the piano as an important component in Stravinsky's orchestra has never been fully explored. But here, as in so many Stravinsky scores, its employment as a member of the ensemble should not be neglected in examining the individual colors that collectively contribute to the composer's overall sense of a textural and timbral spectrum. Indeed, it is specifically in such a capacity that the piano would serve Stravinsky from this point forward.

The 15 years that followed the 1944 *Two Piano Sonata* were perhaps one of the most compositionally turbulent in Stravinsky's career. He continued to produce a new work at the rate of about one composition a year, though *The Rake's Progress* naturally consumed his attention over a larger span (1948–1951). Signs of a burgeoning serial inclination continue to surface in works like the 1947 *Orpheus,* the 1952 *Cantata,* and, as suggested earlier, most significantly in the 1953 *Septet.*[27] If there is a single turning point in one specific composition, surely it occurs in Stravinsky's notated charting of what constitutes an embryonic matrix for the 16-note series used in the passacaglia of the *Septet.*[28] As beautifully reprinted in *Pictures and Documents,* Stravinsky was obviously intrigued by the compositional possibilities that resulted through submitting his tonally anchored series to the standard retrograde, inversion and retrograde-inversion permutations. Here Stravinsky appears as a neophyte, for the manipulation of the series seems to have been so unfamiliar to him that not only was the RI form understandably written out, but curiously, he first constructed an IR form as well, perhaps not realizing the redundancy of this form as a transpositional equivalent before he later crosses out this version.

Craft reports that he and Stravinsky played a four-hand version of the "newly completed" *Septet* on June 28, 1953, though the work was not premiered until January 1954.[29] In addition to the two-piano arrangement, which looks as much like an original two-piano work as anything Stravinsky ever wrote for that medium, the piano plays a central role in the ensemble scoring. Indeed, now that works specifically written for piano no longer served the composer's interests, the keyboard as part of his orchestral ensembles increased in stature. *Agon* (1957), *Threni* (1958), *The Flood* (1962), *Variations* (1964), and even *Requiem Canticles* (1966) all utilize the piano in very focused, coloristic ways, not unlike the instrument's orchestral employment in the early ballets.

Even in *Movements for Piano and Orchestra,* the piano, though clearly elevated to a central role, is exploited not so much as an undaunted virtuoso instrument, but rather as a featured concertante contributor. The work was commissioned by Karl Weber, a Swiss magnate who approached Stravinsky through Nicholas Nabokov. Specifically, the commission as described by Nabokov in a letter of March 11, 1958, called for a work "for piano and orchestra—or, rather, for piano and a group of instruments of your own choice."[30] Weber intended the piece to be performed by his pianist wife, Margrit. Having already completed the first two of the eventual five movements, Stravinsky first met with Mrs. Weber in September of 1958. During the initial stages of the composition, Stravinsky had apparently conceived the work as a "Concerto for Pianoforte and Group of Instruments," taking his cue no doubt from the original request as delivered by his friend Nabokov. But by April, the title as it is known today had been decided.

Craft reports Stravinsky's apprehension regarding the Webers' possible reservations about what may have been construed as music differing from their expectations. Stravinsky states that "if the style and technique of the music are alien to you . . . I will return the advance on the commission," an amazingly magnanimous offer it seems, given the fact that by the time of this communication, Stravinsky had now completed the third movement and sketched the fifth.[31] The fourth movement was the last to be written. It was finished on July 30, the date appearing at the conclusion of the printed score, though the four interludes were not completed until August 16, 1959. There are other indications, too, that perhaps negotiations continued between Stravinsky and Weber while the piece was actually being written. From an April 17 entry in his *Chronicle of a Friendship,* Craft reports, "As a result of a letter this morning from the Webers in Zurich . . . I.S. says, 'I think I will have to add another minute or two of music'. To which Vera's comment is: 'So much for "all-encompassing conceptions of form.' "[32]

The 78-year-old Stravinsky conducted the first performance at Town Hall and the work was recorded a year later, but with Charles Rosen, the illustrious pianist who has continued to champion Stravinsky's piano music. Stravinsky had declared that *Movements* was a culminative work, the "cornerstone" of his late works, as he referred to it, marking the arrival of his serially oriented journey through the early years of the decade. His exuberance over this accomplishment magniloquently bursts forth in *Memories and Commentaries:*

> I have discovered new (to me) serial combinations in the *Movements for piano and Orchestra,* however (and I have discovered it in the process that I am becoming not less but more of a serial composer; those younger colleagues who already regard "serial" as an indecent word, in their claim to have exhausted all that is meant by it and to have gone far beyond, are, I think, greatly in error), and the *Movements* are the most advanced music from the point of view of construction of anything I have composed. No theorist could determine the spelling of the note order in, for example, the flute solo near the beginning, or the derivation of the three Fs announcing the last movement simply by knowing the original order, no matter how unique the combina-

torial properties of this particular series. Every aspect of the composition was guided by serial forms, the sixes, quadrilaterals, triangles, etc. The fifth movement, for instance (which I had to rewrite twice), uses a construction of twelve verticals. The *gamma* and *delta* hexachords in this movement are more important than the A and B, too. Five orders are rotated instead of four, with six alternates for each of the five, while at the same time, the six work in all directions, as though through a crystal.

Now that I have mentioned my new work, I should add that its rhythmic language is also the most advanced I have so far employed; perhaps some listeners might even detect a hint of serialism in this too. *My* polyphonic combinations are meant to be heard vertically, however, unlike those of my younger colleagues. Though parallels are not equivalents, look at Josquin for a parallel: That marvelous second *Agnus Dei* (the three-voice one) in the *Missa l'Homme armé,* or at Baude Cordier's *pour le deffault du dieu acchus,* or, for even more remarkable examples, at the Cyprus Codex.

Each section of the piece is confined to a certain range of instrumental timbre (another suggestion of serialism?), but the five movements are related more by tempo than by contrasts of such things as timbre, "mood," "character"; in a span of only twelve minutes, the contrast of an *andante* with an *allegro* would make little sense; construction must replace contrast. Perhaps the most significant development in the *Movements,* however, is the tendency towards antitonality—in spite of long pedal point passages such as the clarinet thrill at the end of the third movement, and the sustained string harmonics in the fourth movement. I am amazed at this myself, in view of the fact that in *Threni* simple triadic references occur in every bar.[33]

If Stravinsky had initially been reticent in adopting these "serial combinations," here he speaks as an unshrinking exponent, going so far as to chide those who have erred in prematurely abandoning its untapped resources. Could this be the same person who once stated that "Theory in musical composition is hindsight. It doesn't exist." Craft reports that Stravinsky always was intrigued by analysis and theories of music, though it was a *sub rosa* interest. Here, however, Stravinsky's epexegesis smacks of one redeemed through conversion, who having witnessed some epiphany, is now blinded by radiance, sanctimoniously defying would-be analysts to explain his sovereign control of the work's "combinatorial properties." Even his ostentation in invoking the serialists' jargon, his intimations of total serialism, pridefully announce his complete governance over his new compositional estate. But who could resist, or for that matter take too seriously, the composer's call to discover the arcanum of the work's pitch language? Inevitably, a swarm of analyses dealing with the work's pitch collections were to follow.[34] Babbitt's comments from his aforementioned essay are still perhaps the most lucid in addressing Stravinsky's proclivity for hexachordal rotations to which the composer had referred in the quotation above.[35] Stravinsky seems purposely to have set out to undermine the tonal pillars of his earlier serially organized works in his excogitative "tendency toward antitonality." As Craft reports, the composer was puzzled by a reviewer's reception of *Movements* as a work in which "there is more than a trace of tonal thinking."[36] Robert Moeves would seem to endorse this perception of tonality, analyzing the cadential gesture of the fourth interlude (mm. 137-140) in terms of ninth and thirteenth chords and in another section, analogizing triadic references here with *Les Noces.*[37]

With the understandable and documented attention shown towards the involuted pitch system of the work, there is little need to rehearse here the deployment of Stravinsky's intricately controlled series throughout this brief but highly concentrated ten-minute work. Stravinsky's rhythmic language in *Movements* is no less of a mensural labrythinth; nor was he any less pleased with its indeciperability, as may also be detected in his remarks. His references to Medieval and Renaissance composers and practices were made out of experience with these musical epochs, inasmuch as shortly after his arrival in Hollywood, Stravinsky became an avid devotee to so-called pretonal literature.[38]

In every way it seems, *Movements* has been pored over by an army of analysts in regard to these quantifiable elements; and there can be little doubt that Stravinsky in fact prized quantification as one of the more attractive and controllable aspects of the serial discipline. But what of the piano's contribution to the ensemble? Even a cursory scan of the 193-measure score quickly reveals a pianism predicatably unlike anything Stravinsky had written before. Its appearance provides the timbral constancy at the center of a kaleidescopically changing pattern of instrumental colors. The keyboard sometimes appears alone, but only briefly, and certainly never to such a degree that one could perceive anything remotely associable with a solo, let alone a cadenza. Most often it is found in combinations with one of the orchestral choirs (there is no percussion but a celesta is scored).

Spatially, the pianism, like the orchestra itself, is noticeably Webernesque. All registers of the keyboard are pointillistically explored as illustrated even in the opening measures (ex. 158).

Here one observes the full initial statement of the original series (mm. 1-2, E flat-F flat-B flat-A flat-A-D-C-B-C♯-F♯-G-F) as announced by the piano in different strata of the keyboard's range. The performance indications are precise with slurs, an accented grace note, and staccatos, immediately suggesting the differentiation of articulation to be expected by the pianist throughout the work. At other places, and interestingly, Stravinsky still marks specific fingerings (mm. 22-24, measure 167) and the distribution of notes between hands (which often involve some treacherous crossings), clearly implying that although he was never to perform the work, Stravinsky continued to write with such practical considerations in mind. Yet the specificity of some of his notations, even now,

Example 158.　*Movements*, mm. 1-4

continued to be enigmatic at times. Karl Kohn's remembrance of having played *Movements* with Craft conducting in 1965 is indicative of this:

> During the rehearsal of Movement I, we played the closing measures exactly as notated, with special care, in fact, to preserve the proportions of weight and emphasis neatly indicated for up- and down-beats. Stravinsky who sat with score in hand, asked, by singing the rhythms, that the last measure be done so that the sixteenths become grace notes, or at least, sixty-fourth notes! I have never known how to regard this arbitrary change from the deliberately notated effect except as a sign of divine free will.[39]

The absolute intensity of this remarkably vibrant work could not but help to impress favorably a public who continued to marvel at Stravinsky's seemingly boundless imagination. But unfortunately, for most pianists and ensembles, *Movements* seems to have become an impractical work to program—a *success d'estime*. Not only does it shun the scintillation that most soloists demand, but even under optimum conditions employing players conversant with the idiom, it remains an extremely prodigious task to perform satisfactorily. Two decades after its appearance, *Movements* is still a difficult work to present, as well as for most audiences to accept. Ultimately it must be admitted that had not Stravinsky been so handsomely commissioned to produce such a specified work, it is unlikely that the piano would have occupied a role higher than that of the keyboard as used in the other ensemble works written around that time. Thus in this instance at least, it seems not so much by design as by fortune that this particular piano work may be viewed as central to the attainment of yet another and perhaps even final plateau in the long compositional evolution of the still growing, still keenly acquisitive composer.

After *Movements* Stravinsky never completed another piano work. But far from showing signs of any impending creative impuissance, the first half of the 1960s was still a compositionally vital one for the indefatigable octogenarian who now turned his energies to orchestral and theatrical works, and finally, to the astonishingly powerful *Requiem Canticles* finished in August 1966, a work viewed by the composer himself as his *coronet opus*.[40] Even now the piano continued to be the essential physical tool in Stravinsky's constructive workshop. Only a few months after the completion of *Requiem Canticles,* Stravinsky seems to have contemplated a solo piano work, which, had it been completed, would have been his first genuinely serious solo piano effort since the *Serenade* of some 40 years earlier. In this regard, Francis Routh writes in one of the numerous general surveys of Stravinsky's life:

> The following year (1967) saw something of a resumption of the normal pattern of his life. He had begun to compose some piano pieces in December 1966; now he abandoned these, and in January 1968 he had in mind a bigger piece.[41]

As presented, these facts are a compilation of a few pieces of information aimed towards a reconstruction of events based upon Craft's diary comments as reported in his aforementioned *Chronicle of a Friendship*. For example, Routh's reference to the December 1966 piano pieces probably stems from Craft's entry of February 14, 1967 (which subsequently appeared as the captions for Arnold Newman's photographic album *Bravo Stravinsky*). At that time, Craft wrote

> During the morning of December 13, 1966, Stravinsky, who always knows exactly when his imagination is at the starting line, expressed "the need to put an idea in order." About thirty-five minutes later he had completed a sketch, which, however, did not extend from that "idea."
> Stravinsky has identified the sketch as "part of a string passage in the middle section of a symphonic piece," and the presence of instrumental indications (violas and cellos) in this initial stage argues that the springs of his invention are concrete. . . .[42]

Routh's conclusion that the work was originally intended for piano may have been based on a later entry recorded by Craft on January 25, 1968, in which Stravinsky reveals that he "does not want to go on with his piano opus because he has 'a bigger piece in mind.' " The composer further states that in this piano work, "I had no sooner forbidden myself to use octaves in one piece than I saw what richness I could extract from them, and I used them in the next piece all the time."[43]

But what does Stravinsky's December 1966 reference to a string passage of a symphonic work have to do with a projected piano work? Could there have been two works in progress or are these two references in some way connected? The fact that Stravinsky was indeed working on a piano opus gains credence through other sources as well.[44] Moreover, upon inquiring about this piece (or pieces) in November of 1972, this author was informed by Mr. Craft that Stravinsky did in fact leave two completed short sections of a larger work for piano as well as some sketches.[45] Indeed, the two completed sections, entitled "Two Sketches for a Sonata" had already been publicly performed (unannounced) at Brandeis University. Through the generous permission of both Mrs. Stravinsky and Mr. Craft, this author was permitted an examination of these manuscript sources.[46] Two sections were virtually completed and already notated on transparencies, which in effect were tantamount to a fair copy. Numerous sketches were examined, including what appeared to be the original serial charts subsequently reprinted on page 484 of Pictures and Documents. From a study of these published sketches (though all of the sketches this author examined are not included in the collection of published plates), hexachordal rotations so common in Stravinsky's late works may be ovserved. Curiously, however, two of the sketches that do appear in *Pictures and Documents* (pp. 484-85) and listed as variations of the row, clearly demonstrate that Stravinsky was thinking in terms of instrumentation. Yet the two completed sections of the "Sonata" that were dated 1966 (though Craft has determined that these sections were completed in early 1967) bear no instrumental indications.

Stravinsky may have initially planned his sketches for a piano work. Upon examining the second of the two completed sections, one would note, for example, that the use of octaves to which Stravinsky referred in one of the piano pieces are present everywhere. But if indeed a piano opus had once been seriously contemplated, obviously he quickly changed his mind. Then, too, it is known that Stravinsky would often prepare piano reductions of sections of a composition just completed rather than wait until the entire work was conceived. Since the "Two Sections for a Sonata" correspond almost identically to the published sketches, it would appear that these completed sketches are in fact the piano reduction of a symphonic work in progress.

Whatever the conceptual origins of this work, it is clear that Stravinsky still cherished, indeed needed, the physical touch of the keyboard as much in his declining years as he did nearly three quarters of a century earlier when he first began formal piano study. The sketches for this 1967 work, as well as the reduction, are as pianistically Stravinskyan as many previous compositions that betray a similar reliance upon the keyboard. His instrumentations in April and May of 1969 of several preludes and fugues from the *Well-Tempered Clavier* continue to attest to his musical union with the piano. Finally, the score of the Bach E flat Minor Prelude, Book I, still open on the music rack, and which according to Craft had been played by Stravinsky only a few days before his death, provides an appropriate capstone to a career profoundly and indissolubly associated with the piano at every step of the journey.

7

The Piano as Stravinsky's
Compositional "Fulcrum"

It is unlikely that history will ever commemorate Stravinsky on the memory of his piano music. Crassly put, it lacks appeal. Yet such a provincialism not withstanding, and regardless of whatever station we choose to assign this music, the impartible association of the instrument itself with the composer far exceeds the boundaries of the piano literature. "I don't care if you count out tone color altogether and simply give me a piano," he declared. "Cannot everything be said on the piano that needs to be?"[1] Uttered in 1925 at the very height of his objectivistic polemic, one must of course question the sincerity of such rhetoric. Yet as an indispensability in at least certain stages of the compositional process, the piano did in fact assume a primacy that may eventually prove to be quite informative. Throughout these pages, allusions to such a connection have been made—allusions to what he himself referred to as a "sort of Pavlovian reaction in which the piano acts as a catalyst on the raw materials in the creative process."[2] Moreover from the very dawn of his interest in music, Stravinsky openly admits to his reliance upon the instrument as a vademecum. His early remembrance of Rimsky's reply to his youthfully expressed anxiety concerning the advisability of "sowing the seeds of musical ideas" at the keyboard, speaks directly to the issue.

> I asked him whether I was right in always composing at the piano. "Some compose at the piano," he replied, "and some without a piano. As for you, you will compose at the piano." As a matter of fact I do compose at the piano and I do not regret it. I go further; I think it is a thousand times better to compose in direct contact with the physical medium of sound than to work in the abstract medium produced by one's imagination.[3]

The recurrence of similar proclamations in one way or another emphasizing his "direct contact" preference in writing is encountered repeatedly throughout the many descriptions of his composing habits. Stravinsky's elder son, Theodore, in his *Le Message d'Igor Stravinsky,* restates the essence of his father's earlier description, reaffirming that despite Stravinsky's experience even by 1948, the composer still was wary of creating sound in an abstract way.[4] Ramuz, Dushkin, Nabokov, Craft, and others all relay the same impressions. Pictorially captured views of the elder Stravinsky seated at the nightclub piano of a Venetian Hotel as late as 1957 composing the initial bars of *Threni*; or even 10 years later, the awaited arrival of a muted piano in the Hotel Pierre where as Craft reports, Stravinsky "is impatient to play the notations made in the last few days, when he was without an instrument"—surely these glimpses attest to the abiding faith Stravinsky placed in the piano as a physical medium.[5] Particularly illuminating is Stravinsky's own statement of the keyboard's significance.

> Whether or not I am a pianist, however, the instrument itself is the center of my life and the fulcrum of all my musical discoveries. Each note that I write is tried on it, and every relationship of notes is taken apart and heard on it again and again.[6]

Inasmuch as linguistic morphology was a particular passion of Stravinsky's, one may assume that when the word fulcrum is used, it is used as a *mot juste,* and enunciated with distinctively Stravinskyan precision. Just so, a fulcrum is an agency "by means of which vital powers are exercised," and nowhere were Stravinsky's powers more consistently exhibited than at and through the piano. At the risk of preciosity, it seems advisable to seek a sharper definition of Stravinsky's use of the piano, his reliance upon its use, and more broadly, to what extent the elemental bond existed between the piano as a tool in the sculpting of primordial ideas, and as an ongoing force in subsequent compositional stages.

As suggested earlier, Stravinsky's attachment to the piano arose from both its utility in auralizing new configurations of sound, as well as in the sheer organoleptic artisanship of personally, physically shaping musical ideas by his own hand. He spoke of being satisfied only upon having discovered the "auditive shape" of an idea.[7] In confirming that such protoplasmic forms were conceived at the keyboard, one begins to sense the kinesthetic origins of his compositional process. Surely such a fundamental, even casual relationship constitutes a pianistic reliance that is too often underestimated if indeed it is not completely overlooked.

It may be recalled that as early as the 1902 piano Scherzo, certain pianistically awkward passages were in evidence. Apparent in the work's coda, for example, were abrupt hand shifts and numerous chordal spacings clearly unmanageable without the aid of the pedal (see ex. 4). Nor can such an instance be conveniently dismissed as an error of youth. Even after Stravinsky had acquired experience, as he had by the time of the 1908 *Four Studies,* the pianistic lay is still occasionally unconventional. In fact with few exceptions, Stravinsky's piano literature often displays the image of an orchestral reduction more than an idiomatically designed keyboard piece. The middle movement of the 1924 Sonata, the romanza of the 1925 *Serenade,* and the cinematically conceived moderato of the 1944 *Sonata for Two Pianos*—all are often justifiably compared to some of the instrumental effects associated with the composer's orchestral textures. But the point is, such writing was as natural an aspect of Stravinsky's keyboard style as other pianistically tailored ideas are idiomatically Debussyan. Stravinsky's pianism is in fact so personally, so eccentrically conceived, that it is not merely judged difficult or awkward among pianists, but is often found to be obstructive, and thus surely contributes to the literature's general neglect.

With this in mind, consider the possibility that some of Stravinsky's most identifiably orchestral sonorities may owe their patent auditive shapes to a pianistic impulse. Perhaps no sonority, for instance, is more recognizable than the "Petrouchka chord," known to all the world as the juxtaposition of two triads at a tritone's length. Whether one chooses to perceive such an insignia sonority as a hexachordal subset of a symmetrical scale, or prefers to regard it more simply as an instance of bitonality, the fact remains the discovery of this chord probably owes more to the natural division of the black and white keys of the piano than to any subsequently extrapolated octatonic structure. Nor are these concepts necessarily incompatible, for Stravinsky addresses the order of his method with explicitness:

> [The] exploration of possibilities is always conducted at the piano. Only after I have established my melodic or harmonic relationships do I pass to composition. Composition is a later expansion and organization of material.[8]

If the enlistment of *Petrouchka* is found to be inadmissible because of its *ab origine Konzertstücke* heritage, then consider next the equally, if not even more exalted "Augurs" sonority of *Sacre.* Much of the interest drawn by this invocatory chord has revolved around establishing an all-inclusive pitch complex that would unite the chord's constituent parts. But additionally, as with *Petrouchka,* the chord is pianistically divisible. White, for one, is direct in suggesting that such a monumental moment in the whole of music literature may simply, that is to say naturally, have come into existence as a result of its "conveniently having fitted [Stravinsky's] two hands."[9] Now surely our etiologic being will seethe at what might first be construed as simplism. Could it be that this cataclysmic *complexe sonore* was the child of spontaneity? In his prefatory remarks to the Andre Meyer sketchbook of *Sacre,* Craft states that the "Augurs chord" was indeed the first idea Stravinsky notated. Moreover he contends that despite Stravinsky's publicly professed disdain for the very notion of bitonality, the composer regularly thought in such terms, though not in any theoretical sense.[10] Yet if not theoretically, then how did he think of the concept? Perhaps more simply in terms of sound, drama, even affect? In any event, it seems that Stravinsky's fingers—those "great inspirers" as he once referred to them—may have more to do with the creation of his ideas than we care to admit.

As a third example of these "passport" chords, to use still another Stravinskyan epithet, consider next another *cause célèbre.* Example 159 reprints the piano reduction of the *Symphony of Psalms* opening chord (the reduction actually duplicates the same voice distribution as the harp and two pianos of the full ensemble).

Example 159.   *Symphony of Psalms* (piano reduction)

The imagination of this chord, by virtue of its orchestral spacing and doubling, has been the focus of many analyses, two of which are especially enlightening:

> . . . the celebrated "Psalms chord" is like no E-minor triad that was ever known before, but if its uniqueness should be considered by anyone to free it from tonal association, its implications do not; for its implicated indirectly with the fate of C minor through that special registration that exposes the octave doublings of G in the quasi-mirror arrangement of intervals. Whenever the "Psalms chord" punctuates the movement, it not only asserts E priority but prefigures the alternate G priority which will eventually serve as a dominant of C Minor.
>
> Thus the "Psalms chord" is involved, either directly or indirectly, with all three of the principal structural issues of pitch-class priority with which the first movement is concerned . . .[11]

Or even more informative:

> . . . Recall the celebrated recurrent chord of the first movement of the *Symphony of Psalms*; it is ever structurally the same: the same absolute intervals in the same spatial

distribution with the same instrumental assignments. It is not merely what would be termed conventionally a root position E minor triad, but is so uniquely a specific representation of such a triad that it is possible for Stravinsky throughout the entire movement to use no root position triads other than E minor triads. . . . The very instrumental sound which is termed "Stravinskyan" cannot arise from techniques separable from the particular compositional conception or inferrable from purely instrumental properties; it derives from this concern with each interval in its spatial placement, the relation not just of each note to its adjacent note, or between extrema, but the relation of every note to every other note within and between timbral groups, and with the structural role of orchestration. The same E-minor chord of the *Symphony of Psalms* is not, in instrumental spacing or pitch assignment, closely similar to any other simultaneity in Stravinsky's music; its relation is to the structure of the movement in which it occurs. For its uniqueness resides in the distribution of G's, emphasized by the number of its occurences and its exposed octave representation within the chord; thus does the first chord adumbrate the destination of the movement, G.[12]

The investiture of this single incantatory sonority with such a grave structural incumbency is an issue chiefly dependent upon penetrating the syntactic organization of the work's pitch system. Nor can there be any doubt that its spatiality, especially as attended in the latter set of remarks, is indeed a prime consideration in grasping the uniqueness of its instrumental context. But as a preorchestral idea, viewed in its most primitive state, the "Psalms chord" is hardly unprecedented in the Stravinskyan literature. In terms of his dependency upon the keyboard, the same textural array that sanctifies this chord is frequently encountered in earlier works whose history springs directly from a pianistic source.

Accordingly, first consider the *Symphonies of Winds* written a decade earlier than the *Symphony of Psalms*. Certainly its instrumentation is no less colorful, no less Stravinskyan than the 1930 work. Yet in comprehending the innovativeness of this 1920 work, some understanding of the composition's early development is valuable. Several crucial points regarding Stravinsky's compositional habits are offered by Craft, and momentarily, will be brought to bear upon the current discussion:

> Stravinsky's creative processes are no less mysterious than those of any other great artist, but some of their patterns contradict the composer's own statements about them. Thus he said that as a rule his works were composed straight through, though his sketchbooks show that this was seldom the case, and that he rarely began at what was ultimately to be the actual beginning. He claimed, too, that his musical ideas always came to him in specific timbres, which he seldom changed in later stages. But his sketchbooks belie him.
>
> At his first press conference in America in 1925, Stravinsky stated that "Les Symphonies d'Instruments a Vent was designed as a grand chant, an objective cry of wind instruments, in place of the warm human tone of the violins." [New York Times, January 6, 1925] But the music was not designed as such at first, and the earliest notations . . . are scored for harmonium; thus the anomaly of Stravinsky's wind-instrument masterpiece is that it was not originally intended for winds.[13]

The preliminary ideas for the work to which Craft refers are found amidst sketches for the 1919 *Piano-Rag-Music*. Indeed, the well-known chorale of the *Symphonies* was shown to share some fundamental linear and harmonic commonalities with that work, as suggested in chapter 4. This chorale, which was eventually to serve as the closing section of the 1920 work, was originally published as a short piano piece, simply described as "Fragment des *Symphonies pour instruments a vent* a la memoire de Claude Achille Debussy" (ex. 160). It had been offered as one of 10 testimonials by various composers as a tombeau to Debussy and was printed in a special number of the December 20 *La Revue Musicale*. The initial sonority of what is often labeled as a piano reduction, but in fact preceded the wind score, is spatially identical to the "Psalms chord."

Example 160. Fragment des *Symphonies pour instruments a vent*

If in fact Stravinsky physically carved such unusually spaced chords at the keyboard, then one must consider matters as basic as the anatomy of his hands. He was a small man; but his hands were disproportionately large. Certainly the expanses characterizing numerous passages in his piano literature demonstrate this. Moreover Soulima's homophylic resemblance further attests to the largeness of his father's hands. Soulima himself was once advised by a teacher to avoid playing a particular composition since his hands were too big, his fingers too large to negotiate some of the intricate chromatic passages of the piece.[14] Appearances of such an identifiable sonority as our original "Psalms chord" are not relegated to orchestral works or a few sketches. Other pre-Psalms instances are evident in one of the solo piano works.

As mentioned in chapter 5, the cadenza finala of the 1925 *Serenade* was actually composed first, though published fourth in order. Little need be added to even a glance at the recurring right hand chords as marked by the asterisks in example 161.

The quiescence of this reiterative chord, motionlessly suspended as a textural stasis, obviously was attractive to the composer. Nor is its use limited to this movement. As example 162 shows, its appearance in the opening Hymne similarly functions as a textural mainstay.[15]

Example 161.   *Serenade*, Cadenza Finala

Example 162.   Hymne, mm. 59 and 70-71

As a third pre-Psalms instance, and once again apparent within the context of a piano work, reconsider the passage first offered in chapter 5 and reprinted as example 163.

Example 163.   *Capriccio*

These two measures are, as will be recalled, a transcription of a rather fully drafted portion of the *Capriccio's* middle movement cadenza. Written in July 1929, less than a year before the first movement of the *Symphony of Psalms* was begun, the spacing of the rising right hand chords of the example's initial bars is of course by now familiar. Finally, even after the *Symphony of Psalms*, Stravinsky continued to favor this same sonority, as for example in the 1945 *Symphony in Three Movements*, where it is to be found as a persistent idea in the orchestral piano's part (refer to ex. 157).

In examining the initial phases of Stravinsky's compositional process and especially in attempting to understand better how an unrefined idea is developed, the history of the "Psalms chord" may provide one clue. In all of the pre-1930 instances, the spatial distribution of the four pitches display the intervallic array (lowest to highest) of a sixth between the bottom two chordal members, and a third between the others. Moreover, the chord had appeared only in the treble, that is (dare one say it?), the more commonly pianistic register of each example. Yet its articulation in the *Symphony of Psalms* expands to include both the treble and bass orchestral ranges as most clearly seen in its occurence in both pianos (refer once more to ex. 159). In effect, the spatial array of the treble stated chord has now been projected symmetrically downward in a "quasi-mirror" fashion, as it was previously termed. Thus, what seems to have been originally and naturally one of Stravinsky's pianistically engendered auditive shapes has now been consciously extended in what is equivalent to a texturally structural development.

One wonders how much more the sketches for this movement would reveal about the already plainly pianistic nature of passages beyond this central sonority. Consider next the series of arpeggiated gestures immediately following this initial chord, reprinted in its piano reduction as example 164.

Our conditioned perception of such a refulgent opening will no doubt resist separating these measures from the colorful oboe and bassoon instrumentation. After all, Stravinsky adamantly insisted that the specific timbre of a motive was inseparable from the motive itself. Yet here, as in the *Symphonies of Winds,* Stravinsky's first orchestral conception of this work was not the one eventually employed. As a single page from the work's sketchbook illustrates (included on p. 295 of *Pictures and Documents*), the inclusion of a full complement of strings was once contemplated. While we cannot determine whether the music of example 164 was associated with a particular timbre from the start, it is clear that the textural gesture itself finds numerous antecents in Stravinsky's piano literature: the mechanical etude style of the 1923 Piano Concerto; the rapidly shifting and rather ungainly arpeggiated tetrachords of the 1925 *Serenade's* rondoletto; the spatial doubling of a line at the distance of two octaves as in the 1924 Sonata's opening; and later in the piano writing of the 1932 gigue (middle section) from the *Duo Concertante.* So common are these fingerprints that their natural transference to nonpiano works is assumable in a classic *abeunt studia in mores* tradition.

As mentioned in chapter 5, the 1923 *Octet,* memorialized as frequently as any Stravinsky opus for its vivid ensemble scoring, was begun as a piano work. Nor can this birthright be disguised, as is easily detectable in such passages as the first section of the finale (ex. 165).

Example 164. *Symphony of Psalms* I., mm. 1-8

Example 165. *Octet*, Finale, mm. 1-12

The similarity of this bassoon dialogue with another earlier illustrated one from the Piano Concerto is clear (see ex. 105). In the case of
the Concerto as previously discussed, the bassoon writing had to have
been originally conceived as the piano part in the same passage, for the
woodwinds merely reinforce and embellish the solo line. Returning to the
Octet, even the initial motive of the second movement's variation E (perhaps the single most premonitory moment in foreshadowing the eventual
stress of octave displacement in the composer's variational technique),

the first designed as a piano passage, then scored for the same bassoon combination (ex. 166).[16]

Example 166.   *Octet*, Variation E, mm. 1-4

Even in *Sacre,* as infrangibly orchestral as any work one could imagine, the elemental influence of the piano should not be undervalued. Far beyond the "Augurs chord" its effects are traceable. Stravinsky's own comments begin to suggest the precipitating potency of the piano in bringing forth such a tour de force as the Danse Sacrale, "which I could play, but did not, at first, know how to write." More tangible evidence has recently come to light through the aforementioned Meyer sketchbook of *Sacre.* Many of the sketches are written in two staff notation conducive to a quick pianistic rendering as perhaps an aural check of a seminal idea. Other sections are more fully drafted, including at times a suggested instrumentation. In such instances, one would like to believe that Stravinsky, as he apparently wished to be portrayed, was the innocent "vessel," as he referred to himself, through which these ideas flowed unmeditated onto the page. But this is more often mythical than actual. Those passages exhibiting specified instrumental assignments frequently are preceded by some pianistically fashioned jots. The notion in example 167, notated at the top of the sketchbook's first page, appears with several other instrumentally unspecified bars in advance of the same passage that is orchestrated in later drafts (and eventually used at rehearsal 14 of the original orchestral score).

Example 167.   *The Rite of Spring* (transcription)

Other sections that likewise bear no early hint of their future timbral reference are rather meticulously worked out in a notation very close to the four-hand score, which was nearly complete by the end of 1912. Example 168, taken from this duet arrangement, reprints the passage beginning four bars after rehearsal 28 and here only slightly different than the sketch for this passage as it first appears in the "Des Adolescentes" section in the Meyer notebook.

Example 168.   *The Rite of Spring*, "Des Adolescentes"

The contention is not that Stravinsky possessed no inkling of what he might desire in terms of an orchestral sound, but rather that often he had not yet decided, even as the compositional process moved forward. Even in those relatively few instances where no preliminary piano sketch previews an instrumental draft, one must not conveniently assume that Stravinsky immediately envisioned a specific orchestral idea. For it is unlikely that the composer in any case did not initially and sensorially (meaning both tactiley and aurally) repeatedly test his ideas at the piano before notating them. As described by Taruskin in his admirable study of the *Sacre* sketches,

> This situation is clearly the result of Stravinsky's well-known working methods. The real development of material took place empirically at the keyboard, and by the time an idea was entered in the sketchbook, it had no doubt already gone through many unrecorded stages of crystallization.[17]

Taruskin justifiably observes that because of these frequent prenotational trials, the sketchbook does not reveal all that we might have hoped it would. Soulima Stravinsky in this regard remembers, too, that his father's sketchbooks were exceptionally clean, and that his father would often repeat a chord over and over, adjusting a voice, an octave register, a doubling, before notating it. Thus, though the very notion may invite a charge of profanation, the study of Stravinsky's sketches, while obviously invaluable, may in some instances at least, be no more revealing than his so-called piano reductions. In the case of *Sacre,* the reductions certainly prove more revealing than the orchestral score in tracing certain aspects of its creation.

Pierre Monteux, entrusted with the premiere of the ballet, remembered Stravinsky at the piano rehearsing the work for the first time:

> With only Diaghilev and myself as an audience, Stravinsky sat down to play a piano reduction of the entire score. Before he got very far I was convinced he was raving mad. Heard this way, without the color of the orchestra which is one of its greatest distinctions, the crudity of the rhythm was emphasized, its stark primitiveness underlined. The very walls resounded as Stravinsky pounded away, occasionally stamping his feet and jumping up and down to accentuate the force of the music.[18]

Stravinsky had completed this solo version by November of 1912 and played it for Ravel and others in Paris early that same month. The four-hand score, not only finished but also published before the ballet's premiere in May 1913 was read with Debussy also in November 1912—a performance that prompted Debussy's quotable oxymoron, "a beautiful nightmare," in later describing his reaction to the work. Moreover, it would be specious to conclude that by the time this four-hand score was performed (undoubtedly to be used for the ballet's rehersals) that all details of orchestration had been settled. Instrumental drafts for *Sacre* were forthcoming months after the four-hand version was completed, thus further suggesting that the specific sound of *Sacre* continued to evolve after the basic ideas had been "reduced" for piano.

Not only the duet version of *Sacre* but the entire sum of Stravinsky's piano reductions provide a treasure of potentially valuable materials virtually ignored. Even the term reduction itself immediately casts these scores in a prejudicial light. "Is a piano reduction to be used for reading, or for playing?" Schoenberg once asked. "For playing to others, or for accompaniment? Should it be a reduction, transcription, arrangement, paraphrase, or re-arrangement? How is it to be all of these things at once?"[19] But for Stravinsky, the piano reduction was all of these things and often even more

The usefulness of his reductions is traceable to as early a work as *The Firebird.* The piano score of this his first full ballet was used in rehearsal with Stravinsky himself acting as the accompanist. Tamara Karasavina, who in fact premiered the part of the *Firebird* in the original production, recalled that the young Stravinsky often came to the hall before the scheduled rehearsal to help her with some of the unfamiliar rhythms and adjustments to the changing tempi. "How interesting it was to see him at the piano. His body seemed to vibrate to the rhythm of his own music."[20] More than 25 years later in preparing *Jeu de Cartes* during the winter of 1936, for example, Lincoln Kirstein, whose subvention had enabled Balanchine's American Ballet Company to add a new Stravinsky work to its repertory, reported that Stravinsky would take the rehearsal pianist home with him to work on tempi.[21] Leo Smit was in fact this unidentified pianist and in the tributes that followed Stravinsky's death, Smit has bequeathed an interesting account of Stravinsky's own performance of the reduction during an early rehearsal.

> Stravinsky grinned his sardonically innocent grin and in a bass bullfrog whisper offered to play the whole of *The Card Game* for me. . . .
>
>   In some unaccountable way, without technique (he sometimes glissandoed what should have been fingered scales), without beauty of tone (he poked the keys with his large bony fingers, muting the dynamics with the left pedal while tapping rhythmically on the right pedal), and keeping time by vigorous gasping counting, he succeeded in conveying the meaning of his musical thought with extraordinary clarity. . . . By the time he finished playing, I felt I had been initiated into the most secret of Mysteries.[22]

Smit also reported that the proofs of the engraved reduction had arrived towards the end of December 1936, while Kirstein remembered "The orchestration and piano score of *Jeu de Cartes* were finished simultaneously in November 1936."[23] But according to Craft, the sketch score was dated December 3.[24] Either way, given the fact that the piano score was reprinted, engraved, and shipped all within a few weeks after the composition was completed, it is doubtful that a piano reduction could have been fully prepared in such a short period. More likely, the reduction was very close to the sketch score and probably needed little revision in adapting it for piano, much in the manner of the transcription of *Ragtime* discussed in chapter 3. Finally, the very first sketches for the ballet, dated December 2, 1935, approximately one year earlier, indicate no instrumental reference, though all of Stravinsky's initial ideas are here innately pianistic. All of this suggests that Stravinsky's piano reduction was a natural end-product resulting from his day to day composing at the keyboard, rather than some appurtenant afterthought.

Stravinsky's familiarity with his own piano reductions is described by Elliott Carter who heard Stravinsky perform the reduction of his 1934 melodrama *Persephone* only a few days before its public premiere:

What impressed me most, aside from the music itself, was the very telling quality of attack he gave to piano notes, embodying often in just one sound the very quality so characteristic of his music—incisive but not brutal, rhythmically highly controlled yet filled with intensity so that each note was made to seem weighty and important.[25]

But surely Stravinsky played from the sketch score rather than the piano reduction prepared later by his son Soulima. Moreover, just how indistinct the boundaries become in distinguishing a sketch score from a piano reduction may be sensed in briefly examining a few pages from this same work. Plate 17 reprints the two bars before rehersal 27 through the first measure of rehearsal 32, while plate 18 reproduces the passage begun at rehearsal 138 through the second bar of rehearsal 139. Both reproductions, reprinted from what is listed as the holograph piano reduction at the Pierpont Morgan Library, are in fact part of the sketch score.[26] In the first of the two plates, the instrumentation for a sizeable section is already determined, while elsewhere Stravinsky only pencils in his suggestions as well as Gide's text. In the second plate, Stravinsky pauses to sketch a specific string divisi. But in both cases, the congruence between these two pages and Soulima's piano reduction is clear. A section of this reduction corresponding to the music illustrated in plate 18 is reprinted in example 169. Both of the lower staves of the reduction were eventually given to the piano itself as part of the orchestral tutti. Even the chordal passage of the top staff (eventually scored for all the orchestral choirs) is markedly pianistic, including the unusually spaced sonorities of the example's final two measures. Moreover, the writing is generally both unmistakenly reminiscent of sections of the first movement of the 1935 *Concerto for Two Solo Pianos* (written just before *Persephone*), as well as predictive of the three other movements of the *Concerto* written after.

These of course are isolated cases capable only of suggesting the potential harvest to be reaped in further studying Stravinsky's reductions. Thus as a final example, a more extended investigation of a single work is now undertaken.

The Morgan Library holds several manuscript materials of *The Firebird*. Included in this collection is the composer's personal copy of the published piano reduction, actually engraved by Jurgenson before the orchestral score, though such an order was not unusual. But beyond its obvious aura as a relic, the score proves valuable by virtue of Stravinsky's added annotations, of which there are many. Frequently, Stravinsky's alterations, as usual, seem rooted in very practical matters and are often aimed towards facilitating his own performance of the rehearsal score. His concern, perhaps even his obsession with the metric and rhythmic

Plate 17. *Perséphone*, autograph pages of piano reduction

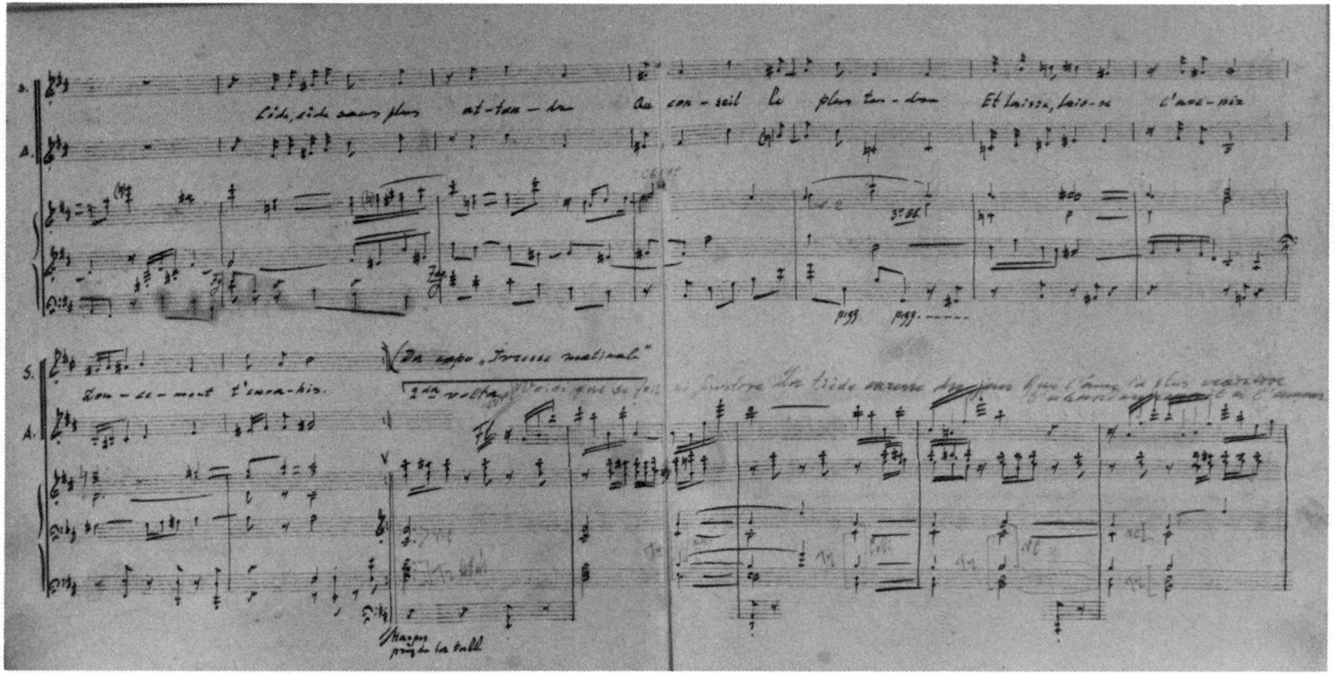

Mary Flagler Cary Music Collection,
The Pierpont Morgan Library

Plate 18. *Perséphone*, autograph pages of piano reduction

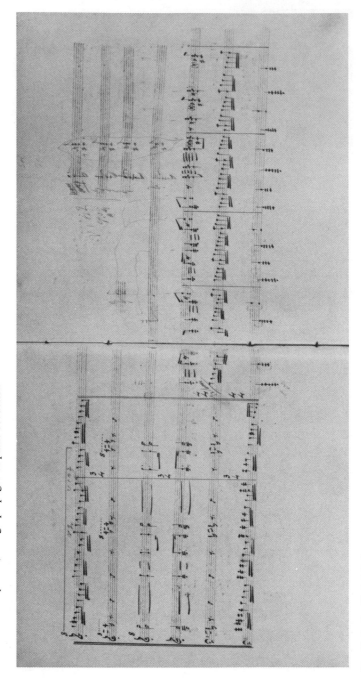

Example 169.   *Persephone*

framework of the ballet is signified by the *notae bene* insertions seen in
plate 19.

Stravinsky itemizes as exactingly as possible the duration sought at
this point of the action, going so far as to define the value of the fermata
rest, and warning about the "unfulfilled" prolongation of a certain metric
change. These cautions are notated on what appears to be an ordinary
index card and directly taped to the binding of the printed score.

Numerous other performance concerns are indicated. Tempo changes,
interpretive signs, and even suggested fingerings (and strange fingerings
they are by any standard of pianism other than the composer's) are inserted throughout the score. In noting these alterations, one must consider that these refinements would have been entered during the time the
work was in rehersal, in all probability, and must reflect to some degree
the necessary changes occasioned by the addition of the choreography.
Moreover, it is quite conceivable that such variables as tempo felxibility,
may well have exceeded Stravinsky's control and simply could have been
dictated by Fokine and others.

Plate 20 offers the final page of another manuscript in the Morgan
collection, the autograph piano reduction. To be observed are the textual

Plate 19.   *The Firebird*, addendum to Stravinsky's personal copy
of the published piano reduction

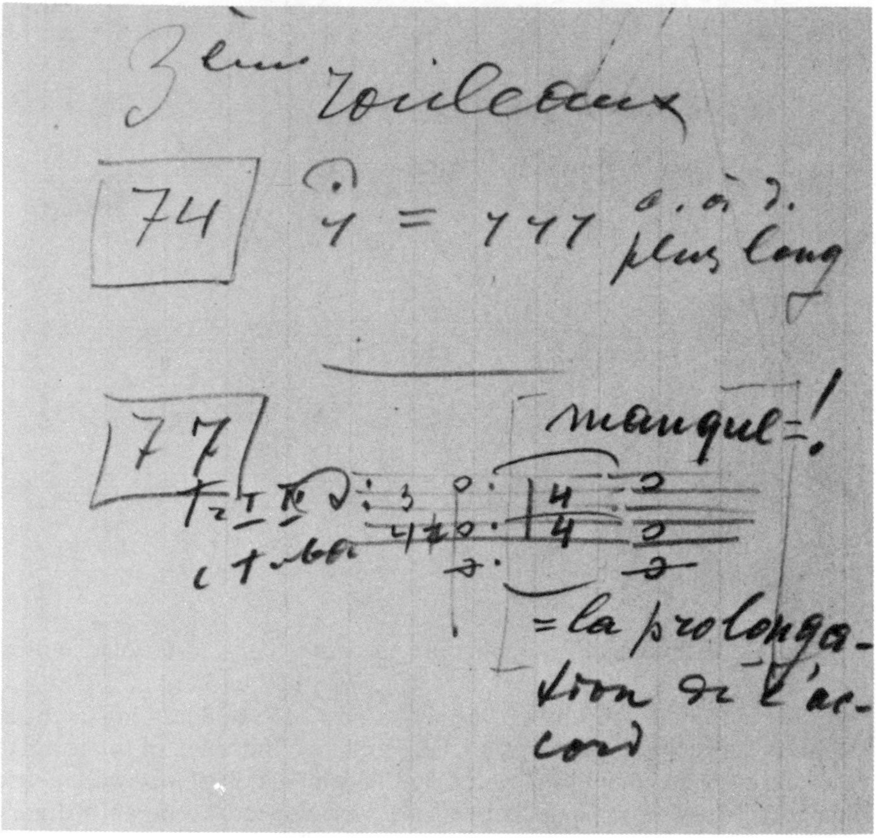

The Robert Owen Lehman Collection, on deposit in
The Pierpont Morgan Library

additions describing the final scene, as well as numerous erasures and
other pencil markings again concerning tempo. When "Tempo I" is reached
towards the end of the second system, a 6/4 metric pattern is introduced.
A similarly notated closure appears in the autograph orchestral manuscript (long held by the Conservatoire de Musique, Geneva) prepared in
April, shortly after the March 21 date of the piano reduction as evident
in the plate.

Next, compare this final autograph page with the Jurgenson publication of the same passage reprinted as plate 21. Here Stravinsky apparently continues to ponder several issues. Again, these changes surely
resulted from the composer/pianist's rehearsing of the score. Several re-

Plate 20. *The Firebird*, final page of the autograph piano
reduction

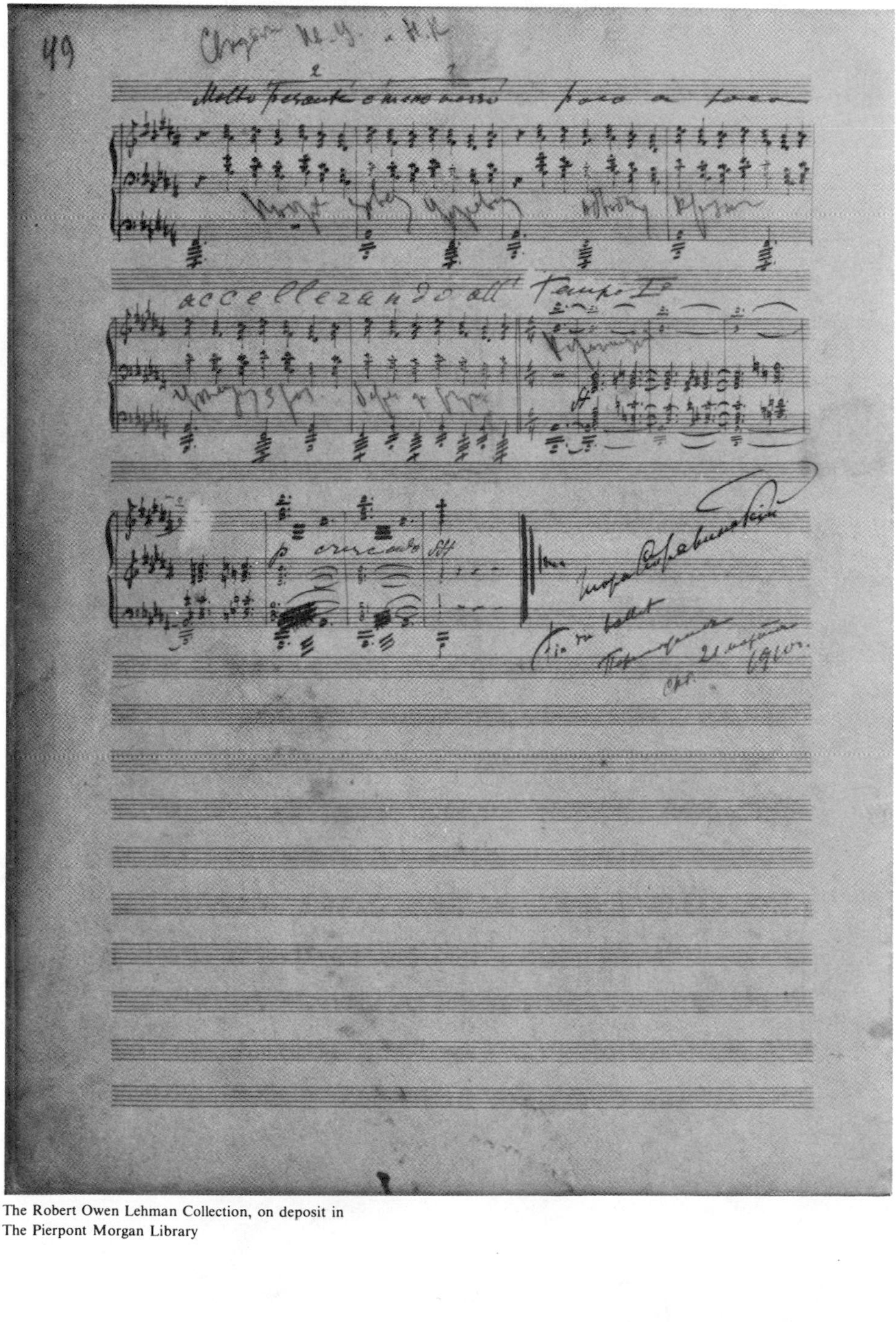

Plate 21. *The Firebird*, final page of Stravinsky's personal copy
of the Jurgenson published piano reduction

gistral adjustments are made, indicating that certain octaves are to be added or that existing ones should be played in a higher register so as to create a truer impression of the orchestral sound envisioned. At rehearsal 202, Stravinsky is so discriminating (by his own volition or otherwise) as to reject the qualifying "molto" of the original direction, though by the time the 1919 *Suite* was prepared, it is reinstated while the "meno moso" is now struck. Curiously, in the autograph piano reduction (refer to pl. 20) the designation, "poco a poco accellerando" to tempo I appears (though the tempo I indication itself may have been the product of a reconsideration since it occurs over an earlier erasure). But by the time the manuscript passed to Jurgenson, it had been diametrically altered to "poco a poco allargando," a fundamental, musical reconception unlikely to have been made by the composer's hand without some external influence. In this regard it is interesting to note that Stravinsky's performance of this closing passage on his own prepared piano roll, as discussed earlier, does not retard to such an exaggerated degree as do most orchestral performances. Other variances are apparent such as the consistently expanding dynamic range in the printed score (*ff* to *fff*, *pp* to *ppp*) as well as Stravinsky's correction of the obvious pitch misprint one bar after rehearsal 208.

Of all these changes, perhaps the most interesting involves the printed 6/4 metric shift mentioned earlier and here encircled as is the entire concluding passage. The pencil line emanating from this circled system leads off the page itself, as reprinted in plate 21. As illustrated in plate 22, the line leads to an addendum notated on the inside back cover of the binding. Not only does Stravinsky suggest a new reduction at this point, but he also changes the original 6/4 meter to 2/2. While such a seemingly inconsequential change would not drastically alter the interpretation, the subtlety was obviously important enough to incorporate in the later engraved orchestral score by which we recognize the passage today.

Perhaps such alterations are more biographically informative than compositionally revealing. For the most part they seem to deal more with the circumstances of Stravinsky's role in the ballet than with matters of a genuinely independent structural re-examination of the music. Ultimately however, how can the situational aspects of Stravinsky's involvement be separated from a study of his music? In this case at least, it is the piano reduction rather than the final orchestral score that provides an insight perhaps otherwise lost.

While the engraved piano reduction furnishes a good bit of scrutable material, it is the holograph of the same score that provides a better opportunity to examine some of the more structurally oriented aspects

Plate 22. *The Firebird*, inside back cover notes to the published
piano reduction

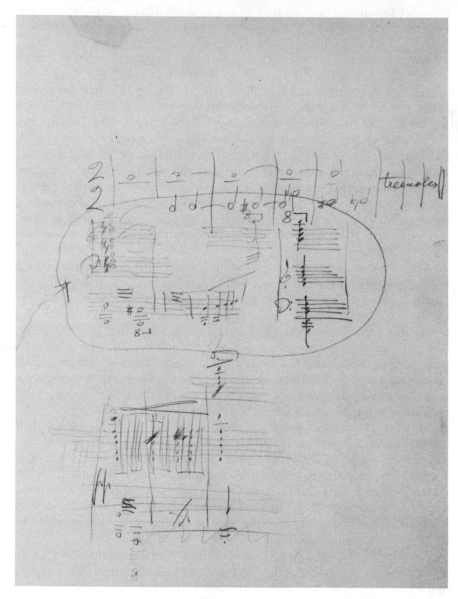

Plate 23. *The Firebird*, "Apparition of the Firebird," autograph piano reduction

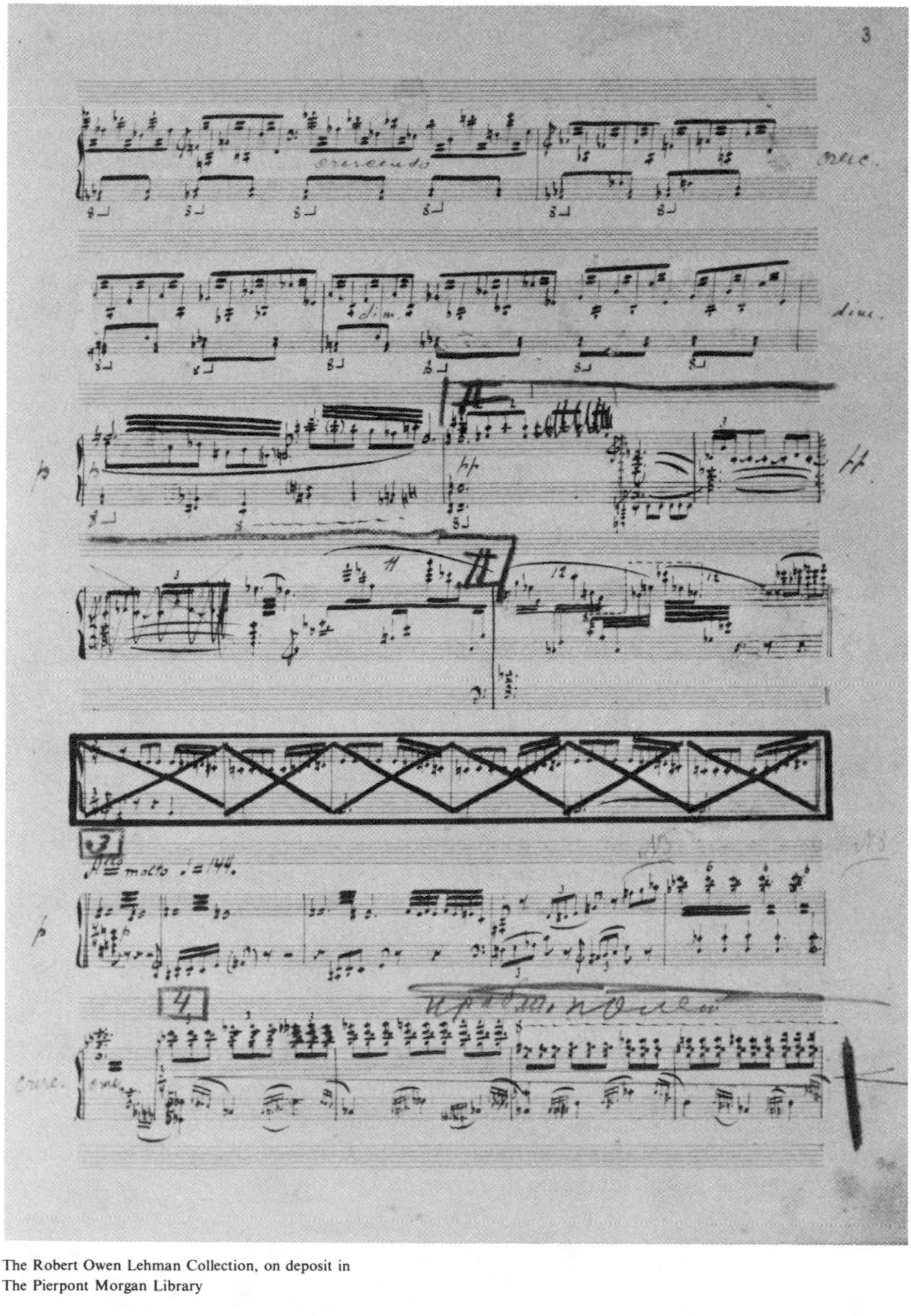

The Robert Owen Lehman Collection, on deposit in The Pierpont Morgan Library

of the work. Plate 23 illustrates the passage preceding the "Apparition of The *Firebird*" as well as the first few measures of that section. The additions seen in the margins (notated in red ink on the autograph itself) serve as flags for Stravinsky's editors, no doubt, since all such indications are included in the Jurgenson reduction previously discussed. More importantly, the passage marked by the bracket and labeled II, demonstrates Stravinsky's ongoing examination of the strategic location of certain passages even after he had entered them in the reduction. For example, in the first bar of the bracketed music, a triplet figure is canceled. So, too, does Stravinsky reject the first figure of the fourth system. While the first deletion holds, the second one is reinstated in the Jurgenson engraving.

Even more revealing is the excision of the entire fifth system that appears just before the allergo molto. But in fact these same measures occured 16 bars earlier as part of "The Enchanted Garden of Kastchei." Conceivably they were first intended to be employed just before the allergo molto as a bridge, based on, by this point, familiar material. Moreover, as typical of Stravinsky's later expressed cutting and pasting method, while the six measures are removed here, they do in fact reappear later in the ballet at rehearsal 46. At that juncture, these same six measures (now transposed) now do indeed function as a transition to the "Apparition of 13 Enchanted Princesses."

Plate 24 reprints the beginning of the "Supplication of the Firebird." The first eight measures, though crossed out here (in blue pencil in the autograph) are actually included in the published reduction. Moreover the passage is lengthened and texturally expanded. The final version of this adagio is in fact twice as long; and pianistically, the revision of the original eight bars incorporates a fuller left hand as well as several octave doublings more closely approximating the sound of the orchestral score. The Jurgenson version of these eight bars are offered for comparison (ex. 170). Finally, one observes that in the autograph, the orchestration is apparently still unsettled as evinced by Stravinsky's vacillation in the first measure as to whether a flute or English horn should be scored, as well as in his cancellation of the bassoon where the allegretto begins.

The final set of plates are the most informative. Plate 25 includes the section of the ballet beginning one bar after rehearsal 99. Among the many changes to be noted there is a metric shift to 9/4 at the end of the second system (corresponding to rehearsal 101 in the printed reduction). While the third system of the autograph displays four measures of this 9/4 meter, by the time Jurgenson printed the reduction (ex. 171), these same four measures had been compressed to three measures of 12/4 before reinstating the 9/4 at rehearsal 102.

Plate 24. *The Firebird*, "Supplication of the Firebird," autograph piano reduction

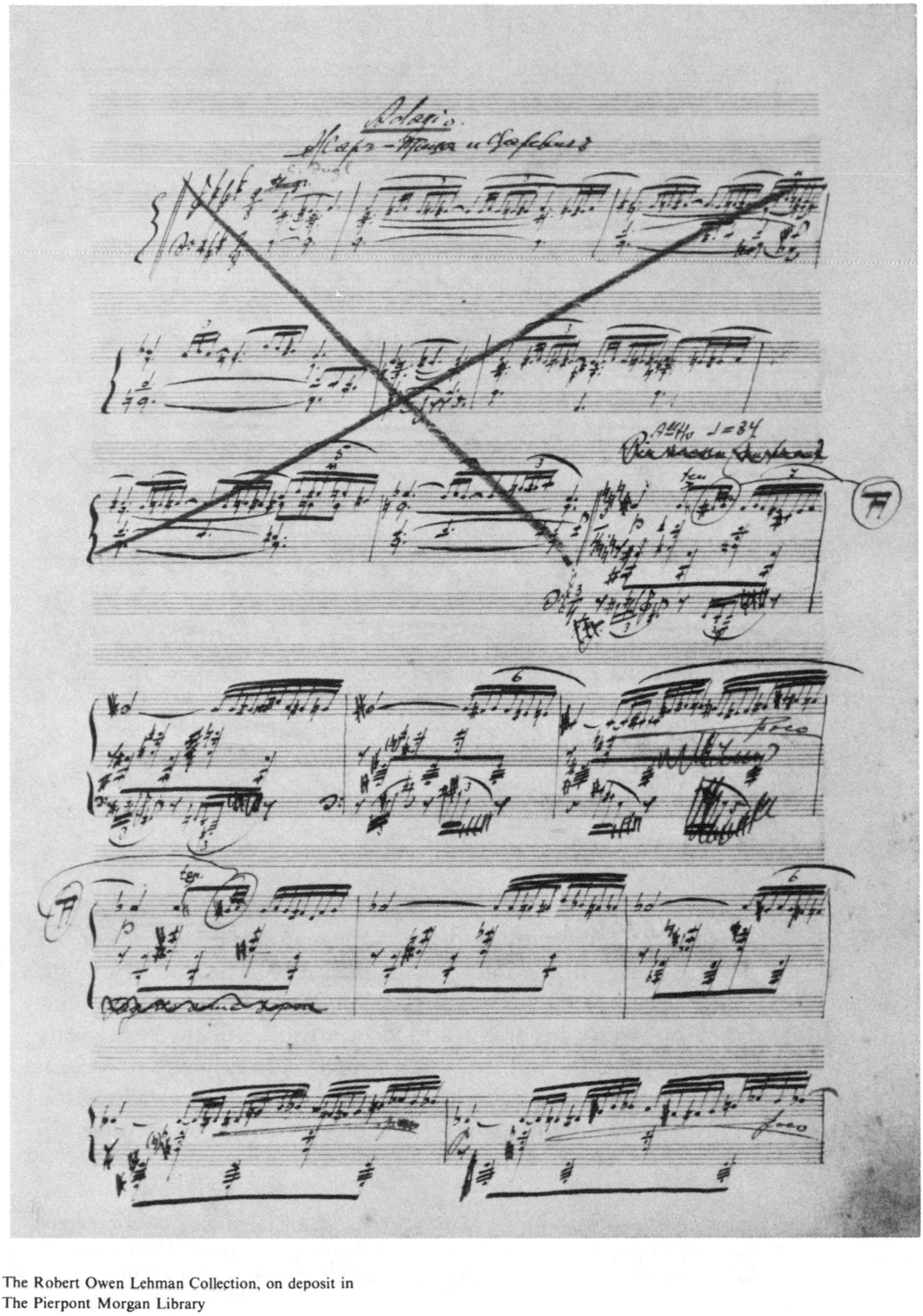

The Robert Owen Lehman Collection, on deposit in The Pierpont Morgan Library

Example 170.   Jurgenson piano reduction, mm. 1-8

Although it is difficult to detect in plate 25, Stravinsky actually had already suggested this metric alteration in the autograph by encircling, in pencil, the first 12 pulses in the initial measure of what he had originally conceived as a 9/4 pattern. Such pencil revisions are common throughout the autograph. Many were no doubt added in advance of the rehearsals begun in the spring of 1910. Indeed, such revisions may well have been those described by Brussel, who with Diaghilev and others, witnessed Stravinsky read through the piano score the previous winter in St. Petersburg.

At the appointed hour, we all met in the little ground-floor room on Zamiatin Peren-lokm which saw the beginnings of so many magnificent productions. The composer, young, slim, and uncommunicative, with vague meditative eyes, and lips set firm in an

Plate 25. *The Firebird*, (rehearsal 99), autograph piano reduction

The Robert Owen Lehman Collection, on deposit in
The Pierpont Morgan Library

Example 171.   Jurgenson piano reduction

energetic looking face, was at the piano. But the moment he began to play, the modest and dimly lit dwelling glowed with a dazzling radiance. By the end of the first scene, I was conquered: by the last I was lost in admiration. The manuscript on the music-rest, scored over with fine pencillings, revealed a masterpiece.[27]

Furthermore, a study of this same autograph page with the published reduction, confirms the fact that Stravinsky initially planned a shorter section and only later interpolated eight additional measures. Specifically, compare the last measure of plate 25's next to the lowest system, and the first measure of the final system, with the bracketed measures of example 172. The explanation of this variance is to be found in the autograph's margin, where Stravinsky (originally in red ink again) adds the direction "insert." Indeed, the passage corresponding to what eventually came to be the section between rehearsal 103 and 104 appears on a loose sheet of manuscript paper and is taped into the binding of the autograph. The addendum is reprinted as plate 26.

Example 172.   Jurgenson piano reduction

Several observations emerge: first, the passage is incontrovertibly pianistic and noticeably similar, in fact, to the first of the 1908 *Four Studies* (especially the coda, as discussed in chapter 2); second, the music of the uppermost staff presents an augmentation of the basic motive which, as indicated by Stravinsky's marking (again in pencil on the autograph page) was eventually assigned to the horns; third, the insertion itself is completely compatible, for it derives from the motivic shape just preceding rehearsal 103 (see ex. 172, top staff), thereby demonstrating how organically sewn various sections of the ballet really are. Perhaps most conspicuously, this same figure generates the principal melodic material for Kastchei's "Infernal Dance." Upon examining plate 27, one imme-

Plate 26. *The Firebird*, Stravinsky "Insert," in autograph piano reduction

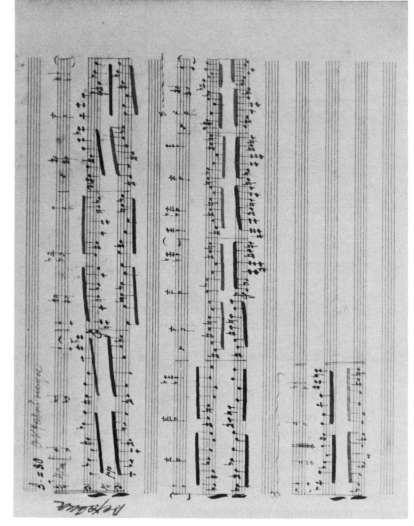

Plate 27. *The Firebird*, "Infernal Dance," autograph piano reduction

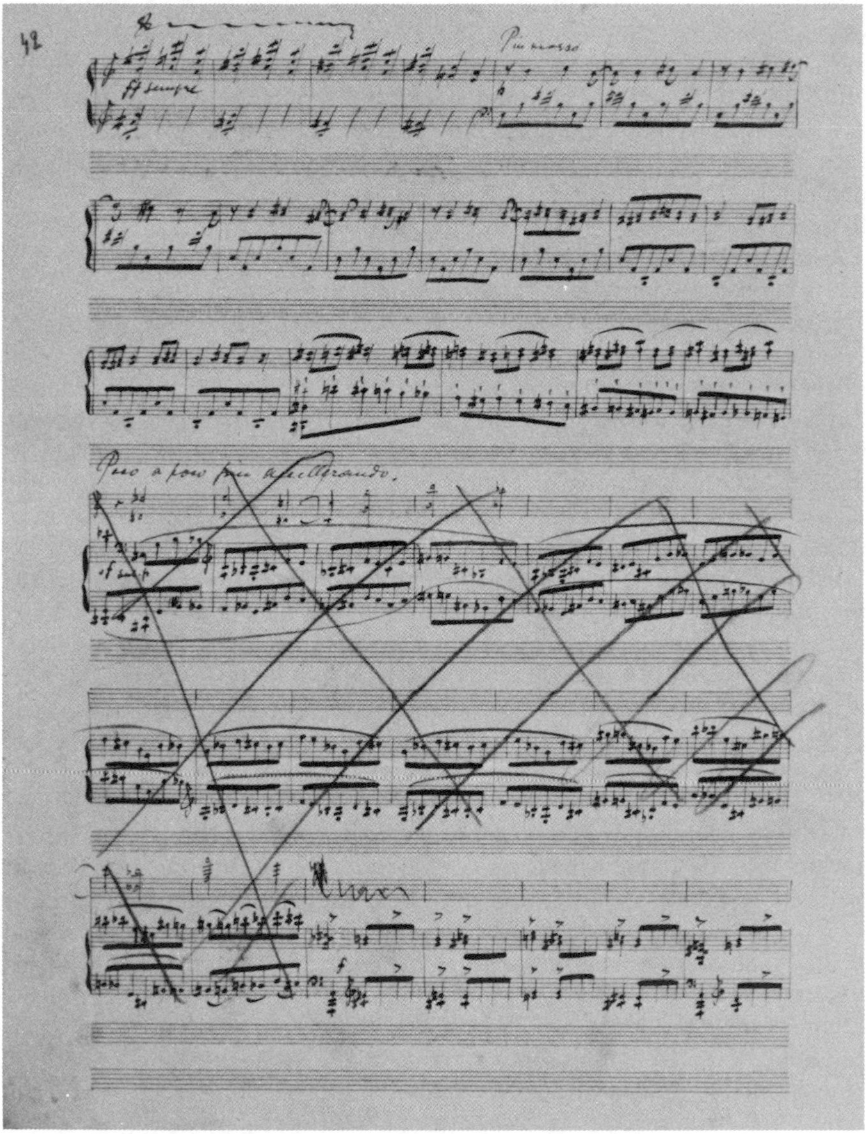

The Robert Owen Lehman Collection, on deposit in
The Pierpont Morgan Library

diately realizes that the interpolated passage discussed above had originally appeared (though twice the length) in the "Infernal Dance" itself, just before what was ultimately marked rehearsal 169 (and analogous to the last system of the plate).

As before, one must keep in mind the possibility that such a significant architectural relocation may be attributable to a committee action whereby the coherence of the compositional structure was judged less essential than the choreographic plan for that particular scene. Moreover, certainly the young Stravinsky would have recognized his own vulnerability and the damaging consequences an impolitic protest against such a structural change could bring. Obviously, at this early point of his career, he was not in a bargaining position and so could not raise too vehement an objection: "I had not yet proved myself as a composer, and I had not earned the right to criticize the aesthetics of my collaborators. . . ."[28] Yet Stravinsky goes on to add that in fact he did criticize them "and arrogantly, though perhaps my age (twenty-seven) was more arrogant than I was." Whether or not such a structural alteration was in fact the result of a behest, cannot of course be ascertained. But in point of fact, the transfer of the material canceled in plate 27 then inserted at the ballet's earlier juncture, makes absolute architectural sense. Not only is the preservation and extension of the motive before rehearsal 103 guaranteed, but the additional measures enhance the accumulating rhythmic thrust. Conversely, had the 16 deleted measures been retained, a questionable suspension of the implicit duple to triple meter change at rehearsal 169 would have resulted, thus compromising the poignancy of the rhythmic shift. In the end, even though such a structural change might have been foisted upon him by Diaghilev, Fokine, and the others involved, it is unlikely that Stravinsky would have been oblivious to what he later neologistically termed the "chrononomy" of his music. The fact that all of the revisions reviewed here are structural improvements surely is more than a product of coincidence.

Stravinsky probably would have been dismayed at the prospect of others poring over the unpublished, private deliberations that constitute part of his creative process. But in fact the piano reductions examined here, as well as the other hypotheses concerning his use of the piano submitted in this final chapter, still have less to do with the true conundrum of his creativity than with tracing certain consistently methodic aspects of his compositional procedures. The gray line that separates the transubstantiation of a creative impulse into a viable compositional idea is, of course, forever elusive. Yet in Stravinsky's case, his clear dependency upon the piano as the fulcrum of his compositional method, may permit us to see more perceptively than would otherwise have been possible, the actual order of development, that is, literally, just how his ideas took shape.

The likelihood that works of such trenchancy, such specific identity as those discussed here, might indeed owe their existence in some significant way to a pianistic origin, should not be confused with the compositional logic with which each work is endowed. Nor should the fact that such non pareil orchestral monuments as the *Danse Sacrale, Histoire,* the *Symphonies of Winds,* and all the other magnificent creations of his seemingly limited imagination were in some very fundamental ways generated through the vibrant dynamism of Stravinsky's peculiar pianistic approach, mitigate our esteem for the ultimate accomplishment. Appropos, one is reminded of Hindemith's sage counsel, in which he advised Stravinsky that often the ignorance of an instrumental idiom, its capabilities, its limits, may actually lead to a poetic latitude that might foster otherwise unfathomable ideas.[29] Indeed one wonders if many of Stravinsky's most audacious orchestral thoughts would have been conceived had he intended the idea for a specific orchestral timbre from the first. Often the ingenuity of his instrumental scores, the unorthodox chord voicings, the percussive string writing, the awkward woodwind configurations, the cumbersome registral shifts—all of these, while beyond the boundaries of orchestral conventionalism, most often fall squarely within the composer's own individualistic brand of pianism. It would, of course, be ludicrous to suggest that Stravinsky's orchestral imagintativeness was completely epiphenomenal. But given the source materials currently available, it would also seem dangerously myopic to disregard the shaping influence effected by the piano in contributing to this same inventiveness.

The certainty of Stravinsky's artistic immortality as an inimitable master of orchestral color may eventually outdistance our current dianoetic attempts to grasp the more easily taxonomical schemata of what Asaf'yev summarized as Stravinsky's "intonational sphere." Even within the last few years, notable progress has been made in uncovering those Rosetta Stones that reveal certain pitch paradigms and the accretion of larger, structural patterns. But as we continue our natural search for a sharper perspective within which to admire the complexity, the totality of Stravinsky's genius, we must cautiously avoid overlooking those phenomena in his career that seem already so obvious as to no longer deserve inquiry. Thus the apparency of such a grossly stated observation as "Stravinsky composed at the piano" may be a deceptively subsumptive epitome that actually conceals more than it informs. Only through a continuing study of his piano literature, his reductions, and, when released, his sketches, drafts, and revisions can the full span of Stravinsky's association with and reliance upon the piano be more accurately measured. Even now, it is clear that the significance of this association is as vital a part of his legacy as any. As such, surely it warrants a higher distinction than history has heretofore adjudged.

Notes

Chapter 1

1. Valerii V. Smirnov, *Tvorcheskoe formirovanie I. F. Stravinskogo* [Creative Formative Years of I. F. Stravinsky].

2. Igor Stravinsky, *An Autobiography*, p. 4.

3. Igor Stravinsky and Robert Craft, *Memories and Commentaries*, p. 25.

4. Vera Stravinsky and Robert Craft, *Stravinsky in Pictures and Documents*, p. 44.

5. See the description of *F. Stravinsky: Stat'i, Pis'ma, Vospominaniya* [F. Stravinsky: Essays, Letters, Memoirs], compiled and annotated by Larisa Kutateladze, edited by A. Gozenpud (Leningrad, 1972), in *Pictures and Documents*, p. 562.

6. Robert Craft, ed., *Stravinsky: Selected Correspondence Volume 1*, p. 3.

7. Ibid., p. 16.

8. Stravinsky, *Autobiography*, p. 6.

9. Nicolas Nabokov, *Igor Strawinsky*, p. 12.

10. Igor Stravinsky and Robert Craft, *Expositions and Developments*, p. 24.

11. Eric Walter White, *Stravinsky*, p. 556.

12. Stravinsky, *Autobiography*, p. 5.

13. Igor Stravinsky and Robert Craft, *Conversations with Igor Stravinsky*, p. 16.

14. V. Stravinsky and Craft, *Pictures and Documents*, p. 22.

15. Stravinsky and Craft, *Expositions*, p. 46.

16. Ibid.

17. Nabokov, *Strawinsky*, p. 12.

18. See Robert C. Ridenour, *Nationalism, Modernism, and Personal Rivalry in Nineteenth-Century Russian Music*, for a monographic study of this subject.

19. Stravinsky and Craft, *Memories*, p. 24.

20. Ridenour, *Nationalism*, p. 34.

21. Mikhail S. Drushkin, *Igor Stravinsky,* p. 149.

22. V. Stravinsky and Craft, *Pictures and Documents,* p. 50.

23. Stravinsky and Craft, *Memories,* p. 25.

24. Walter Piston, "A Reminiscence," *Perspectives of New Music* 9 (1971):6.

25. V. Stravinsky and Craft, *Pictures and Documents,* p. 20.

26. Stravinsky and Craft, *Conversations,* p. 43.

27. Igor Stravinsky and Robert Craft, *Dialogues and a Diary,* pp. 99-100.

28. Stravinsky and Craft, *Expositions,* p. 27.

29. Craft, ed., *Selected Correspondence,* p. xi. Two additional volumes of Stravinsky's letters are to be forthcoming.

30. This brief romance for piano and voice is known to be held by Soviet scholars and in fact was recorded several years ago on disc.

31. Smirnov, *Creative Formative Years.*

32. V. Stravinsky and Craft, *Pictures and Documents,* p. 19.

33. Ibid.

34. Stravinsky, *Autobiography,* p. 11.

35. V. Stravinsky and Craft, *Pictures and Documents,* p. 22.

36. Stravinsky, *Autobiography,* p. 14.

37. Ibid., p. 15.

38. Stravinsky and Craft, *Expositions,* p. 49.

39. Stravinsky, *Autobiography,* pp. 15-16.

Chapter 2

1. I wish to thank Mr. White for kindly sharing with me the prepublication proofs of the work in 1973.

2. The plate is reproduced from Smirnov's *Creative Formative Years of I. F. Stravinsky.*

3. Nicolas Nabokov, *Igor Strawinsky,* p. 12.

4. Robert C. Ridenour, *Nationalism, Modernism, and Personal Rivalry in Nineteenth-Century Russian Music,* p. 45.

5. Ibid.

6. Edward Gorden, "Classic and Romantic in Russian Music," *Music and Letters* 50 (January, 1969): 153-57, provides an interesting essay in regard to Rimsky-Korsakov's assimilation of stylistic traits from both historical periods.

7. Alfred Cortot, "Igor Strawinsky, le piano et les pianistes," *La Revue Musicale* 190 (May-June, 1939):274.

8. Vera Stravinsky and Robert Craft, *Stravinsky in Pictures and Documents,* p. 411.

9. Robert Craft, ed., *Stravinsky: Selected Correspondence Volume 1*, p. vii.

10. Cortot, "Strawinsky, le piano," p. 274.

11. Ridenour, *Nationalism*, p. 217.

12. Igor Stravinsky and Robert Craft, *Conversations with Igor Stravinsky*, p. 48.

13. Again, Mr. White was generous in forwarding the page proofs of the Sonata in 1973. A facsimile page of the Sonata appears in the Stravinsky entry in the latest edition of *Groves*.

14. Igor Stravinsky, *An Autobiography*, p. 20.

15. V. Stravinsky and Craft, *Pictures and Documents*, p. 22.

16. There are a few other commonly known minor works from this period. See my "Stravinsky's Piano Scherzo (1902) in Perspective: A New Starting Point," *The Musical Quarterly* 67 (January, 1981):82, in which these works are listed in the first footnote.

17. Clive Barnes, "City Ballet Triumphs in Stravinsky Fête," *New York Times,* 19 June 1972, p. 1. However, Mr. Craft has informed me in a letter of May 19, 1983, that Mme. Malraux did not play the Scherzo movement of the Sonata, but rather the little 1902 Scherzo discussed earlier. Indeed, Craft reports that he actually taught the piece to Mme. Malraux.

18. The manuscript is held by the Bibliotheque Nationale.

19. V. Stravinsky and Craft, *Pictures and Documents*, p. 49.

20. Igor Stravinsky and Robert Craft, *Expositions and Developments*, p. 49.

21. V. Stravinsky and Craft, *Pictures and Documents*, p. 629.

22. The fourth Etude in $F^{\sharp}$ Major is missing.

23. Igor Stravinsky and Robert Craft, *Memories and Commentaries*, p. 63.

24. Ibid.

25. V. Stravinsky and Craft, *Pictures and Documents*, p. 605.

26. Boris Asaf'yev, *Kniga o Stravinskom* [A Book About Stravinsky], trans. Richard F. French, p. 17.

Chapter 3

1. I wish to thank J. Rigbie Turner, curator of music manuscripts at the Pierpont Morgan Library, for providing me with this information.

2. Igor Stravinsky, *An Autobiography*, p. 25.

3. Stravinsky, *Autobiography*, p. 53.

4. Much of the information throughout this study was gained from an interview with Soulima Stravinsky on February 10, 1974, conducted in Urbana, Illinois. Having had the privilege of studying piano with him for two years, Mr. Stravinsky was very kind in sharing several remembrances of his father with me. Moreover in his "Russian Folk Melodies in *The Rite of Spring*," *Journal of the American Musicological Society*

23 (1980):501-43, Richard Taruskin makes several references to the fact that Stravinsky was quite familiar with numerous folkloristic anthologies by this time. See especially n. 15, p. 508 in Taruskin's essay.

5. Vera Stravinsky and Robert Craft, *Stravinsky in Pictures and Documents,* p. 44.

6. Robert Craft, ed., *Stravinsky: Selected Correspondence Volume 1,* p. 410.

7. The premiere of this work took place at the International Stravinsky Symposium, September 13, 1982, at La Jolla, California. Charles Wuorinen, the pianist on that occasion, also premiered a "Berceuse à 2 mains" which apparently was composed in 1940, shortly after Stravinsky came to America.

8. It is held by the Music Division of the Library of Congress. Apparently the Stravinsky estate also holds a manuscript version of the work, though not an autograph.

9. V. Stravinsky and Craft, *Pictures and Documents,* p. 661.

10. Ibid.

11. Ibid., p. 610.

12. The duets were later orchestrated as two separate instrumental suites between 1917 and 1925.

13. Craft, ed., *Selected Correspondence,* p. 412.

14. Ibid., Craft details some specific changes in this version, including the addition of glizzandi and the alteration of certain pitches.

15. Igor Stravinsky and Robert Craft, *Dialogues and a Diary,* p. 72.

16. According to Craft, Stravinsky's talents as an illustrator were exhibited in providing caricatural titivations upon the march manuscript that satirize various wartime images: cannons, flames, detonations, etc.—all of which indicate his awareness of the conflict around him.

17. In editing some of his father's piano music for the collection *Stravinsky: The Short Piano Pieces* (Boosey & Hawkes, 1977), Soulima Stravinsky chose to arrange both the polka and valse but not the march for solo piano. In each instance, he editorially adds the extra measures that Stravinsky was later to incorporate into the instrumental transcriptions of these works.

18. Craft, ed., *Selected Correspondence,* p. 413.

19. Ibid., p. 412.

20. Stravinsky and Craft, *Dialogues,* p. 73.

21. The piece is included in Soulima Stravinsky's collection mentioned above. Also, a reprint of the work appears in White's biography, p. 248.

22. Craft, ed., *Selected Correspondence,* p. 414.

23. Mikhail S. Drushkin, *Igor Stravinsky,* p. 18.

24. Robert Siohan, *Stravinsky,* p. 68.

25. V. Stravinsky and Craft, *Pictures and Documents,* p. 176.

26. Roman Vlad, *Stravinsky,* p. 55.

27. Those readers familiar with Allen Forte's analytic ideas as outlined in *The Structure of Atonal Music* will recognize these pitch-class sets as cell *A* = 3-7, cell *B* = 3-9, and cell *C* = 4-23. Similarly, those acquainted with Howard Hanson's earlier system of intervallic identification as presented in *The Harmonic Materials of Modern Music*, will recognize these same cells respectively as PMN, P²S, and P³NS². Though Hanson's terminology is perhaps easier to apply at first, demanding less understanding of the intense relationships, Forte's application is preferable, and as regards Stravinsky, is especially appropriate in grasping the complex network of pitch relatedness in larger compositions. For example, see Forte's *The Harmonic Organization of "The Rite of Spring."* No knowledge of either Hanson's or Forte's theories has been assumed here; thus the necessity for establishing an accessible analytic apparatus to employ in discussing the pitch content of the march. Nonetheless, only the simplest of fundamentals are presented here and the reader is encouraged to familiarize himself with sections 1.1 through 1.10 of Forte's *The Structure of Atonal Music*. A summary of Forte's principles is presented in David Beach's "Pitch Structure and the Analytic Process in Atonal Music: An Interpretation of Sets," *Music Theory Spectrum* 1 (1979):7-22.

28. Taruskin discusses such a usage in his *JAMS* article (see n. 4, above).

29. Edward T. Cone, "Stravinsky: The Progress of a Method," in *Perspectives on Schoenberg and Stravinsky,* ed., Benjamin Boretz and Edward T. Cone, pp. 155-64.

30. These fundamental properties of pitch organization have been addressed through several theories over the last few years. Arthur Berger's pioneering, and by now classic study "Pitch Organization in Stravinsky," first published in *Perspectives of New Music,* 1963, sought to expostulate a preliminary theory of pitch structure that extended beyond a single work. Since this admirable first step, surely the most exhaustive and serious strides have been taken by Pieter van den Toorn in his monographic investigation "Some Characteristics of Stravinsky's Diatonic Music," *Perspectives of New Music* 14 (1975) and 15 (1977). These ideas have recently been given even fuller exposure in the same author's *The Music of Igor Stravinsky* (Yale University Press, 1983). (I wish to thank Mr. van den Toorn for permitting me to study the prepublication proofs of his landmark study.) In seeking to codify a "useful set of binding theoretical propositions," van den Toorn in his *PONM* articles, rejects "appeals to a 'basic cell' rationale whereby 'coherence' is attributed to the unfolding of some intervallically conceived cohesiveness." Since it is, in fact, a cellular approach that I have chosen to employ in examining the march, some comment upon van den Toorn's compelling ideas seems appropriate. His theory rests upon the pervasive octatonicism of Stravinsky's music, primarily founded upon two symmetrical pitch resources ("Model A and B"), along with the "interpenetration" of diatonic elements. In covering a representative sampling of the Stravinsky literature, van den Toorn goes a considerable distance in unraveling the paralogistic mysteries of the so-called wrong note syndrome so prevalent still in explicating Stravinsky's pitch configurations. Considering the piano literature's much maligned past, the author chooses not to include a piano work in his study—an understandable exclusion based upon history's vantage point. His decision to examine only Stravinsky's "most significant works" is likewise reasonable, though as a consequence, this obviates some of those less known compositions written during crucially transitional periods. To the point, a work such as the march incorporates representative techniques found in the children's piano literature of this time and displays many of the salient aspects of pitch structure alluded

to by van den Toorn in several of Stravinsky's grander creations. More importantly perhaps, the duet reveals these very techniques in a formative stage, and certainly far in advance of *Histoire du Soldat,* a work that van den Toorn employs as a summary composition in his *PONM* essays. In many ways, van den Toorn wisely eschews the basic cell approach, for his is a concerted efforted to separate the cellular trees from the larger forest—indeed, a path that has usually not been cut in approaching the topic. Yet while this tact is admirable in attempting to construct an inclusive theory of pitch construction, it does not invalidate an examination of the small intervallic units of Stravinsky's music; rather it only subsumes them. Indeed it is the basic cell that animates the whole of such larger theories of pitch language. Van den Toorn's theory is, of course, an inductive one, ultimately concluding that the use of certain cells is an inherent aspect of an incontestable use of the octatonic scale (as colored by other elements). But it is the unfolding of various germinal subsets of the parental octatonicism that seems, in the instance of the duets at least, to resemble more closely the way in which Stravinsky likely plotted his pitch strategy within the limited sphere of these miniatures.

31. Craft, ed., *Selected Correspondence,* p. 413.

32. See for example the opening gesture of Schoenberg's Opus 19, No. 6, in which both cell *A* and *B* play an important generative role.

33. Taruskin, "Russian Folk Melodies."

34. Leo Kraft, "Stravinsky and Tradition: First Thoughts," *Perspectives of New Music* 9 (1971):140.

35. Frank Onnen, *Stravinsky,* trans. Mrs. M. M. Kessler-Button, p. 19.

36. This according to Craft, whose "A Catalogue of Manuscripts (1904–1952) in Stravinsky's Possession" is included in White's biography. (The catalogue itself is dated, as will be discussed in chap. 5.) Also, see Asaf'yev's *A Book About Stravinsky,* pp. 120-26 for a discussion of basic cells used in *Renard,* one of the few occasions upon which the author entered into an analytic discourse.

37. See Menachem Zur, "Tonal Ambiguities as a Constructive Force in the Language of Stravinsky," *The Musical Quarterly* 68 (October, 1982):516-26, for a recent discussion that also includes such cells as an analytic cornerstone.

38. Allen Forte, *The Harmonic Organization of "The Rite of Spring,"* p. 28.

Chapter 4

1. Igor Stravinsky and Robert Craft, *Expositions and Developments,* p. 104.

2. White quotes both of these examples in his biography, p. 263, suggesting that the later "Berceuse" was not published since it duplicated the pitches of the earlier song.

3. Robert Craft, ed., *Stravinsky: Selected Correspondence Volume 1,* p. 138.

4. Vera Stravinsky and Robert Craft, *Stravinsky in Pictures and Documents,* p. 163.

5. Stravinsky Previsions a New Music," *Current Opinion* 71 (March 1925): 329-30.

6. V. Stravinsky and Craft, *Pictures and Documents,* p. 164.

7. Ibid., p. 622.

8. Ibid., p. 60.

9. Plates 6 and 7 were made from photographs taken of the rolls as they were unfolding on the player-piano owned by the Music Division of the Library of Congress. Please also note that the valuable listing of Stravinsky's "Arrangements for Player-Piano" included as appendix D of White's biography has recently been supplanted by Rex Lawson's compilation of the composer's complete "Music on Piano Roll." This new and full catalogue was distributed at the International Stravinsky Symposium at La Jolla (September 1982) and should appear in the proceedings of that symposium, to be published by the University of California, Berkeley, within the next few years.

10. Edward Berlin, *Ragtime,* p. 15.

11. V. Stravinsky and Craft, *Pictures and Documents,* p. 623.

12. Alfred Cortot, "Igor Strawinsky, le piano et les pianistes," *La Revue Musicale* 190 (May-June 1939):281.

13. V. Stravinsky and Craft, *Pictures and Documents,* p. 102. For a recent essay dealing with the composer's interest in rag, see Barbara B. Heyman, "Stravinsky and Ragtime," *The Musical Quarterly* 63 (October 1982):557-58, where the author discusses other similarities with Debussy.

14. Craft, ed., *Selected Correspondence,* p. 130.

15. Igor Stravinsky, *An Autobiography,* p. 78.

16. See Wilfrid Mellers, "Stravinsky and Jazz," *Tempo* 81 (Summer 1967):29.

17. "Great American Composer—Will He Speak in the Accent of Broadway?" *Current Opinion* 63 (November 1917):317.

18. Stanley C. Wise, " 'American Music Is True Art,' Says Stravinsky," *New York Tribune* 16 January 1916, sec. 5, p. 3.

19. Stravinsky and Craft, *Expositions,* p. 103.

20. Robert Craft, "The Composer and the Phonograph," *Hi-Fidelity* 7 (June 1957): 35.

21. Ibid.

22. Soulima Stravinsky, private interview, February 10, 1974.

23. Richard Middleton, "Stravinsky's Development: A Jungian Approach," *Music and Letters* 54 (July 1973):295.

24. Stravinsky, *Autobiography,* pp. 71-72.

25. V. Stravinsky and Craft, *Pictures and Documents,* p. 175.

26. Berlin, *Ragtime,* p. 2.

27. Stravinsky, *Autobiography,* p. 78.

28. V. Stravinsky and Craft, *Pictures and Documents,* p. 152.

29. Ibid., p. 620.

30. Ibid.

31. Igor Stravinsky and Robert Craft, *Dialogues and a Diary,* p. 87.

32. V. Stravinsky and Craft, *Pictures and Documents,* p. 646.

33. Ibid., p. 175.

34. Craft, ed., *Selected Correspondence,* p. 91. Actually Picasso prepared six such drawings, three of which appear in the British edition of *Memories and Commentaries.*

35. Ibid., p. 144.

36. V. Stravinsky and Craft, *Pictures and Documents,* p. 631.

37. Ibid., p. 169.

38. Ibid., p. 175.

39. Ibid., p. 618.

40. Robert Winter and Bruce Carr, eds., *Beethoven, Performers, and Critics,* p. 138.

41. Craft, ed., *Selected Correspondence,* p. 413.

42. Stravinsky, *Autobiography,* p. 82.

43. Craft suggests that it was once again the affluent Chilean, Madame Errazuriz, who being on cordial terms with Stravinsky since his earlier trip to Madrid, actually commissioned the *Piano-Rag-Music,* though the work is officially dedicated to Rubinstein. It was Rubinstein himself who commissioned the *Petrouchka* piano solo, and in providing a larger sum for the arrangement than Diaghilev "had given for the whole ballet," as Stravinsky once complained, presented the composer in *Expositions* with the opportunity to recall this inequity.

44. Stravinsky, *Autobiography,* p. 82.

45. Craft, ed., *Selected Correspondence,* p. 144.

46. Ibid., p. 160.

47. V. Stravinsky and Craft, *Pictures and Documents,* p. 631.

48. Ibid., p. 169.

49. Eric Walter White, *Stravinsky's Sacrifice to Apollo,* p. 94.

50. Arthur Rubinstein, *My Many Years,* p. 85.

51. Eric Walter White, *Stravinsky,* p. 281.

52. Roman Vlad, *Stravinsky,* p. 57.

53. V. Stravinsky and Craft, *Pictures and Documents,* p. 193. The statement originally appeared in *Le Vingtieme Siècle* May 27, 1930.

54. A. R. Danberg Charters, "Negro Folk Elements in Classic Ragtime," *Ethnomusicology* 5 (September 1961):174-83, though Berlin disputes this in his study.

55. Igor Stravinsky, *Poetics of Music,* p. 28.

56. Igor Stravinsky and Robert Craft, *Conversations with Igor Stravinsky,* p. 20.

57. I have addressed elsewhere a potentially deeper architectonic substratum founded upon the binding strength of recurrent pitch-class sets that correspond to the articulation of the partitions outlined in table 1. See my "Structural Coherence in Stravinsky's *Piano-Rag-Music,*" *Music Theory Spectrum* 4 (1982):76-91. I wish to express

my gratitude to the editor of this journal, Lewis Rowell, for permitting me to use some of the illustrations first appearing in that study.

Chapter 5

1. Vera Stravinsky and Robert Craft, *Stravinsky in Pictures and Documents*, p. 209.

2. A more complete listing of the Pergolesi source materials appears in Eric Walter White's *Stravinsky*, p. 285.

3. V. Stravinsky and Craft, *Pictures and Documents*, p. 217.

4. Igor Stravinsky, *An Autobiography*, p. 91.

5. V. Stravinsky and Craft, *Pictures and Documents*, p. 630.

6. Ibid.

7. From the prefatory remarks to the Boosey & Hawkes edition (1977).

8. V. Stravinsky and Craft, *Pictures and Documents*, p. 630.

9. Igor Stravinsky and Robert Craft, *Themes and Episodes*, p. 30.

10. Stravinsky, *Autobiography*, p. 99.

11. As reprinted in White's biography, pp. 581-82.

12. V. Stravinsky and Craft, *Pictures and Documents*, p. 629.

13. Ibid., p. 630.

14. Arthur Rubinstein, *My Many Years*, pp. 101-2.

15. V. Stravinsky and Craft, *Pictures and Documents*, p. 217. Also see page 15 of *Igor and Vera Stravinsky: A Photograph Album* (photographs selected by Vera Stravinsky and Rita McCaffrey with captions by Robert Craft) wherein Stravinsky is reported to have commented, ". . . I have taken three episodes from *Petrouchka* and arranged them according to the three traditional movements of the sonata. . . ."

16. Rubinstein, *My Many Years*, p. 148.

17. Ibid., p. 139.

18. V. Stravinsky and Craft, *Pictures and Documents*, p. 621.

19. Igor Stravinsky and Robert Craft, *Dialogues and a Diary*, p. 71.

20. V. Stravinsky and Craft, *Pictures and Documents*, p. 631.

21. In a paper by Mr. Craft delivered *in absentia* to the International Stravinsky Symposium, sketches for the *Octet* were made available. Craft also confirmed the fact that some of the material for the fugato was drafted for piano four-hands, a rather typical Stravinskyan setting.

22. Reprinted in White's biography, pp. 576-77.

23. Mikhail Drushkin includes these remarks in his biography of Stravinsky.

24. From the *"Octour"* article. See White, pp. 574-75.

25. Stravinsky, *Autobiography*, p. 119.

26. Reprinted in White, p. 576.

27. V. Stravinsky and Craft, *Pictures and Documents,* p. 197.

28. Joachim Kaiser, *Great Pianists of Our Time,* p. 183.

29. Robert Craft, ed., *Stravinsky: Selected Correspondence Volume 1,* p. 214.

30. Ibid., pp. 170, 177, 179. But naturally, Stravinsky had been playing the work much earlier than March. From an interview in Antwerp (and reprinted in *Igor and Vera Stravinsky: A Photograph Album* p. 14), the composer comments that "I am working on a Concerto for piano and orchestra, which I force myself to play every day without employing the pedals. . . ." The interview took place on January 10, 1924, that is, months before his letter to Ansermet.

31. Such a summary itinerary was not unusual. This author remembers, for example, Soulima Stravinsky's personal score of *Three Movements from Petrouchka* upon which the pianist logged the dates and places of his frequent performances, even into the 1970s.

32. Eric Walter White's reissue of Craft's "A Catalogue of Manuscripts (1904–1952) in Stravinsky's Possession," an inventory taken shortly after Craft's arrival in the Stravinsky household, is largely dated. The autograph full score of the Piano Concerto, for example, is no longer part of the Stravinsky archives as listed therein, having been donated to the Library of Congress collection on November 7, 1967. A register of the numerous post-1954 manuscript deposits at the Library of Congress, as well as those at the Pierpont Morgan Library in New York, is compiled in my article, "Stravinsky Manuscripts at The Library of Congress and The Pierpont Morgan Library," *The Journal of Musicology* 1 (July 1982):327-37. In regard to the Piano Concerto, while Craft's catalogue once listed 52 pages of summary sketches for the work, these materials also seem to have exchanged hands. In a letter to this author dated July 3, 1981, Mr. Craft mentions that among the manuscripts of the piano works still in the Stravinsky archives, none remain for the Concerto.

33. The use of the original manuscript for performances was of course quite common, and Stravinsky seems often to have entrusted the well-being of the autograph to the reliability of the registered mails. In another letter to Ansermet, dated October 22, 1924, Stravinsky states: "Today I sent my manuscript orchestral score of the Concerto to you by registered mail." (From Craft, *Stravinsky: Selected Correspondence,* p. 182.)

34. The revised score reflects minor changes for the most part, rather than any structural reformation in comparison to the 1931 publication. However, a rather consistent re-evaluation of tempi is evident. A comparative table of such tempo variances is included in White's biography, pp. 318-19.

35. In this regard, see two studies: William S. Newman, "Beethoven's Fingerings as Interpretive Clues," *The Journal of Musicology* 2 (April 1982):171-97; Jeanne Bamberger, "The Musical Significance of Beethoven's Fingerings in the Piano Sonatas," *The Music Forum,* Volume 4, pp. 237-80.

36. See for example, William E. Benjamin, "Tonality without 5ths: Remarks on the First Movement of Stravinsky's Concerto for Piano and Wind Instruments," *In Theory Only* 2 (November-December 1977):53-70, and a response in, Robert P. Morgan's "Dissonant Prolongations, Perfect 5ths and Major 3rds in Stravinsky's Piano Concerto," *In Theory Only* 4 (April 1978):3-7.

37. V. Stravinsky and Craft, *Pictures and Documents,* p. 215.

38. See two additional studies: Joseph Straus, "Stravinsky's Tonal Axis," *The Journal of Music Theory* 26 (1982):261-90; Robert P. Morgan, "Dissonant Prolongations: Theoretical and Compositional Precedents," *The Journal of Music Theory* 20 (1976):46-91.

39. Igor Stravinsky and Robert Craft, *Expositions and Developments,* p. 51.

40. In an early letter to Craft dated October 7, 1947, Stravinsky addresses a specific misprint in this section: "No, the last eighth of the fifth measure after rehearsal 86 in my Piano Concerto is a G$^\#$, only in the next bar comes the G natural." Indeed, a G natural does appear in the 1924 two-piano score, though G$^\#$s appear in other voices of the same vertical. The addition of the sharp would have amounted to a precautionary indication; but Stravinsky was always concerned about such reminders (as will be discussed in conjunction with the *Serenade en La*). In the same missive to Craft, Stravinsky acknowledges receipt of a French recording of his Piano Concerto as played by Soulima, mentioning his son's fine playing, though the tempi were taken "too hurriedly." See page 331 of *Stravinsky: Selected Correspondence* for a reprint of the full letter.

41. V. Stravinsky and Craft, *Pictures and Documents,* p. 218.

42. Ibid.

43. Ibid., p. 252.

44. J. F. Cooke, "Chronological Progess in Musical Art," *The Etude* 44 (August 1926):559-60.

45. These reviews are collected in, Eugene Goosens, *Overtures and Beginners,* p. 274. For a more detailed and contemporary view of the premiere in 1924, see Adolph Weissmann, "Strawinsky spielt sein Klavier Konzert," *Anbruch* 6 (1924): 407-9. One is reminded here too of the account of a 1959 performance in Moscow by the New York Philharmonic wherein the piece was judged "a manifesto of musical coldness, dryness, and anemia," as reported in Boris Schwarz' "Stravinsky in Soviet Russian Criticism," *The Musical Quarterly* 48 (July 1962):340-61. Even Prokofiev in a 1924 letter to Miaskovsky states that the work is like Bach and Handel and "I do not like it very much," though he begrudgingly adds that "it is very strongly sewn together. . . ." (See *Pictures and Documents,* p. 626).

46. V. Stravinsky and Craft, *Pictures and Documents,* p. 629.

47. Stravinsky and Craft, *Expositions,* p. 51.

48. Robert Siohan, *Stravinsky,* p. 105.

49. Stravinsky, *Autobiography,* p. 113. Moreover, Stravinsky's unmitigated devotion to Czerny seems to have been inherited by his son Soulima, who regularly assigned the use of these exercises not only as a pedagogic aid for his students during his tenure at the University of Illinois, but even as programmed recital pieces for some of his advanced graduate piano students.

50. V. Stravinsky and Craft, *Pictures and Documents,* p. 629.

51. Rubinstein, *My Many Years,*, pp. 150-51.

52. Ibid., p. 283.

53. In this regard see Stravinsky's letters to Ansermet dated October 2 and 22, as reprinted in *Selected Correspondence*. In the latter message to Ansermet, Stravinsky writes: "I finished my Sonata and am now practicing the piano. Maybe I will play the piece on my tour if I feel able to do it at that time."

54. From the February 10, 1974, interview with Soulima Stravinsky.

55. V. Stravinsky and Craft, *Pictures and Documents*, p. 629.

56. Stravinsky and Craft, *Dialogues*, p. 9.

57. I wish to thank Rex Lawson for his aid regarding information concerning Stravinsky's piano rolls.

58. This author also wishes to acknowledge the generous help of Messrs. James Smart and Sam Brylawski of the Division of Recorded Sound, the Library of Congress in making these piano rolls available to me.

59. V. Stravinsky and Craft, *Pictures and Documents*, p. 259.

60. Ibid., pp. 310-11. Also, certain aspects of the Stravinsky-Prokofiev connection, including some remarks on each composer's pianism, was addressed in a paper entitled "Stravinsky and Prokofiev: Sizing Up the Competition," by Malcolm Brown, delivered at the La Jolla Stravinsky Symposium.

61. From a review of a League of Composers concert, *New York Herald Tribune*, October 26, 1925.

62. Eric Walter White, *Stravinsky's Sacrifice to Apollo*, pp. 104-5.

63. Stravinsky, *Autobiography*, p. 116.

64. Halsey Stevens, in one of the more enlightening secondary sources, addressed the relationship of Stravinsky's slow movements of the 1920s and 1930s and Beethoven's keyboard adagios. See "Critical Years in European Musical History 1915–1925," *International Musicological Society* 10 (1969):221-33.

65. Stravinsky and Craft, *Dialogues*, p. 71.

66. For a recent article about Boulanger, see Allen Shawn, "Nadia Boulanger's Lessons," *The Atlantic* 251 (March 1983):78-85, in which some of these concepts are discussed.

67. From *La Revue Musicale* 10 (1925):103. Lourie's essays seem to have attracted Stravinsky more than most. Craft reports that Stravinsky held Lourie in uncommonly high esteem and entrusted him with many assignments, including proofreading and the piano reductions of some of his most recent works, such as the *Symphonies of Winds* and the *Octet.*.

68. In his *Craft of Musical Composition*, Volume 1, Hindemith includes this opening passage as an example in applying his own harmonic theories of chord fluctuation.

69. In a 1926 colloquy at the Rice Institute, Boulanger dealt largely with tracing such transformations. Other examples of such augmentation in the movement occur at mm. 41, 49, 64, and 117.

70. It is not the purpose here to argue for a strict concurrence with the basic precepts of the Fibonacci theorem, though some similarities are in fact quite clear. However, other Stravinsky compositions have been tested more rigorously against the idea of

golden proportions. See, for example, Clive B. Pascoe, "Golden Proportion in Musical Design," (D. M. E. diss., University of Cincinnati, 1973), in which the *Ragtime for Eleven Instruments* and the 1946 *Concerto en Re* are discussed.

71. This article is reprinted in Paul Henry Lang's *Stravinsky: A New Appraisal of His Work*, p. 25.

72. Ibid., p. 26.

73. Ibid., p. 28. Also consult Cone's diagram of the entire movement reprinted in the essay.

74. Ibid., p. 29. Also see B. M. Williams "The Structure of Stravinsky's *Symphony in C*," *The Musical Quarterly* 59 (July 1973):355-69 for another discussion of the temporal elements of the work.

75. Stravinsky, *Autobiography*, pp. 123-24.

76. V. Stravinsky and Craft, *Pictures and Documents*, p. 261.

77. Mr. Craft was kind enough to share this information with me in advance of his publication of "The Chronology of the *Serenade en La*," to appear in his second volume of Stravinsky's correspondence.

78. According to Craft, an earlier and "possibly incomplete" performance of the work was given to a private audience the previous month at the home of Werner Reinhart. Moreover, in a lecture delivered at Trinity University (San Antonio) on November 13, 1982, Craft suggested that it may have been a work other than the *Serenade* that was originally intended for a gramophone cutting, a work that was never completed. In this regard, see the photograph album of Vera Stravinsky mentioned in n. 15 above (page 15). There Stravinsky comments, "I am composing/finishing a piano Sonata." This is dated March 25, 1925, that is too late for the earlier Sonata and quite possibly a work undertaken before the *Serenade* was completed.

79. Craft, ed., *Selected Correspondence*, p. 4.

80. From Craft's (currently in press) essay regarding the *Serenade's* chronology.

81. Years ago, for example, Claudio Spies pointed out perhaps the most obvious of these obtrusions in the very first measure of the Hymne, wherein the D of the second right hand chord should of course be a conforming C. Other blatant blunders include the incorrect note value for its corresponding metronomic indication preceding the Hymne, and the failure to include a 7/8 metric change at bar 64. See Claudio Spies, "Editions of Stravinsky's Music," in *Perspective on Schoenberg and Stravinsky*, eds., Boretz and Cone, p. 253.

82. The letter is reprinted courtesy of the Paul Van Katwijk Collection, Fine Arts Library, Southern Methodist University, Dallas, Texas. The translation is provided by Professor Ilya Mamitov of that institution's Department of Foreign Languages.

83. The reissue of the originally pressed two 78 rpm discs of the French Columbia recording, is by Seraphim's "Great Recordings of the Century." Mono 60183, and includes several other Stravinsky piano performances as well.

84. From the prefatory remarks to the Boosey & Hawkes publication.

85. Walter Piston, "A Reminiscence," *Perspectives of New Music* 9 (1971):6.

86. Craft, see n. 77, above.

87. Igor Stravinsky, *Poetics of Music,* pp. 36-37.

88. Arthur Berger, "Neoclassicism Reexamined," *Perspectives of New Music* 9 (1971):85.

89. Stravinsky, *Autobiography,* p. 125.

90. Eric Walter White, *Stravinsky,* p. 324.

91. V. Stravinsky and Craft, *Pictures and Documents,* p. 264.

92. Wilfrid Mellers, "Stravinsky's Oedipus as 20th Century Hero," pp. 34-46, included in the Lang collection cited in n. 71, above.

93. V. Stravinsky and Craft, *Pictures and Documents,* p. 276.

94. Lawrence Morton, "Stravinsky and Tchaikovsky: *Le Baiser de la fée,*" pp. 47-60, also see Lang collection above.

95. Stravinsky, *Autobiography,* p. 159.

96. The third movement was finished first; the second movement on September 13; and the first movement was the last to be composed, probably within the last few weeks of the month. Craft reports that Stravinsky wrote to Paidchadze on October 23, "In a few days, I will finish the instrumentation of the first part of the *Capriccio,*" which in fact he did on October 26.

97. See *Pictures and Documents,* p. 292, for a fuller account of the premiere as well as a later review by Ezra Pound.

98. Stravinsky and Craft, *Dialogues,* p. 54.

99. Stravinsky, *Autobiography,* p. 159.

100. Stravinsky and Craft, *Dialogues,* p. 66.

101. V. Stravinsky and Craft, *Pictures and Documents,* p. 215.

102. Samuel Dushkin, "Working with Stravinsky," in *Igor Stravinsky,* ed. Edwin Corle, pp. 179-92.

103. Ibid., p. 190.

104. Some interesting sketches for the Dithyrambe of the *Duo* are reprinted on p. 309 of *Pictures and Documents.*

105. In an interview that took place in Oslo on September 27, 1935, Stravinsky mentioned, "Incidentally, this piece [referring to the *Concerto for Two Solo Pianos*] is not quite finished, but I have completed a sonata for piano and violin, inspired by Virgil—a strenuous piece, since it is to some extent athematic." This is reported on p. 27 of *Igor and Vera Stravinsky: A Photograph Album.*

106. Stravinsky, *Autobiography,* p. 169.

107. Sketches for the work are held by the Stravinsky estate (89 pages of summary sketches, if Craft's 1954 catalogue is still accurate), while the holograph, dated le 1 Sept/35, is held by the Library of Congress.

108. Stravinsky and Craft, *Dialogues,* p. 74.

109. Soulima Stravinsky, private interview. However, Mr. Craft has informed me that the work was actually begun in Paris rather than Voreppe. Moreover there is evidence to indicate that the *Two Piano Concerto* was begun immediately after the premiere of the *Duo Concertante*. See the second volume (forthcoming) of Mr. Craft's compilation of Stravinsky's correspondence for a more detailed account of the *Concerto's* history.

110. Stravinsky and Craft, *Dialogues,* p. 74.

111. The lecture, as reprinted in the original French, appears in appendix A of White's biography. According to Craft, Stravinsky recorded the lecture in Los Angeles, April 7, 1949; but still later in *Dialogues,* the composer stated "I would not care to see [the lecture] reprinted."

112. V. Stravinsky and Craft, *Pictures and Documents,* p. 326.

113. I wish to gratefully acknowledge the help of Professor Marcus in having shared these memories with me during an interview in New York, the summer of 1981.

114. V. Stravinsky and Craft, *Pictures and Documents,* p. 629.

115. One of the earliest writers to comment on this issue was Robert Tangeman in "Stravinsky's Two Piano Works," *Modern Music* 22 (1945):96-97.

116. Andre Schaeffner, "Stravinsky's Two-Piano Concerto and other Parisian Novelties," *Modern Music* 13 (1936). Schaeffner was one of Stravinsky's earliest biographers and seems to have enjoyed a good relationship with the composer around this time.

117. Robert U. Nelson, "Stravinsky's Concept of Variations," in the Lang collection of essays, pp. 61-73.

118. Ibid., p. 62.

119. V. Stravinsky and Craft, *Pictures and Documents,* p. 340.

120. Tangeman, "Stravinsky's Two Piano Works," p. 94.

121. Ingolf Dahl, "Symphony in 3 Movements," *Modern Music* 23 (1946):161.

122. Stravinsky and Craft, *Dialogues,* p. 75.

Chapter 6

1. Letter from Ellis B. Kohs to Stravinsky. See Vera Stravinsky and Robert Craft, *Stravinsky in Pictures and Documents,* p. 352.

2. Alexis Kall, "Stravinsky in the Chair of Poetry," *The Musical Quarterly* 26 (1940):283-96.

3. Frank Onnen, *Stravinsky,* p. 34.

4. V. Stravinsky and Craft, *Pictures and Documents,* p. 368.

5. The plate is reproduced courtesy of the Music Division of the Library of Congress and Theodore Presser Company.

6. V. Stravinsky and Craft, *Pictures and Documents,* p. 369.

7. Igor Stravinsky and Robert Craft, *Dialogues and a Diary,* p. 85.

8. See George Brinton Beal's "Entr'acte: Stravinsky and the Elephants," *Concert Bulletin of the Boston Symphony Orchestra,* January 1944, in which a description of the rehearsals and production of the ballet appears. Also see Lawrence Morton's "Incongruity and Faith," in Edwin Corle's *Stravinsky,* in which the author discusses Stravinsky's transmogrification of the simple, even trivial musical ideas and quotes into the "dream quality" of the work. Finally, in his collection of Stravinsky's letters (*Stravinsky: Selected Correspondence* Volume 1), Craft reports that in 1945, General de Gaulle specifically requested a score of the *Circus Polka*—surely a request as bizarre as the music itself.

9. V. Stravinsky and Craft, *Pictures and Documents,* p. 357.

10. Ibid., 646.

11. In this context, one is reminded of Nabokov's anecdote in which he recounts Stravinsky's own description of just how interchangeable passages in one of his compositions were. In explaining the score of *Orpheus* to Nabokov, the composer stated "You can eliminate these harp-solo interruptions, paste the parts of the fugue together, and it will be one whole piece." (The story originally appeared in Nabokov's *Old Friends and New Music.*)

12. In example 142, the pitches are ordered in closest proximity, for comparative ease.

13. Stravinsky and Craft, *Dialogues,* p. 73.

14. Mikhail Drushkin, *Stravinsky,* p. 262.

15. Craft, ed., *Selected Correspondence,* p. 240. Richard Johnston was the other pianist.

16. *Stravinsky and the Theatre,* pp. 66-67.

17. The identification was mentioned during a panel discussion ("Stravinsky in America") in which Morton participated, at the La Jolla Stravinsky Symposium.

18. I am deeply indebted to Professor Taruskin for having first called my attention to Bernard's anthology, *Pensi Russkago Naroda* (Songs of the Russian People), as well as initially providing me with the identifications discussed.

19. V. Stravinsky and Craft, *Pictures and Documents,* p. 373.

20. See Charles Burkhart, "Stravinsky's Revolving Canon," *The Music Review* 29 (1968):161-71, in which the author discusses aspects of the canonically developed theme, its mirror inversion and its pitch structure.

21. See Donal Johns, "An Early Serial Idea of Stravinsky," *The Music Review,* 23 (1962):305-13. Johns clearly addresses the use of the series in the variations in such way that there is no need to rehearse his remarks here. Simply stated, the variations display, with few exceptions, a literal use of the 29-note row.

22. The extent of Craft's intercession in this regard has been a recurrent focus of considerable discussion for a long time. Since Stravinsky's death, and especially in the most recent past, Mr. Craft has on several occasions suggested that his presence in the Stravinsky home was indeed a significant voice, introducing the composer to music that had previously gone unheard, and encouraging the always eager composer to undertake compositional investigations that others would have thought unthinkable. See both the *New York Review of Books,* June 1982, and "Assisting Stravinsky," *The Atlantic* 250 (December 1982):68-74, in which Craft addresses this matter.

23. Milton Babbitt, "Some Remarks on the Recent Stravinsky," in Boretz and Cone *Perspectives on Schoenberg and Stravinsky,* p. 176.

24. Alexandre Tansman, *Igor Stravinsky,* trans. Therese and Charles Bleefield, p. 247.

25. Eric Walter White, *Stravinsky,* p. 426.

26. V. Stravinsky and Craft, *Pictures and Documents,* p. 371.

27. See Merton Shatzkin, "A Pre-Cantata Serialism in Stravinsky," *Perspectives of New Music* 16 (1977):139-43, and, Robert Moeves, "Mannerism and Stylistic Consistency in Stravinsky," *Perspectives of New Music* 9 (1971):97-101.

28. In his "Assisting Stravinsky" article (see n. 22, above), Craft discusses in some detail Stravinsky's first contact with Schoenberg's own *Septet-Suite*: "On February 24, 1952, I conducted a performance of Schoenberg's *Septet-Suite,* with Stravinsky present at all the rehearsals, as well as the concert. This event was the turning point in his later musical evolution," p. 72.

29. V. Stravinsky and Craft, *Pictures and Documents,* p. 395.

30. Ibid., p. 452.

31. Ibid., p. 453.

32. Robert Craft, *Chronicle of a Friendship,* pp. 85-86.

33. Igor Stravinsky and Robert Craft, *Memories and Commentaries,* pp. 100-101.

34. Of these, three are suggested: Andreas Briner, "Guillaume de Machaut 1958–59 oder Strawinsky's *Movements for piano and orchestra," MELOS* 27 (1960):184-86; Claudio Spies, "Impressions After an Exhibition," *Tempo* 102 (1972):2-9; David Ward-Steinman, "Serial Techniques in the Recent Music of Igor Stravinsky" (D.M.A. diss., University of Illinois, 1961).

35. At the International Stravinsky Symposium in La Jolla, Babbitt again used *Movements* as the exemplar in his discussion of "Order, Symmetry and Centricity in Late Stravinsky."

36. V. Stravinsky and Craft, *Pictures and Documents,* p. 454.

37. From Robert Moeves, "Mannerism and Stylistic Consistency," pp. 98-100.

38. V. Stravinsky and Craft, *Pictures and Documents,* p. 645. Craft reports that the composer had been introduced to this music by Manfred Bukofzer and that "the music had a powerful effect on Stravinsky. Later, Bukofzer sent an essay on the isorhythmic motet, which also influenced the composer."

39. Karl Kohn, "Reflections on Igor Stravinsky," *Perspectives of New Music* 9 (1971) p. 67.

40. In his "Some Notes on Stravinsky's Requiem Settings," in *Perspectives on Schoenberg and Stravinsky,* Boretz and Cone eds., Claudio Spies (who was given access to the source materials before the score was released) notes that the four doubling horns of the Libera Me "were originally entrusted to a harmonium. . . ." (p. 234.) Stravinsky did employ both a piano and celeste in the score.

41. Francis Routh, *Stravinsky,* pp. 67-68.

42. Craft, *Chronicle,* p. 303.

43. Ibid., p. 343.

44. See, for example, "Quintet for Igor Stravinsky," *Intellectual Digest* (1972):pp. 83-87. Participants included Robert Craft, Paul Horgan, Vera Stravinsky, and Naomi and Bruce Bliven Jr.

45. Craft to this author, December 11, 1972.

46. This examination took place in the Stravinsky apartment, February 23, 1973.

Chapter 7

1. Vera Stravinsky and Robert Craft, *Stravinsky in Pictures and Documents*, p. 199.

2. Roman Vlad, *Stravinsky*, p. 83.

3. Igor Stravinsky, *An Autobiography*, p. 5.

4. See the translation by Craft and Andre Marion (Boosey & Hawkes, London), pp. 48-49.

5. See *Pictures and Documents* for the *Threni* photograph and Arnold Newman's *Bravo Stravinsky* for Craft's 1967 caption accompanying the picture. For an even more recently released memento of the composer at the piano, see p. 15 of *Igor and Vera Stravinsky: A Photograph Album*.

6. Igor Stravinsky and Robert Craft, *Expositions and Developments*, pp. 51-52.

7. Igor Stravinsky and Robert Craft, *Conversations with Igor Stravinsky*, p. 15.

8. Ibid.

9. Eric Walter White, *Stravinsky*, p. 211.

10. Robert Craft, "*The Rite of Spring*: Genesis of a Masterpiece," in *Igor Stravinsky, The Rite of Spring: Sketches 1911–1913*, p. xvii.

11. Arthur Berger, "Problems of Pitch Organization in Stravinsky," in *Perspectives on Schoenberg and Stravinsky*, Benjamin Boretz and Edward Cone eds., p. 145.

12. Milton Babbitt, "Some Remarks on the Recent Stravinsky," *Perspectives*, Boretz and Cone, p. 168.

13. V. Stravinsky and Craft, *Pictures and Documents*, p. 225.

14. Soulima Stravinsky, private interview.

15. As employed in the *Serenade*, this chord's relationship to the identical sonority of the later *Symphony of Psalms*, was addressed in this author's 1974 doctoral dissertation. Curiously, the same analogy (as well as numerous other ideas first advanced in my earlier study) are duplicated in a recent article by David Evenson, "The Piano in the Compositions of Igor Stravinsky," *The Piano Quarterly* 30 (1982):26-31.

16. Craft released some sketches for parts of the *Octet*, including this one, at the Stravinsky Symposium in La Jolla.

17. Richard Taruskin, "Russian Folk Melodies in *The Rite of Spring*," *Journal of the American Musicological Society* 33 (1980):509.

18. From Minna Lederman, ed., *Stravinsky in the Theatre*, pp. 128-29. One notes, too, that George Antheil received a similar impression in hearing Stravinsky play the piano

version of *Les Noces* (see White's biography, p. 83, for the full account of Antheil's remembrance).

19. Arnold Schoenberg, *Style and Idea,* ed., Leonard Stein, pp. 348-49.

20. Robert Siohan, *Stravinsky,* p. 25.

21. Lincoln Kirstein, "Working with Stravinsky," *Modern Music* 14 (March 1937):143.

22. Leo Smit, "A Card Game, A Wedding, and A Passing," *Perspectives of New Music* 9 (1971):90-91.

23. Kirstein, "Working with Stravinsky."

24. V. Stravinsky and Craft, *Pictures and Documents,* p. 332.

25. Elliott Carter, *Perspectives of New Music* 9 (1971):1-2.

26. Stravinsky had originally presented the manuscript to Victoria Ocampo in 1960. Dated Mai-Juin 1936, the holograph is actually incomplete, and carries Stravinsky's postscript that he hasn't the time to finish it.

27. White, *Stravinsky,* p. 184.

28. Stravinsky and Craft, *Expositions,* p. 146.

29. Stravinsky, *Autobiography,* p. 168.

Bibliography

Adorno, Theodor Wiesengrund. *Philosophy of Modern Music*. Translated by Anne G. Mitchell and Wesley B. Blomster. New York: Seabury Press, 1973.

Antheil, George. *Bad Boy of Music*. Garden City, New York: Doubleday, Doran & Co., 1945.

Apel, Willi. *Harvard Dictionary of Music*. 2nd rev. and enl. ed., Cambridge, Mass.: Harvard University Press, Belknap Press, 1972.

Armitage, Merle, ed. *Stravinsky*. New York: G. Schirmer, 1936.

Asaf'yev, Boris. *Kinga o Stravinskom* [A Book About Stravinsky]. Translated by Richard F. French. Ann Arbor: UMI Research Press, 1982.

Austin, William. *Music in the Twentieth Century*. W. W. Norton & Co., 1966.

Babbitt, Milton. "Order, Symmetry and Centricity in Late Stravinsky." Paper read at the International Stravinsky Symposium, September 13, 1982, La Jolla, California.

————. "Remarks on the Recent Stravinsky." In *Perspectives on Schoenberg and Stravinsky*, pp. 165-85. Rev. Edited by Benjamin Boretz and Edward T. Cone. New York: W. W. Norton & Co., 1972. Originally in *Perspectives of New Music* 2 (1964):35-55.

Bamberger, Jeanne, "The Musical Significance of Beethoven's Fingerings in the Piano Sonatas." In *The Music Forum*, Volume 4. Edited by Felix Salxer. New York: Columbia University Press, 1976.

Barnes, Clive. "City Ballet Triumphs in Stravinsky Fete." *The New York Times*, 19 June 1972, p. 1.

Beach, David W. "Pitch Structure and the Analytic Process in Atonal Music: An Interpretation of the Theory of Sets." *Music Theory Spectrum* 1 (1979):7-22.

Beal, George Brinton. "Entr'acte: Stravinsky and the Elephants." *Concert Bulletin*, Boston Symphony Orchestra, January 13-15, 1944.

Beliaiev, Viktor Mikhailovich. *Igor Stravinsky's "Les Noces": An Outline*. Translated by S. W. Pring. London, 1928.

Benjamin, William E. "Tonality without 5ths: Remarks on the First Movement of Stravinsky's Concerto for Piano and Wind Instruments." *In Theory Only* 2 (November-December 1977):53-70.

Berger, Arthur. "Neoclassicism Reexamined." *Perspectives of New Music* 9 (1971):79-86.

————. "Problems of Pitch Organization in Stravinsky." In *Perspectives on Schoenberg and Stravinsky*, pp. 123-54. Rev. Edited by Benjamin Boretz and Edward T. Cone. New York: W. W. Norton & Co., 1972. Originally in *Perspectives of New Music* 2 (1963):11-42.

Berlin, Edward A. *Ragtime: A Musical and Cultural History*. Berkeley and Los Angeles: University of California Press, 1980.

Blitzstein, Marc. "The Phenomenon of Stravinsky." *The Musical Quarterly* 21 (1935):330-47.

Boretz, Benjamin, and Cone, Edward T. *Perspectives on Schoenberg and Stravinsky.* Revised edition. New York: W. W. Norton & Co., 1972.

Boulanger, Nadia. *Lectures on Modern Music.* Houston: Rice Institute, 1926.

Briner, Andreas. "Guillaume de Machaut 1958-59 oder Stravinsky's 'Movements for piano and orchestra.' " *MELOS* 27 (1960):184-86.

Brown, Malcolm. "Stravinsky and Prokofiev: Sizing up the Competition." Paper read at the International Stravinsky Symposium, September 11, 1982, La Jolla, California.

Burkhart, Crarles. "Stravinsky's Revolving Canon." *The Music Review* 29 (1968):161-64.

Carter, Elliott. *Perspectives of New Music* 9 (1971):1-5.

Charters, A. R. Danberg. "Negro Folk Elements in Classic Ragtime." *Ethnomusicology* 5 (1961):174-83.

Collaer, Paul. *Stravinsky.* Brussels: Editions 'Equilibres,' 1930.

Cone, Edward T. "Stravinsky: The Progress of a Method." In *Perspectives on Schoenberg and Stravinsky,* pp. 155-64. Rev. Edited by Benjamin Boretz and Edward T. Cone. New York: W. W. Norton & Co., 1972. Originally in *Perspectives of New Music* 2 (1962):18-26.

Cooke, J. F. "Chronological Progress in Musical Art." *The Etude* 44 (1926):559-60.

Corle, Edwin, ed. *Igor Stravinsky.* New York: Duell, Sloane and Pearce, 1949.

Cortot, Alfred. "Igor Strawinsky, le piano et les pianistes," *Le Revue Musicale,* Number 190 (1939):264-308.

Craft, Robert. "A Personal Preface." *The Score,* Number 20 (1957):11-13.

_____. "Assisting Stravinsky." *The Atlantic* 250 (December 1982):68-74.

_____. "The Composer and the Phonograph." *High Fidelity* 7 (June 1959):35.

_____. "The Chronology of the 'Serenade en La.' " Forthcoming.

_____. "Genesis of a Masterpiece." In *The Rite of Spring: Sketches, 1911-1913.* London: Boosey & Hawkes, 1969.

_____. *Stravinsky: Chronicles of a Friendship.* New York: Alfred A. Knopf, 1972.

_____. *Stravinsky: Selected Correspondence, Volume 1.* New York: Alfred A. Knopf, 1982.

Dahl, Ingolf. "Symphony in 3 Movements." *Modern Music* 22 (1946):159-65.

Drushkin, Mikhail S. *Igor Stravinsky: His Character, Creative Work, Opinions.* Leningrad, 1974. German translation, Leipzig: Verlag Philipp Reclam jun., 1976.

Dushkin, Samuel. "Working with Stravinsky." In *Igor Stravinsky,* pp. 179-92. Edited by Edwin Corle. New York: Duell, Sloane and Pearce, 1949.

Evenson, David. "The Piano in the Compositions of Igor Stravinsky." *The Piano Quarterly* 30 (1982):26-31.

Forte, Allen. *The Harmonic Organization of 'The Rite of Spring.'* New Haven: Yale University Press, 1978.

_____. *The Structure of Atonal Music.* New Haven: Yale University Press, 1973.

Gillespie, John. *Five Centuries of Keyboard Music.* Belmont, California: Wadsworth Publishing Co., 1965.

Goldman, Richard Franko. "Current Chronicle." *The Musical Quarterly* 46 (1960):260-64.

Goosens, Eugene. *Overture and Beginners.* London: Methuen and Co., 1951.

Gorden, Edward. "Classic and Romantic in Russian Music." *Music and Letters* 50 (1969):153-57.

Gozenpud, A. ed. *F. Stravinsky: Stat'i Pis'ma Vospominaniya* [F. Stravinsky: Essays, Letters, Memoirs]. Leningrad, 1972.

"Great American Composer—Will He Speak in the Accent of Broadway?" *Current Opinion* 63 (1917):317.

Hanson, Howard. *Harmonic Materials of Modern Music.* New York: Appleton-Century Crofts, 1960.

Heyman, Barbara B. "Stravinsky and Ragtime." *The Musical Quarterly* 63 (1982):557-71.

Hindemith, Paul. *Craft of Musical Composition.* Translated by Arthur Mendel. New York: Schott Music, 1937.

Hopkins, G. W. "Stravinsky's Chords." *Tempo* 76 (1966):6-12.

Horgan, Paul. *Encounters with Stravinsky.* New York: Farrar, Strauss, Giroux, 1972.

Jacobi, Frederick Jr. "Harvard Soirée." *Modern Music* 17 (1939–1940):47-48.

Johns, Donald. "An Early Serial Idea of Stravinsky." *The Music Review* 23 (1962):305-13.

Joseph, Charles M. "Stravinsky Manuscripts in The Pierpont Morgan Library and The Library of Congress." *The Journal of Musicology* 1 (1982):327-37.

_____. "Stravinsky's Piano Scherzo (1902) In Perspective: A New Starting Point." *The Musical Quarterly* 67 (1981):82-93.

_____. "Structural Coherence in Stravinsky's *Piano-Rag-Music.*" *Music Theory Spectrum* 4 (1982):76-91.

Kaiser, Joachim. *Great Pianists of Our Time.* Translated by David Woolridge and George Unwin. New York: Herder and Herder, 1971.

Kall, Alexis. "Stravinsky in the Chair of Poetry." *The Musical Quarterly* 26 (1940):283-96.

Karsavina, Tamara. "Recollection of Stravinsky." *Tempo* 58 (1948).

Keller, Hans. "No Bridge to Nowhere." *Musical Times* 102 (1961):156-58.

Kirby, F. E. *A Short History of Keyboard Music.* New York: The Free Press, 1966.

Kirchmeyer, Helmut. *Igor Strawinsky: Zeitgeschichte im Personlichkeitsbild.* Regensburg: Gustav Bosse Verlag, 1958.

Kirstein, Lincoln. "Working with Stravinsky." *Modern Music* 14 (1937):143.

Kohn, Karl. "Reflections on Igor Stravinsky." *Perspectives of New Music* 9 (1971):66-67.

Kraft, Leo. "Stravinsky and Tradition: First Thoughts." *Perspectives of New Music* 9 (1971):140-41.

Lang, Paul Henry, ed. *Stravinsky: A New Appraisal of His Work.* New York: W. W. Norton & Co., 1963.

LaRue, Jan. *Guidelines for Style Analysis.* New York: W. W. Norton & Co., 1970.

Lederman, Minna, ed. *Stravinsky in the Theatre.* New York: Pelegrini & Cudahy, 1951.

Libman, Lillian. *And Music at the Close: Stravinsky's Last Years.* New York: W. W. Norton & Co., 1972.

Lourie, Arthur. "La Sonate pour Piano de Strawinski." *La Revue Musicale,* Number 10 (1925):100-104.

Mellers, Wilfred. "Stravinsky and Jazz." *Tempo* 81 (1967):29-31.

_____. "Stravinsky's Oedipus as 20th-Century Hero." In *Stravinsky: A New Appraisal of His Work,* pp. 34-46. Edited by Paul Henry Lang. New York: W. W. Norton & Co., 1963.

Middleton, Richard. "Stravinsky's Development: A Jungian Approach." *Music and Letters* 54 (1973):289-301.

Moeves, Robert. "Mannerism and Stylistic Consistency in Stravinsky." *Perspectives of New Music* 9 (1971):97-101.

Morgan, Robert P. "Dissonant Prolongations: Theoretical and Compositional Precedents." *The Journal of Music Theory* 20 (1976):46-91.

_____. "Dissonant Prolongations, Perfect 5ths and Major 3rds in Stravinsky's Piano Concerto." *In Theory Only* 4 (April 1978):3-7.

Morton, Lawrence. "Incongruity and Faith." In *Igor Stravinsky,* pp. 193-200. Edited by Edwin Corle. New York: Duell, Sloane and Pearce, 1949.

_____. "Stravinsky in America." Paper read at the International Stravinsky Symposium, September 12, 1982, La Jolla, California.

—————. "Stravinsky and Tchaikovsky: Le Baiser de la fée." In *Stravinsky: A New Appraisal of His Work,* pp. 47-60. Edited by Paul Henry Lang. New York: W. W. Norton & Co., 1963.

Muir, Malcolm. "Stravinsky and Stravinsky." *Newsweek,* 21 August 1948, p. 72.

Nabokov, Nicolas. *Old Friends and New Music.* London: Hamish Hamilton, 1951.

—————. *Igor Strawinsky.* Berlin: Colloquium Verlag, 1064.

Nelson, Robert U. "Stravinsky's Concept of Variation." In *Stravinsky: A New Appraisal of His Work,* pp. 61-73. Edited by Paul Henry Lang. New York: W. W. Norton & Co., 1963. Originally in *The Musical Quarterly* 48 (1962):327-39.

Newman, William S. "Beethoven's Fingerings as Interpretive Clues." *The Journal of Musicology* 2 (1982):171-97.

Nobel, Jeremy. "Debussy and Stravinsky." *The Musical Times* 108 (1967):22-25.

Ogdon, John. "Stravinsky and the Piano." *Tempo* 81 (1967):36-41.

Onnen, Frank. *Stravinsky.* Translated by Mrs. M. M. Kessler-Button. Stockholm: The Continental Book Company A. B., 1948.

Pascoe, Clive B. "Golden Proportion in Musical Design." D.M.E. dissertation, University of Cincinnati, 1973.

Perle, George. *Serial Composition and Atonality.* 5th rev. ed. Berkeley: University of California Press, 1981.

Piston, Walter. "A Reminiscence." *Perspectives of New Music* 9 (1971):6-7.

Philipp, Isidor. *Complete School of Technic for the Pianoforte.* Bryn Mawr, Pennsylvania: Theodore Presser Co., 1908.

"Quintet for Igor Stravinsky." *Intellectual Digest,* August 1972, pp. 83-87.

Rajna, Thomas. "Stravinsky's Piano Works." *Composer* 29 (1968):5-9.

Ramuz, Charles F. *Souvenirs sur Igor Strawinsky.* Paris: Nouvelle Revue Francaise, 1929.

Ridenour, Robert C. *Nationalism, Modernism, and Personal Rivalry in 19th-Century Russian Music.* Ann Arbor: UMI Research Press, 1981.

Rimsky-Korsakov, Nikolay Andreyevich. *My Musical Life.* Translated from the 5th revised edition by Judah A. Joffe. New York: Alfred A. Knopf, 1942.

Routh, Francis. *Stravinsky.* London: J. M. Dent & Sons Ltd., 1975.

Rubinstein, Arthur. *My Many Years.* New York: Alfred A. Knopf, 1980.

—————. *The Young Years.* New York: Alfred A. Knopf, 1973.

Schaeffner, Andre. "Stravinsky's Two-Piano Concerto and other Parisian Novelties." *Modern Music* 13 (1936):37-38.

Schloezer, Boris de. *Igor Stravinsky.* Paris: Editions Claude Aveline, 1929.

Schoenberg, Arnold. *Style and Idea: Selected Writings of Arnold Schoenberg.* Edited by Leonard Stein. London: Faber and Faber, 1975.

Schonberg, Harold. *The Great Pianists.* New York: Simon and Schuster, 1963.

Schwarz, Boris. "Stravinsky in Soviet Russian Criticism." In *Stravinsky: A New Appraisal of His Work,* pp. 74-96. Edited by Paul Henry Lang. New York: W. W. Norton & Co., 1963. Originally in *The Musical Quarterly* 48 (1962):340-61.

Sessions, Roger. "Thoughts on Stravinsky." *The Score* 20 (June 1957):32-36.

Shatzkin, Merton. "A Pre-Cantata Serialism in Stravinsky." *Perspectives of New Music* 16 (1977):139-43.

Shawn, Allen. "Nadia Boulanger's Lessons." *The Atlantic* 251 (March 1983):78-85.

Siohan, Robert. *Stravinsky.* Translated by Eric Walter White. New York: Grossman Publishers, 1965.

Slonimsky, Nicolas. *Lexicon of Musical Invective.* New York: Coleman-Ross, 1953.

Smalley, Roger. "Personal Viewpoints." *Tempo* 131 (1967):21.

Smit, Leo. "A Card Game, A Wedding, and A Passing." *Perspectives of New Music* 9 (1971):87-92.

Smirnov, Valerii V. *Tvorcheskoe formirovanie I. F. Stravinskogo* [Creative Formative Years of I. F. Stravinsky]. Leningrad, 1970.

Spiess, Claudio. "Editions of Stravinsky's Music." In *Perspectives on Schoenberg and Stravinsky,* pp. 250-67. Edited by Benjamin Boretz and Edward T. Cone. New York: W. W. Norton & Co., 1972.

_____. "Impressions After an Exhibition." *Tempo* 102 (1972):2-9.

_____. "Some Notes On Stravinsky's Requiem Settings." In *Perspectives on Schoenberg and Stravinsky,* pp. 233-49. Edited by Benjamin Boretz and Edward T. Cone. New York: W. W. Norton & Co., 1972.

Stein, Erwin. "Stravinsky's Septet (1953) . . . An Analysis." *Tempo* 31 (1954):7-11.

Stevens, Halsey. "Critical Years in European Musical History 1915–1925." *International Musicological Society* 10 (1967):221-33.

Straus, Joseph. "Stravinsky's Tonal Axis." *The Journal of Music Theory* 26 (1982):261-90.

Stravinsky, Igor. *An Autobiography.* New York: Simon and Schuster, 1936.

_____. *Poetics of Music: In the Form of Six Lessons.* Translated by Arthur Knodel and Ingolf Dahl. Cambridge, Massachussets: Harvard University Press, 1942.

"Stravinsky Previsions a New Music." *Current Opinion* 71 (1925):329-30.

Stravinsky, Igor, and Craft, Robert. *Conversations with Igor Stravinsky.* Berkeley and Los Angeles: University of California Press, 1980.

_____. *Dialogues and a Diary.* London: Faber and Faber, 1961.

_____. *Expositions and Developments.* London: Faber and Faber, 1959.

_____. *Memories and Commentaries.* Garden City, New York: Doubleday and Company, 1960.

_____. *Themes and Episodes.* New York: Alfred A. Knopf, 1966.

Stravinsky, Soulima. *Stravinsky: The Short Piano Pieces.* New York: Boosey & Hawkes, 1977.

Stravinsky, Theodore. *Catherine and Igor Stravinsky: A Family Album.* London: Boosey & Hawkes, 1973.

_____. *Le Message d'Igor Strawinsky.* Lausanne: Librarie F. Rouge, 1948. English translation by Robert Craft and Andre Marion. London: Boosey & Hawkes, 1953.

Stravinsky, Vera, and Craft, Robert. *Stravinsky in Pictures and Documents.* New York: Simon and Schuster, 1978.

Stravinsky, Vera, and McCaffrey, Rita. *Igor and Vera Stravinsky: A Photograph Album 1921–1971.* Captions by Robert Craft. New York: Thames and Hudson, 1982.

Strobel, Heinrich. *Stravinsky: Classical Humanist.* Translated by Hans Rosenwald. New York: Merlin Press, 1955.

Sutton, Wadham. "Stravinsky and Synthetic Melody." *Musical Opinion* 91 (November 1967):81-83.

Tangeman, Robert. "Stravinsky's Two-Piano Works." *Modern Music* 22 (1945):93-98.

Tansman, Alexandre. *Igor Stravinsky: The Man and His Music.* Translated by Therese and Charles Bleefield. New York: G. P. Putnam and Sons, 1949.

Taruskin, Richard. "Russian Folk Melodies in The Rite of Spring." *Journal of the American Musicological Society* 33 (1980):501-43.

Terry, Walter. "Balanchine's Ballet Tribute to Stravinsky." *Saturday Review,* July 15, 1972, p. 66.

van den Toorn, Pieter C. *The Music of Igor Stravinsky.* New Haven: Yale University Press, 1983.

_____. "Some Characteristics of Stravinsky's Diatonic Music." *Perspectives of New Music* 14 (1975) and 15 (1977).

Vlad, Roman. *Stravinsky.* 2nd ed. Translated by Frederick and Ann Fuller. London: Oxford University Press, 1967.

Wade, Carroll D. "A Selected Bibliography of Igor Stravinsky." In *Stravinsky: A New Appraisal of His Work,* pp. 97-109. New York: W. W. Norton & Co., 1963. Originally in *The Musical Quarterly* 48 (1962):372-84.

Ward-Steinman, David. "Serial Techniques in the Recent Music of Igor Stravinsky." D.M.A. dissertation, University of Illinois, 1961.

Weiser, Bernard. *Keyboard Music.* Dubuque, Iowa: William C. Brown Co., 1971.

Weissmann, Adolph. "Strawinsky spielt sein Klavier Konzert." *Anbruch* 6 (1924):407-9.

Wharton, Edith, ed. *The Book of the Homeless.* London: Macmillan & Co., 1916.

White, Eric Walter. *Stravinsky: The Composer and his Works.* 2nd rev. ed. Los Angeles: University of California Press, 1979.

————. *Stravinsky's Sacrifice to Apollo.* London: The Hogarth Press, 1930.

Williams, B. M. "The Structure of Stravinsky's Symphony in C." *The Musical Quarterly* 59 (1973):355-69.

Winter, Robert, and Carr, Bruce, eds. *Beethoven, Performer and Critic.* International Beethoven Congress, Detroit, 1977. Detroit: Wayne State University Press, 1980.

Wise, Stanley C. " 'American Music is True Art,' Says Stravinsky." *New York Tribune* 16 January 1916, sec. 5, p. 3.

Yarustovsky, B. M., ed. *I. F. Stravinsky: Stat'i Materialy* [I. F. Stravinsky: Essays and Materials]. Moscow: Sovietsky Kompositor, 1973.

Yastrebtzev, V. V. *Nikolay Andreyevich Rimsky-Korsakov: Vospominaniya* [Reminiscences of N. A. Rimsky-Korsakov]. Leningrad, 1959-1960.

Zur, Menachem. "Tonal Ambiguities as a Constructive Force in the Language of Stravinsky." *The Musical Quarterly* 68 (1982):516-26.

Index